CEASE BUZZER!

LIFE AS A U.S. NAVY EA-6B PILOT IN THE ERA OF TOP GUN

J. P. SPRINGETT II

COMMODORE'S RIDGE PUBLISHING - LURAY, VIRGINIA

Copyright © 2023 by J. P. Springett II

All rights reserved.

No part of this book may be reproduced in any form or by any electronic or mechanical means, including information storage and retrieval systems, without written permission from the author, except for the use of brief quotations in a book review.

This book is a memoir. It reflects the author's present recollections of experiences that occurred in the past. Some names and characteristics have been changed, some events have been compressed or combined, and any dialogue has been recreated.

The views expressed in this publication are those of the author and do not necessarily reflect the official policy or position of the Department of Defense or the U.S. government. The public release clearance of this publication by the Department of Defense does not imply Department of Defense endorsement or factual accuracy of the material.

Commodore's Ridge Publishing

www.commodoresridge.com

Library of Congress Control Number: 2023902122

Paperback ISBN: 979-8-9859023-7-2

Ebook ISBN: 979-8-9859023-6-5

Hardcover ISBN: 979-8-9879757-1-8

V1.03

Front Cover Photo: VAQ-133 Tanking from KC-135, U.S. Air Force photo by Master Sgt. Lance Cheung

Rear Cover Photo: Prowlers on Flight Deck, U.S. Navy Photo

TABLE OF CONTENTS

Introduction	v
Prelude	1
1. Aviation Preflight Indoctrination	7
2. Primary Flight Training	21
3. Intermediate Jet Training	27
4. Advanced Jet Training	44
5. "Welcome to the Fleet!"	67
6. "Rooks, Rooks, Rooks"	85
7. Life on the Boat - A Thumbnail	101
8. USS America (CV-66) 1991-1992	116
9. Peacetime Flying at Sea	138
10. USS America (CV-66) 1993 - 1994	147
11. The Maintenance Department - The Beating Heart of a Squadron	176
12. USS Abraham Lincoln (CVN-72) 1994-1995	185
13. USS Theodore Roosevelt (CVN-71) and USS Enterprise (CVN-65)	205
14. VAQ-133 Executive Officer: Bagram Air Base, Afghanistan 2006	226
15. VAQ-133 Commanding Officer: Bagram Air Base, Afghanistan 2007	253
16. Commander, Electronic Attack Wing, U.S. Pacific Fleet	265
About the Author	275
About Self-Publishing	277

INTRODUCTION

Prowlers on Flight Deck, U.S. Navy Photo

As I introduce this book, it is important to note that this memoir isn't just about flying the EA-6B. The story begins as I enter flight training and includes descriptions of life on the carrier, humorous port visits, training detachments, exercises with the other services, and several wonderful experiences on liberty. In addition, the book provides a few accounts of combat actions over Serbia, Kosovo, and Iraq, and a unique perspective of land-based EA-6B combat support in Afghanistan. That said, it is a memoir that contains some selected highlights and some lowlights from a long naval career. If you are looking for a story about electronic warfare tactics, or a detailed narrative of a senior aviator's life, this is not your book.

The thirty-six-year stretch between the release of the first "Top Gun" movie in 1986, and its sequel in 2022 was an exceptionally busy period for Naval Aviation. The public knows that Navy fighter pilots flew hundreds of thousands of combat sorties and employed millions of pounds of ordnance on enemy targets in the Middle East and elsewhere. What most will not be familiar with are the extensive operations of the EA-6B community during this period and the fact that no Navy fighter went into harm's way without dedicated Electronic Warfare support.

Our job as EA-6B crews was not to make it into the movies. The EA-6B "Prowler" was an Electronic Warfare aircraft flown by both the Navy and the Marine Corps that was designed to "Deny, Degrade, Deceive, or Destroy" the enemy air defense systems that were used to target American, allied, and partner forces. When you saw footage of a strike mission on TV, we were there too, but we operated in the background so that our fighter and bomber crews could get to the target, deliver their ordnance, and return safely.

As the Global War on Terror became an extended period of counter-insurgency operations, the EA-6B community discovered a new role. All of the Navy's carrier-based Prowler squadrons supported the troops from the sea. However, some of us left the carrier and, along with the Marine Corps, began to operate our expeditionary squadrons from air bases across Iraq and Afghanistan. While this new obligation meant that the small EA-6B community was stretched to its limit, it was done without complaint. We were saving lives and ensuring that more of the young Americans who had volunteered to serve their nation could return home when their job was done.

About the title: I initially considered calling this book "Not Top Gun," but that was just too self-deprecating. Although I was a career EA-6B pilot, I have exactly as many air-to-air kills as 99.9% of the Navy fighter pilots that ever lived and have collected more flight time, combat missions, and traps than many of them. With this in mind, it will be helpful to understand that the term "Cease Buzzer" is an urgent request for an EA-6B to stop jamming; this is not very glamorous. My friends in the fighter world lived to hear radio calls like "Fox Two," a term that accompanied the launch of an air-to-air missile. This is clearly exciting stuff and is the kind of phrase that you have come to expect to be yelled by the hero in the movies as they shoot down an enemy fighter and then do an aileron roll.

The radio call "Cease Buzzer," on the other hand, epitomizes life in the EA-6B community. When you have people urgently demanding that you stop doing your mission because it bothers them, it can be a bit deflating. While things have changed over time, early in my career it seemed to me that the radio call "Cease Buzzer" was the only feedback that an EA-6B crew would ever receive, and for a long time, a mission did not seem complete until someone, anyone, asked us to turn the jammers off. Essentially, if someone cried "uncle" we had done our job. So, although it is pretty clear that the term is not nearly as exciting as others that may have been heard on the radio, it will have to do.

NOTE: It should be very clear that this is **not** intended to be a comprehensive retelling of my aviation career. I tell my favorite sea stories and describe some of the key events that stuck in my memory. Despite the breadth of the narrative, this book barely scratches the surface of the immensely rewarding experiences that took place over three decades of working with the best officers and enlisted sailors in the world's most capable Navy. I do apologize to those who are looking for electronic warfare tactics, techniques, or procedures. This book does not contain any - for obvious reasons. Perhaps someday we can tell those stories, but I doubt it.

Many of the sea stories in this book seem to revolve around alcohol. First, I will say that times have changed and the old culture of the Navy is long gone. I also feel that it is necessary to point out that this book is a distillation, (ahem), of three decades worth of experiences around the globe. Yes, when we were young we played hard and alcohol was part of that lifestyle. However, booze wasn't the center of our lives - flying was. There were many, many more placid days on deployment, on liberty, or at home than there were crazy, boozy trips around the world - but they don't make good sea stories.

Because this is a work of memory, the book contains flaws, bias, and the other inevitable artifacts of being a product of an aging brain. It has been appropriately cleared by the Department of Defense as long as I tell you that all the views are my own…and that some of this narrative might not be factually correct. It is self-published - since finding an agent and getting through the "normal" process of publishing these days is nearly impossible. Being self-published also means that it was largely self-edited, I take all the blame for any typos or grammar issues - I find a few more every time I read it.

Finally, I appreciate the help of my pre-readers and their editorial assistance. I have done what I can to make these stories interesting and entertaining without burning any bridges with the people with whom I shared these adventures (and it is worth noting that the fellow aviators with whom I have maintained contact have enjoyed the book). Thanks for reading, I hope that you enjoy it!

PRELUDE

USS Theodore Roosevelt (CVN-71), U.S. Navy Photo

Ionian Sea, April 1999

The atmosphere aboard the USS Theodore Roosevelt (CVN-71) was tense, but the crew was excited. The ship had departed from its homeport Norfolk, Virginia, on the 26th of March, 1999, to begin a regularly scheduled six-month deployment. Two days before the Roosevelt's departure, NATO had begun combat operations against the Federal Republic of

Yugoslavia. This meant that the United States was now involved in an air war over Europe for the first time in decades.

Quite a few of the air wing's pilots were already familiar with the region. We had flown dozens of reconnaissance sorties around Bosnia-Herzegovina and the area near Sarajevo on earlier deployments supporting Operation Deny Flight. However, we were now potentially headed into combat against an adversary that had been trained and equipped by the Russians – a situation that would be much different from the relatively benign Operation Southern Watch missions we had been planning to conduct before this new conflict had begun. Despite the news headlines suggesting that the carrier was heading to war, we had not yet been ordered to participate, and there was still a fair amount of uncertainty about our schedule. On the good side, the USS Theodore Roosevelt was steaming toward the fight at high speed. On the bad side, there clearly was some doubt at higher levels of the nation's defense leadership about the necessity for the carrier to contribute. Operation Allied Force was essentially an Air Force mission led by an Army General and high-level service politics were definitely in play as the carrier headed across the ocean.

Regardless of the uncertainty, we prepared for combat. In the eight years since Operation Desert Storm, the Navy's Carrier Air Wings had flown thousands of combat sorties over Iraq. As a result, many of us were pretty familiar with "the drill." As aircrew, we needed to think about our personal preparation. There was extra survival equipment that needed to be incorporated into our flight gear, regional charts to dig up, and "Blood Chits" to distribute (if we were shot down, these documents told the locals that they would be rewarded if they helped us). We needed to prepare holsters for our sidearms, program our GPS (if you had one), and refresh our training with the special survival radios that would replace the normal ones we carried.

In our squadron, we followed the results of the Air Force strikes through intelligence reports, parsing the classified message traffic like old-timers huddled near a radio listening to war news. We refreshed our understanding of the Air Tasking Order (ATO) and put in a lot of time to familiarize ourselves with intelligence assessments of Yugoslavian air defenses. Along the way, we did some normal flying. The air wing needed to maintain currency with both daytime and nighttime arrested landings while we waited for the order. My log book shows a few normal sorties as we transited to the Mediterranean, including one on the 5th of April. As we got closer to the fight, the decision was finally made, and we were ordered to participate in Operation Allied Force. As is typical with such bureaucracy, the notice was last minute. We had about eight hours to plan for our first air strikes on Yugoslavian military forces, the first two of which were intended to take place on the night of the 6th.

When it comes to combat missions, there is a certain unwritten hierarchy to how they are planned and scheduled in an air wing. Every aviator worth their salt wants to be part of the "first night" of such strikes. However, like many things in the military, these assignments are commonly made in order of seniority.

My squadron, VAQ-141, supplied the Suppression of Enemy Air Defense (SEAD) experts who were assigned to each of the several air wing strike planning teams. These teams were organized to distribute the vast amount of work that strike planning required and enable the air wing to conduct sequential strikes with no pause. As the air wing's involvement continued from day to day, the planning assignments would eventually work their way down the "batting order." My squadron Commanding Officer (CO) was the SEAD lead for the first planning team, and as a result, he and his crew were guaranteed to support the first combat mission the air wing would conduct. In comparison, since I was a junior Lieutenant Commander, I served as the SEAD lead on what I think was probably the seventh or eighth strike team. However, there was an important caveat to this scheme - each mission required multiple EA-6Bs, so there were always additional aviators who would be assigned to support the primary crew (or to stand in as a spare). In this case, my low seniority worked out perfectly; I was scheduled to fly the second EA-6B on the first CVW-8 strike.

While we eventually transitioned to a highly flexible "kill box" style of planning and execution, the first events that the air wing conducted were classic "Alpha Strikes." This meant that we applied an updated version of the well-proven tactics that had been employed in Vietnam. Such a strike started with an enemy target (or set of targets) and a block of time during which higher headquarters desired us to conduct the mission. This information was provided to us in the daily ATO. When this data was combined with what our intelligence knew about the adversary's air defenses, it gave us enough information to choose a route and a specific Time on Target, or TOT. Our strike planners then created what amounted to a set-piece plan that outlined the specific flight paths and altitudes of two dozen or more strike and support aircraft; coordinating the individual missions in order to maximize the overall effect. Everything in this type of strike was based on the TOT, and the entire event was intended to be flown without any radio communications.

The first and second strikes of Operation Allied Force for CVW-8 were textbook Navy efforts. We had fighters doing a fighter sweep, we had defensive counter-air, we had strike-fighters dropping bombs, and we had a huge SEAD package with F/A-18Cs and EA-6Bs shooting AGM-88, High-Speed Anti-Radiation Missiles (HARM) and jamming Serbian radars. Also of note, these two strikes would be entirely Navy efforts. This meant we would be getting fuel from "organic" tanking, which required that every S-3B that could get airborne would provide fuel for the strike with an aerial refueling package. The timeline was so compressed for this first night that there hadn't been time to establish the "big-wing" Air Force tanking that would later be a key resource for us.

In addition, one of the very unique things about the way our particular squadron of EA-6Bs operated during Allied Force was that my CO had convinced our Air Wing Commander (known as "CAG") that our jets should fly with three jamming pods and two HARM missiles, instead of three jamming pods, an external fuel tank, and a single HARM. While this configuration increased the number of HARM that were available to our strike planners, it also meant that the Prowler crews would fly using internal gas only, essentially making us as fuel-critical as the notoriously "thirsty" F/A-18Cs that we were supporting.

The day raced by as we prepared for our missions. In no time at all, we were putting on our flight gear and walking to our aircraft. I remember launching from the carrier that evening, joining with the tankers, and getting topped off with fuel. We then headed to a rendezvous point off the coast of Montenegro. As the strike was forming, it definitely felt that "Ride of the Valkyries" should be playing at full blast, just as it did in the movie "Apocalypse Now." The opening mission of the war felt surreal; the towns and cities along the Adriatic coast were illuminated as if it were any ordinary Tuesday night, and we could see the glow of the Italian peninsula from our jamming orbits. While it sounds horrible, it crossed my mind that war in Europe was somehow going to be much more civilized than the combat missions we had thought we were going to fly in the Arabian Gulf.

Anyway, as occasionally happened in combat, the strike was delayed. Although we had all launched on time, there had been some of the usual friction that comes with warfare, and the strike leader had "Rolexed" the mission, delaying it for ten minutes. My CO, in the lead EA-6B, asked my fuel state and decided to send me back to the tanker so that I would have enough fuel to cover the delayed egress of the strike. I was disappointed but dutifully went back to the S-3B tanker, got topped off, and headed back toward the jamming orbit, expecting to have missed the entire event. However, after I got my gas, the strike was delayed one more time, and now it was the CO's jet that needed fuel. So, he departed, and I arrived back on station just as the strike "pushed" from their positions over the Adriatic towards the target area.

Now, because our radar-jamming interfered with our own radios and the fact we did not have night vision goggles, the fate of a Prowler crew at that time was to be right in the middle of combat and not really know much about what was going on. We could see missiles fired, anti-aircraft artillery exploding, and the afterburners of various fighters. However, our jamming effectiveness required that we ignore those distractions and operate on a strict route and timeline, hoping that the aircraft we were supporting were where they were supposed to be at the right time. In this case, the original plan had each of the two EA-6Bs in jamming orbits that were stacked on top of one another. While we both would jam, each of us would also fire one HARM missile to suppress or destroy parts of the enemy's air defense. With the CO's jet away getting fuel, I was now the only EA-6B in position to support the strike. This meant that I got to execute a maneuver that we believed a Prowler would never do in combat, shoot one HARM, and then do a timed two-minute circle and fire a second missile from the same spot in the sky. This would be awesome!

As awesome as this was, it is worth noting that prior to this night I had never fired a HARM. I distinctly remember pausing for a moment before I pulled the trigger on the first missile. It certainly occurred to me that the weapon that I was about to fire was intended to destroy equipment and kill people. Like many before me, I didn't justify the use of lethal force based on the high-level "correctness" of the mission. Instead, I pulled the trigger to protect my friends in the fighter aircraft that would soon be over the target and vulnerable to enemy fire.

Watching those thousand-pound missiles arc high into the night sky was spectacular (and surprisingly loud). Each missile flew straight and level for a short period and then pitched high into the sky, where it would look for adversary radar signals and then come down at tremendous speed, ideally destroying the target with a powerful warhead that contained thousands of tungsten cubes. Once both missiles had been launched, we settled into a jamming orbit that covered the egress of all the fighters as they completed their bombing runs. While we couldn't see the effects of the strike from our position, a short series of radio calls confirmed that the mission was a success. With everyone off-target and accounted for, we all flew back down the Adriatic and returned to the carrier for a nighttime arrested landing, an event that was usually stressful, but on this day, it was only a relief.

1

AVIATION PREFLIGHT INDOCTRINATION

Building 633, U.S. Navy Photo

Naval Air Station Pensacola and Forrest Sherman Field are known as the "Cradle of Naval Aviation." When I arrived there in 1988, NAS Pensacola was the gateway to the promised land, a place that held the opportunity to wear a U.S. Navy uniform and fly something, hell, anything with props, rotors, or jets.

The late 1980s was an interesting time to join the military because, as the song says, "the times they were a-changing." The Naval Aviation Schools Command was working through a huge backload of prospective flight students, and there were lengthy delays in a training pipeline that was already almost two years long. The good news for students like myself was that we were all at the tail end of the Reagan Era buildup, and there were a lot of aircraft in the Fleet that needed pilots. The bad news was that we were closer to the end of this buildup than we wanted to be. The next stage of the Navy's history would be characterized by a major drawdown, and the understanding that we were competing for a diminishing number of cockpit seats definitely increased the pressure on us to succeed. So, when we all arrived in Pensacola, there was an implicit understanding that the good-natured rivalry that had always been part of the naval aviation training syllabus had been cranked a couple of levels higher.

When a Student Naval Aviator arrived at NAS Pensacola to start flight school, they reported to Building 633, a large edifice on Chambers Drive that still serves as the headquarters of this phase of naval aviation training. The construction of Building 633 dates back to 1941 and the desperate days at the beginning of World War II, when the building first began to serve as an entryway into naval aviation. This was a period during which the U.S. Navy went from hundreds of naval aviators to tens of thousands in just a few years. When I arrived in 1988, the building was certainly showing its age. I remember walking up the concrete stairs to the Quarter-Deck at the front of the building on my first day. The Quarter-Deck represented the formal entrance to the command, and I had arrived in my Service Dress Blue uniform as I had learned to do in the Reserve Officer Training Corps. In what turned out to be an anticlimactic event, a bored duty officer looked at me, stamped and signed my orders (providing "proof" of the date and time of my official arrival in Pensacola), and told me that my class would begin the next Monday.

As I think about my initial experiences in the building, I seem to recall that the interior was either warm or freezing cold, but never anywhere in between. The HVAC system was not the best, and it clearly hadn't been upgraded in a while. The interior paint was faded and colored by the humid air and decades of cigarette smoke.

The floors were worn vinyl tile, and I am pretty sure that the stairs made creaking sounds as you stepped on them. Although I was hesitant to spend much time looking at them, the walls were covered with old photos of Naval Aviation history. From my lowly perspective, the "patina" of the building was not a negative; it provided a sense of authenticity that appealed to me (and all the Naval Aviation enthusiasts who had ever walked its halls). For me, this atmosphere also provided a real sense of continuity with those who had come before us.

Not only was Building 633 the headquarters for the Naval Aviation Schools Command and its staff, but it was also the home of the first phase of flight training, known as Aviation Preflight Indoctrination (API). This course was the first step in the Naval Aviation training pipeline, and my performance and the decisions made by the staff instructors would set the course for the rest of my career.

The U.S. Navy may look homogenous to outsiders, but the truth couldn't be any more different. The Navy officer corps is made up of several different "tribes," and each of these groups has a very distinct culture. The first division is made between combat arms and staff officers. Staff officers are exactly what they sound like, doctors, lawyers, supply, and other critically important service members, none of whom are trigger pullers. The combat arms officers of the Navy are known as Unrestricted Line officers. Within the Unrestricted Line, there is further division. There are Surface Warfare officers who drive and operate ships; they are known as "black shoes." There are Submarine Warfare officers who drive and operate submarines; they are known as "bubbleheads." And there are Aviators, who are known as "brown shoes." (Yes, there are also Special Warfare types, SEALS, divers, and Explosive Ordnance Disposal, but they are small communities and largely stay out of the fray.)

At the time, one of the peculiarities of Navy uniform regulations was that Surface Warfare Officers wore black shoes with the Navy's Khaki uniform, while Aviators were authorized to wear brown shoes. When I arrived at NAS Pensacola, I was wearing black shoes. I approached the issue of my uniform from a very legalistic perspective. I was not an aviator and therefore had not earned the privilege of wearing brown shoes. I certainly was not the only student to take this position. When we all showed up to our first class, about half of the students had black shoes on. As the days of instruction continued, the transition to brown shoes was slow but steady. There was no order given, and the issue was never officially discussed with the whole class, but the transition to brown shoes gradually progressed across the group. At some point, I was among the last three or four students wearing black shoes. I wasn't intentionally being stubborn about the issue of shoe color, but I was a bit superstitious; I was determined to wear black shoes until API was complete.

One morning I arrived early and was sitting at my desk preparing for whatever we were going to do that day. An instructor walked in, saw me, stopped, and said, "Hey, come on out here for a minute." Now, our direct interaction with the aviators who taught the material was minimal, so being called out like this was alarming. I walked out into the hall with him, and he immediately asked why I was still wearing black shoes. I provided my reasoning and told him that I didn't think I had earned the right until the end of API. He looked at me a little strangely and said something like, "Are you planning to fail?" I said, "No." He then patted me on the shoulder, "We don't hedge in Naval Aviation. You are here because we think you will make it all the way. Go buy brown shoes." This provoked a sudden realization that I was already part of "the team." Sure, I still had to earn my seat, but the instructors wanted me to succeed, not fail. This simple interaction changed the entire tenor of my approach to flight school and naval aviation in general.

Despite the fundamental importance of all the academic material that was covered during API, perhaps the most critical event of the indoctrination period came at the very beginning of the curriculum. In addition to being home to Naval Aviation Schools Command, NAS Pensacola also serves as the home of the Naval Aerospace Medical Institute, an organization that every Naval Aviator knows as "NAMI." NAMI was the living nightmare of all the students in API because of the comprehensive flight physical that was commonly known as the "NAMI Whammy." While we had all undergone physicals in order to qualify for the school, the NAMI exam that we underwent upon our arrival at Pensacola was the gold standard of all the exams that would follow over the course of our aviation career. The real risk of the NAMI Whammy was that it was notorious for the discovery of disqualifying medical issues, and if they found something that disqualified you, there was generally nothing that could be done. While there were a few students who were worried about random health challenges you would find in any large group of people, most of us were as healthy as we could possibly be. What we were concerned about when it came to the NAMI Whammy was our eyesight.

While it has since changed, at that time no student could proceed forward with flight training as a Navy pilot unless their eyesight tested 20/20, uncorrected, by NAMI. This was a standard that the service used as one of the ways to thin the large numbers of applicants that they had, and as a way to divert otherwise qualified students into Naval Flight Officer (NFO) training. NFOs are officers who fly in aircraft but don't pilot them and who therefore were allowed to wear glasses if they needed them. I wanted to fly in the front seat, not ride, so my visual acuity was critically important.

When I think back to this milestone, I only remember one part of the extensive physical exam. After worrying about it for months, and hearing a constant stream of stories about people who had been disqualified, I finally found myself nervously sitting in a chair in the NAMI ophthalmologist's office. Without delay, the doctor entered the room, took my paperwork, and proceeded to check my eyesight. As each eye was covered, I smoothly read line eight on the eye chart and then line nine. After I returned to the exam chair, I was sure that I had gotten all the letters of the eye test right. I was just starting to feel my blood pressure lower when the doctor started looking into the back of my eyes with an instrument that had a very bright light. At some point, he paused and called over another ophthalmologist to look at something curious that he wanted a second opinion on. I desperately wanted to ask about what he had discovered, but I didn't want to force him into making a hasty decision or elevate the significance of the observation in any way. After the men conversed, the doctor turned back to his desk and started making notes on my paperwork. As he turned to look at me, he apparently could tell that I was about to have a coronary. Taking pity on my stress, he had the patience to tell me that I just had an unusual formation of blood vessels in the back of one eye and that, in general, all was well. I was 20/15, and my eyesight would allow me to proceed as a pilot trainee. The utter relief provided by this brief discussion was indescribable.

Although it was a critical part of our move to the next stage of the process, the academic syllabus in API was not particularly difficult. During the six or so weeks in the program, we sat in uncomfortable chairs in our starched khaki uniforms and learned the basics of meteorology, aerodynamics, navigation, engines, and basic flight rules – literally a "starter set" of information to give all the students the same foundation upon which to build the rest of their aviation career. When it came to the course material, in many cases, I was sure the lessons hadn't changed much since the 1950s; the old diagrams of engines and aircraft on the classroom wall certainly hadn't. The tests were easy but still somewhat stressful, not only because it would be embarrassing to fail any of the courses but because such a failure would inevitably result in disenrollment. However, an academic failure at API was very unusual. The course material wasn't just basic, but it was spoon-fed to us in a way that anyone who had ever served in the military would be familiar with, which is to say that when the instructor thumped his podium or stamped his foot, it was time to pay particularly close attention to that fact or figure because you'd certainly see it again.

Our lives in API were busy, but the training program only operated during the week. As a result, there were a couple of hundred young men who had decent paychecks, weekends off, and who were essentially living at the beach in Florida. This combination of circumstances provided our introduction to the "work hard, play hard" environment that would continue through flight school and into our fleet tours. During API, almost all of us lived on the base. These were the days when it was still a bit unusual for a young flight student to be married, and most of us lived in what was known as the Bachelor Officer's Quarters, or BOQ. The BOQ rooms in NAS Pensacola were great. They were essentially hotel rooms where we could sleep, eat, and study. There was a housekeeping service, good air conditioning, plenty of parking, and the cost was essentially accounted for in our pay.

Friday afternoons after class would usually find several of us sitting out front of the BOQ, drinking a beer, and considering where we were going to go for the evening ahead. After the first few days of class, I ran into a fellow Virginia Tech graduate, and we began to explore the town as a team. Pensacola had three main areas of opportunity for flight students. The first was obvious, downtown Pensacola. The downtown area was only a few miles away from the base, and the bars were always full of young aviators and college kids from around the region. A bar called Seville Quarter was generally a good place to start a weekend evening and was always a "target-rich" environment for young naval aviators looking to meet their first ex-wife. McGuire's was also a popular hangout that was a few hundred yards down the road from Seville. It was more relaxed than the frenzied atmosphere of downtown, with good bar food, cheap beer, dollar bills pasted all over the ceiling, and confusing bathroom doors. Trader Jon's was also an option; it was a famous bar with a Naval Aviation theme. Trader Jon's was always packed, but it was the semi-official home of the Blue Angels, and as a student, it always seemed to be a bit cheeky to hang out there, so we didn't.

The second area to try was out to the west of Pensacola, down the beach towards Perdido Key and Gulf Shores. One of the advantages of this area was that even though it was a bit of a drive, the base had a back gate that cut the transit time by half when it was open. The bar of choice in this area was the Flora-Bama. Now huge and unrecognizable, at that time, the old Flora-Bama was a low-ceilinged dive bar connected to a great deck that was built right on the beach. The bar was noted for the annual mullet toss, a drink called the Bushwhacker, awesome weekend parties, and its reputation among Navy flight students as a great place to meet women.

I distinctly remember entering the bar from the parking lot. You would quickly transition from the hot, bright Panhandle sun to the dark and cool interior. It would take a few moments for your eyes to adjust, but if you paused near the entryway by the cigarette machines, you would see that the wall was covered with photos of Flora-Bama fame. There were framed pictures from past events, regional bands, and autographed photos of Kenny Stabler and Jimmy Buffet. At some point, an entrepreneurial friend of mine managed to get his portrait on the wall. As a young aviation student, he spent some time as an intern with NASA. During his stay, he managed to get a photo of himself taken in a NASA flight suit while standing in front of a T-38 jet trainer. When autographed and placed in a frame, the photo matched the format of mementos provided by actual astronauts that were commonly seen in a variety of establishments all along the Gulf Coast. Somehow, he convinced the Flora-Bama management to hang the picture, or perhaps he placed it on the wall himself. Regardless, this photo served as an invaluable component of his attempts to meet women. If and when the astronaut photo failed to impress a young lady, his backup plan of having business cards made up attesting to his occupation as a "dolphin trainer" served as a somewhat hysterical conversation piece. I have fond memories of those very late evenings at "the Bama" and can tell you that this was the first place I learned that sleeping on the beach was not all that it is cracked up to be.

The third location for a good night out took a little more effort but was always worth the trip, and this was Pensacola Beach. The primary complication of traveling to the bars on Pensacola Beach was the distance from the base and the bridge that divided the beach area from the mainland. Despite the extra time that it took to get there, the beach bars were awesome; they collected young people from all over the nation. As our time in Pensacola progressed, I gradually learned that my friend had a nose for establishments like biker bars or strip clubs, and while I can't for the life of me remember the name of the place, there was one establishment on the beach that we visited several times. It was a low-ceilinged bar that had attractive waitresses, cheap beer, and good food. The primary challenge of going all the way to Pensacola

Beach was the police that patrolled between the beach and the town, and drunk driving, while very common in a state that still had drive-through liquor stores, was a sure way to be disenrolled. The primary choke point for the drive home was the bridge across the bay. If you made it back across the bridge, the odds of law enforcement interception greatly diminished. Rather than employ a designated driver in the manner intended, my friend and I "cleverly" split the risk. On one night, I'd drive my Blazer; on another night, he'd drive his RX-7. This practice didn't necessarily keep either of us from drinking but theoretically cut our individual risk by fifty percent.

In the regular breaks between lessons, the students would gather outside Building 633 and shoot the breeze on some picnic tables that had been placed in the space between buildings. In addition to the discussion about the academics (and debriefs of our weekend adventures downtown), two prevailing questions were discussed at length by the students during their participation in API. By far, the most common inquiry was, "What do you want to fly?" This was a surprisingly tricky question to answer. There were three major flight school pipelines in the Navy; rotary wing (helicopters), maritime patrol (large multi-engine aircraft), and jets. There was a definite hierarchy to these pipelines. Students were sorted into these programs based on their desire and their flight grades. There was also an allowance for the service's necessity to occasionally fill the required quotas with students who had the scores that qualified them to move to their desired pipeline, but the service needed them elsewhere (a much-dreaded decision known as "quality spread"). Rotary students were decided first, maritime students were second, and those who made the final cut went to jets. Of course, I think the majority of us thought that the "right" answer to the question was, "I will fly anything." Few wanted to publicly admit that they had a preference, some of this was to avoid later disappointment, and some was to avoid any bad luck. Despite our highly competitive nature, it seemed to be rather risky to say that you wanted to fly jets before you had even put on a flight suit.

The second most common question among the students was,

"Where do you want to do Primary?" While API was the first stage of training, the next step was Primary Flight Training. There were two locations where Primary training was conducted. The first was Naval Air Station Whiting Field, a base that was just to the north of Pensacola. The second location was found at Naval Air Station Corpus Christi, along the Gulf Coast of Texas. We discussed and debated the merits of each location at length. Much of our discussion was based on hearsay about how hard it was to navigate to and from the airfield, combined with vague stories from students further through the pipeline. I avoided these discussions whenever possible; I didn't care what I flew as long as I was flying and didn't care where I went to learn. The Navy could make the call, and I'd be happy with the result.

The curriculum in API wasn't all classroom material. In addition to the coursework, there were significant physical and physiological challenges to be overcome. There was an obstacle course that had an outsized reputation for difficulty, probably as a carryover from the movie "Officer and a Gentleman" that had been released about six years prior. The real obstacle course in Pensacola had a rope wall and a few barriers, but the most significant challenge came from the fact that much of the route was run on soft sand that turned your legs to rubber and sucked the life from you.

There were other events as well. In what was clearly a throwback to some 1940s concept of war-fighting preparation, we were all required to participate in a boxing match. Notionally, this event was included to eliminate any "shrinking violets" or some such thing. In real life, it was the only event where we experienced the true physicality of the competition that we were engaged in. Of course, the training for this boxing match was minimal. We learned how to spar, dodge, jab, and the essential maneuvers of the ring. Then the instructors paired us up by size and gave us gloves, head guards, and bite protectors. On "fight day," we worked our way through the class roster from shortest to tallest. Now, it should be clear that we aren't talking about a professional fight. All that was required of us was that we keep swinging through a match that consisted of three short rounds. As I am 6' 2", my bout was the final one of the day. When I took my place across the ring from the other tall guy in the class, I had to force myself to disregard my sense of how ridiculous the entire scene was. At the instructor's signal, we both stepped out into the ring and touched gloves; then we started wailing away at each other. While I think we all kind of wanted to be the person who knocked the other student out, it didn't take me long to realize how exhausting boxing was. Each of us got in a couple of solid jabs, hooks, and roundhouse swings early in the match. We did our best to bob and weave, but by the beginning of the last round, we had essentially ceased to move our feet and were just trading punches, more like "Rock 'em Sock 'em Robots" than "floating like a butterfly and stinging like a bee." I remember being very happy when the final bell rang. In the end, the entire class successfully proved that we all embodied the "spirit of the attack," and we moved on to our next event.

As we advanced through the API syllabus, one of the most difficult tasks for many of the students wasn't academic; their challenge came as a result of the fact that they hadn't spent much, if any, time in the water. It shouldn't be surprising that water survival was a significant interest for the Navy, and as a result, we spent a fair amount of time in the huge aviation training pool or Pensacola Bay. The training was thorough but not particularly advanced. We learned to float with our flight gear on, drown-proof ourselves by using uniform parts as flotation devices, and swim the four required "survival strokes." I don't have any particularly good memories of these events. Many of them were done as a group and could be a bit hazardous; imagine the churn of dozens of guys in combat boots kicking for their lives in the crowded pool during a one-mile swim. During these events, I did get my first sinus-clearing experience in the Dilbert Dunker (a device that was also made famous by the movie "Officer and a Gentleman") and participated in a para-sailing event in Pensacola Bay.

Para-sailing in the bay might sound a little like a country club event, but in true Navy style, the entire point was for the student to be dragged a couple of hundred feet into the air and cut loose from the boat so that they would come down in the choppy water underneath a real parachute canopy. This event required us to demonstrate that we could clear ourselves from the parachute without drowning. This may not sound difficult, but the thin nylon fabric and the parachute cords that connect the canopy to the harness are quite dangerous in the ocean. More than one aviator has successfully ejected or jumped from an aircraft, only to be dragged down to a watery grave by a parachute that is filled with tons of water. Despite the risk inherent in the event, I thought it was a blast. The only other thing that I remember about it, aside from the glorious view from high above Pensacola Bay, was that the boat operator helpfully started the event by dragging me and a few of the other students along behind the boat, partially drowning us before getting us airborne and cutting us lose.

Another important component of API was aviation physiology. In aviation physiology, we learned about all the ways that our bodies would try to kill us in an airplane. We learned why we shouldn't fly with a cold or stuffy head. We studied the optical illusions we may experience that were caused by light and shadow. We used spinning stools that trained us to recognize "the leans" and how the vestibular system in our ears could make us feel like we were straight and level when our eyes told us that we were in a turn (or vice versa). Most importantly for my future, we became familiar with how it felt to be deprived of oxygen at altitude and to recognize the symptoms of hypoxia.

Today, hypoxia training is done with a handy desktop system, but at that time, the Navy would put us in a big hypobaric chamber and pump the air pressure down until we got to the required equivalent altitude of somewhere around twenty-thousand feet. Then we'd take off our oxygen masks and do some simple tasks until we demonstrated the appropriate symptoms of hypoxia, and an instructor called out our number or tapped us on the shoulder and told us to put our mask back on. Like the para-sailing event, this training was significantly risky. Despite the entertainment granted by the flatulence that resulted from the decreasing pressure, putting people in a real hypobaric situation resulted in quite a few students hurting their sinuses, or discovering they had a filling in their mouth that contained trapped air, or experiencing one of the other real-world maladies of actual high-altitude exposure. However, the symptoms of hypoxia that I became familiar with in this training (hot flashes, tingling in extremities, and bluish fingernails) would later save my life.

Finally, survival training was also a key component of our API experience. While it is gone now, at the time, there was an excellent Navy Land Survival School on base. Not only did the building have a large classroom, but it was filled with displays of all the ways an aviator could survive across a range of environments. As I recall, it even had living samples of venomous snakes, spiders, and other critters that we would not want to meet if we had to jump out of our airplane over the swamps of Florida. Much like the other lessons, survival school was a combination of classroom and hands-on training. We learned the basics of first aid, wound care, how to find and purify water, how to make fire, and the things that we might eat in an emergency. We learned about the survival gear that was in our aircraft, everything from the small rafts in the seat pan of an ejection seat to the multi-person rafts that could be dropped from a plane. The final section of this training was a multi-day trip into the swamps of Eglin Air Force Base, a huge facility about ninety minutes from NAS Pensacola that houses several different training events for all of the services.

As I recall, this was a two-night adventure. We were taken by bus to a deserted area on the base and given a rudimentary set of survival equipment. On the first day, we had a lot of hands-on time with the instructors, building shelters, turning parachute-cord into fishing lines or traps, and the various skills of survival, all monitored or taught by our instructors. The next day, the instructors left us alone to "survive" with strict orders not to leave the camp. We built shelters and slept on the sand underneath those mylar survival "blankets" that may trap warmth but which are also very noisy (and keep humidity trapped inside). We hunted for food, but I don't think we ate much. This lack of food surely disappointed the Army Ranger students who briefly rampaged through our camp the second night, yelling and screaming, with machine guns blazing with blanks. We were later told that they were probably looking to score some supplies off of the soft Navy guys but were disappointed to find nothing but cold, hungry flight students fitfully sleeping in their parachute lean-tos.

There was no ceremony for graduating from API, although I do vaguely remember standing in formation at some point. However, what I do vividly recall is getting my first set of brand-new flight suits and my official Naval Aviation leather jacket. There was nothing more exciting than getting that highly coveted jacket. I think all of the students knew that it was a token of Naval Aviation that we had not yet earned, I certainly did, but it represented everything that we wanted to be. Today, that same jacket still hangs in my closet. The woven cuffs are trashed, it has a large hole in it, and the leather is as stiff as a board, but for me, it is just as exciting to look at as the day it was issued.

2

PRIMARY FLIGHT TRAINING

T-34C "Turbo Mentor"

At the end of API, we all were notified where we were heading next. I was ordered to move from Pensacola to Naval Air Station Corpus Christi, Texas, and report to VT-27, the "Boomers." VT-27 operated the T-34C, a turbo-prop driven two-seat trainer built by Beechcraft. The first stage of my flying adventure had begun!

In retrospect, my move to Texas was good for lots of reasons. I enjoyed Florida, but there were lots of distractions around Pensacola. This is not to say that there weren't a fair number of ways for a flight student to get into trouble in South Texas, but the environment was different. The beach was fun, but the sand was kind of brown and dirty, the waves weren't very good, and cars were allowed to drive on much of it. As for nighttime entertainment, there were a few fun country bars in town that were worth visiting. There was also a dance club that was a few blocks away from our apartment; it was the kind of late-80s bar that had cheap beer, was always dark inside, blasted Guns-N-Roses at high volume, and had dry-ice fog constantly floating along the floor. The other location we spent a lot of time was a pool hall that was not too far away. We spent hours playing pool, talking about flying, drinking beer, and eating far too much greasy bar food.

After I got to Corpus Christi, I ran into several additional fellow graduates from Virginia Tech, all of whom were beginning Primary at around the same time. I didn't know the guys very well at that point, but our shared college experience gave us a place to start building friendships. While I don't remember how it ended up this way, it wasn't long before six of us had rented a few apartments in the same complex. While I vaguely recall exploring the potential for renting a house on South Padre Island, it was far too expensive an option, and the apartment complex we ended up in turned out to be perfect. It was several miles inland from the base and the beach, had a small pool, and was largely isolated from the primary sources of trouble.

When it came to the academic portion of Primary, things moved fast. Although it seemed to us that we were "just" being prepared to fly, what we were absorbing was an entire organizational methodology of how to learn complex tasks in a very intuitional way. In Naval Aviation, it wasn't enough to just learn to fly an aircraft; we had to understand every plane we flew at a systems level. This meant we studied how the fuel system, electrical system, avionics, flight controls, and engine all worked. We started to learn about the aerodynamics of the aircraft and all the related structural limitations. We memorized our emergency procedures and learned to operate from checklists. Navigation training never stopped, and we continually learned about the weather as we progressed. Every section of training had its own checklist and set of instructions, objectives, and requirements. There was classroom instruction, simulator time, and actual flights. The syllabus was rigorously constructed and was executed in order. It was also a system that had to manage a fair amount of flexibility; we were always subject to bad weather, aircraft maintenance, and other scheduling issues, such as failing students, getting ill, or having other conflicts.

The next most important thing that we were introduced to was grading. Every flight or simulator that I would have for the next three years would be a graded event, and grades were critically important. Each event had its own grading card. Each card had all the maneuvers or objectives listed for that specific event. Some maneuvers were to be introduced or demonstrated by our instructor, but all the rest, including the catchall of "head-work" and "air-work" were graded. Even the solo flights that came later were graded. The grading scheme was simple, our performance was either "average," "above average," or "below average." A "ruler job" was a grade sheet that was all average. A student's objective was to be net positive, as in "I got two above and one below on that flight." A grade of "unsatisfactory" was also possible. This circumstance was known as a "down" or a "pink sheet." A student receiving a down didn't happen frequently, but it was not particularly uncommon. An unsatisfactory event stopped a student's progression through the syllabus and required remediation, usually a bit of extra training. The determination of what would be necessary was usually handled with a visit to the training officer. Students who had an unsatisfactory event were required to trade their flight suits for a khaki uniform, and this experience was known as the "walk of shame." The lesson that was communicated by the public exposure of a personal setback was the same as many programs in the Navy; it pays to be a winner. While API had essentially been a "pass/fail" experience, when we started Primary, we stepped into a competitive environment where our skill would decide what we would fly and where we would go in the Navy.

The aviation training pipeline was so full during this period that every transition to a new squadron resulted in some downtime before class started; this period was known as being in a "pool."

Some of our time waiting for class to start was spent wandering around the beaches of South Texas, but most of us wanted to put this time to good use. As we waited, we were encouraged to start learning about the T-34C aircraft, memorizing procedures, and familiarizing ourselves with the local flight rules. At some point, we were told that we were allowed to go into the squadron on the weekend, find an aircraft, and sit in the cockpit in order to get familiar with the switches and controls, preparing for a "blind cockpit" test that occurred early in the syllabus. As long as we didn't turn on the battery, nothing would function. We were repeatedly warned that anyone who accidentally initiated the engine start sequence would be immediately kicked out of the program.

So, one fine day a fellow Virginia Tech graduate and I went to the flight line, found an empty T-34C, and climbed in. We familiarized ourselves with all the switches, talked our way through the start sequence, and imagined the emergencies that could take place. We swapped places between the front and back cockpit at least once and continued to mentally rehearse things that we hadn't yet officially done in training. During our last run through the checklist, the battery had been inadvertently turned on (by someone who wasn't me!) and not turned off. As a result, as soon as one of us hit the start button, the starter engaged, and the prop started to turn. This initiated one of the scariest moments of my early career. "Battery off! Turn the battery off!" Fortunately, the battery was turned off within seconds, the starter disengaged, and the prop quickly came to a stop. There was a long pause while we waited for someone to grab us and send us home, but apparently, this huge error went unseen; the flightline was totally empty that day. Without speaking, it took only a few seconds for both of us to casually climb from the airplane and head for the flightline exit in as fast a walk as possible. While we both ended up making it to the Fleet, I don't think we ever talked about that event again; it was a secret that was best kept under wraps.

One of the things that the Navy did to manage the speed and intensity of our training in Primary was to assign each student an "on-wing." An on-wing was a flight instructor who served as a dedicated mentor for each student. I flew my first eight flights with a P-3 pilot who seemed rather gruff but was exceptionally professional. We would take off from the Naval Air Station and head to a working area where I learned all the basics of flying. I learned the "course rules," which were essentially the landmarks that we used to navigate out and back. I learned the radio calls, which were very simple but amazingly difficult to master as you were flying. We did stalls and spins and practiced emergency procedures like high or low-altitude power loss, stuck throttles, or malfunctioning props. We did lots and lots of touch-and-go landings. One of the primary skills that my on-wing insisted that I perfect was to correctly trim the aircraft. Each power change required an adjustment to the aircraft's trim to keep the control forces in the stick neutral. A sloppy aviator could get away with not completely trimming the aircraft, but this would affect every subsequent maneuver, making them more difficult to execute. While it was torture at the time, I carried this basic airmanship lesson through my entire aviation career (until I flew a jet that essentially trimmed itself). I always knew I was doing well on a flight when we were heading home, and my instructor started humming the theme from Superman. There was no spare time in this flight progression. My first Naval Aviation solo was completed on my fifteenth flight; it was 1.2 hours long, and I logged seven touch-and-go landings. The next week I went to the Officer's Club along with the rest of the students who had soloed and had my uniform tie ritually cut in half by my on-wing. This was the first rite of passage that I participated in as a Naval Aviator, and it is one of my favorite memories.

    The speed of this syllabus didn't give you much time to sit back and think about how cool it was to fly, but I do remember the wonderful feeling of walking to a T-34C by myself, starting it, calling to taxi, and taking off into the South Texas sky to go out and fly my solo flights. I was astonished at how quickly the Navy was allowing me to take this aircraft out and go do aerobatics, or fly to an outlying field and do touch-and-goes. It didn't quite feel like total freedom, everything we did was essentially part of a script or checklist, but it built our self-confidence very quickly. Although we constantly drilled our emergency procedures, I didn't have any real issues with the airplane, with the exception of one afternoon. I was in the back seat of the aircraft, having jumped on the opportunity to ride along on a mission where an instructor was leading other students through some formation flying. As we were coming home from the working area I started smelling smoke. I looked down below my seat to see a lot of "arcing and sparking." I let the instructor know, and he declared an emergency and landed the aircraft. It was probably fortunate that it was not a graded event because when maintenance came out to look at the aircraft, they quickly discovered that one of the detachable map lights had made it underneath my seat and shorted out on a battery contact. Not necessarily my fault, but it definitely was not my proudest moment.

Primary went by very quickly. In the end, I flew thirty-nine total flights in the T-34C, got about seventy flight hours, and was done with Primary in a little over five months. As I progressed through the program, I realized that I was doing rather well. While I was still hesitant to publicly admit that I wanted to fly jets, it seemed clear that there was an increasing opportunity that I might do so. Grades were everything, and the composite grades that we got were what fed something called the Navy Standard Score (NSS), a weighted average that gave the Navy an idea of where we stood against everyone who had ever been in the program. As the end of Primary approached, I started to allow myself to imagine what it would be like to make it to the jet pipeline and what base I might be sent to. At some point, I somehow learned that my grades were in the top third of the group. This was a great place to be, but it still had its own hazards. The first student was generally guaranteed their first choice of orders, but for those further down in line, well, the Navy reserved the right to send high-scoring students to one of the other training options. At the end of Primary, I wasn't at the top of the list, but I had done well, and received orders to Intermediate Jet Training at Beeville, Texas, where I was going to VT-26 to fly the T-2C "Buckeye" – I had gotten "jets!"

3
INTERMEDIATE JET TRAINING

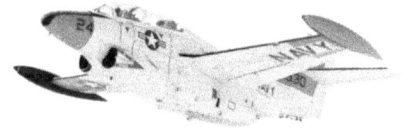

T-2C "Buckeye"

Beeville, Texas, was the perfect place to combine a bunch of student Naval Aviators and fast jets. The small town is about eighty miles to the north of Corpus Christi in the middle of, well, not much. Don't get me wrong, the area surrounding Beeville is a beautiful ranch and agricultural land, but it is lightly populated, the town is small, and homes are few and far between. From my perspective, it was clearly a great area to "turn jet fuel into noise."

When I arrived at VT-26, there was a significant backlog of students and at least a two-month-long delay before I could start the syllabus. At that point in my life, any delay seemed like forever, but rather than sit around in Beeville for a month or six weeks, I arranged Temporary Duty orders to a reserve adversary squadron called VFC-12 that was based at Naval Air Station Oceana. VFC-12 was a good place for a student to hang out. I got to see real aviators brief and debrief flights, and could stare out the window and watch F-14s, A-6s, and A-4s, any time I needed a "fix." The squadron didn't require that I do any real work, but I helped out by learning to be the Urinalysis Officer and sat in the bathroom collecting sample bottles, doing the required paperwork, and shipping them off to wherever they were tested. I also got to spend some time in the fabled Oceana Officer's Club. However, after my first visit to the club, I honestly didn't go there much. The environment was a bit too intimidating for a student who was there by himself, but it was a great place to have lunch.

As a reward for all my patient effort in managing urine samples, somebody in the squadron took pity on me and arranged for a couple of flights before it was time to head back to Texas. The first "good deal" flight was a backseat flight in a T-2C. This jet was used for out-of-control flight training at Oceana, and the pilot who flew it needed some time in the aircraft to stay current. So, they took me down to maintenance, put me in a G-suit, helmet, harness, and oxygen mask, and sat me in the back of the jet on a cold, gray, and overcast day. As a salty veteran of almost forty flights in a T-34, I felt sure that I'd be able to manage whatever was thrown at me. The truth was that when the jet took off, my brain kind of shut down for at least the first ten minutes as a result of being totally overloaded. This was my first flight in an airplane with a helmet and oxygen mask. In T-34s we used a headset with a boom mike. Now that I was wearing this new gear, my most pressing problem was that not only did it seem difficult to breathe and talk, but there was a hose hanging from the front of my face that just got tangled up in everything.

The next thing that caught me by surprise was that after takeoff we went right into the clouds. While I had gotten some basic instrument training in the T-34, all of my flights had been in clear skies, and this new experience was instantly disorienting. Anyway, whether I knew what was happening or not, the flight continued. We flew down the Virginia coast towards Marine Corps Air Station Cherry Point, where we were going to shoot an instrument approach and then come home. I remember some icing on the wings that the pilot was somewhat concerned about, and I was astonished at the fact that he let me fly for a little while on a TACAN approach. We finished the approach with a touch-and-go and then headed back to the north to Oceana. Along the way, the weather had gotten worse, and we shot an instrument approach into the field. As we rolled into parking by the hangar and stopped, the pilot said, "Hey, good job." Whether or not that was true, that single comment made my week, and I felt sure that I could handle my upcoming move into the T-2C.

While the flight in the T-2C was benign, it whetted my appetite for more. Fortunately, I got one more flight. This time I got a flight in the back of a TA-4J. I would become intimately familiar with the jet in the coming year, but at this time, the TA-4J was as exotic as any aircraft I could ever expect to get into. During this mission, we would be operating as a simulated aggressor against a real fleet fighter. I sat through the brief, nodding my head when it seemed appropriate while pretending to understand what we were going to do. I then went down to maintenance to get outfitted with all my flight gear and was assisted with the required connections as I climbed into the back seat of the TA-4J.

While I was now slightly less disoriented by the oxygen mask, the flight itself was a non-stop roller coaster. We launched into the working area off the east coast with another A-4 and, within minutes, were in a fight with aircraft that I barely saw before we were pulling several Gs in air-to-air combat. We did three or four air-to-air setups, and I was lost the entire time, which wasn't long because flights like this burned fuel at a tremendous rate and are very short. After about forty minutes, the pilot asked, "So what do you think?" I don't remember exactly what I said, but it was something like, "I think I need to do that again so that I can see what is happening."

With the time for my temporary duty "good deal" complete, it wasn't long before I made it back to Beeville. Within a couple of days of my return to the base, my class of T-2C students was off at a speedy clip. My group finished ground school and the endless introductory simulators, and then I found myself in the back seat of a T-2C for my first official flight, an instrument hop exactly like the one I had flown in Oceana, with one exception, I was now the one flying the jet from the back seat and was doing the instrument work for a real grade.

As students progressed through the T-2C syllabus, several specific instrument flights were encouraged to be taken outside of the local flying area. These flights were usually flown over a weekend, allowing the student to see new and unique instrument approaches and the instructor to enjoy a Friday or Saturday night in a place that was more fun than Beeville. Ideally, a student would find an instructor who was amenable to travel; they would agree on a location and then let the operations department know. Occasionally, however, an instructor or a staff member would want to go somewhere specific and they would just "draft" a student, using the student's training flights as a way to get to their desired destination. Early one week, I got called into the training office and told that I needed to talk to "Vinny" from the Training Wing. I gave him a call and was told that he needed to go to San Diego the next weekend and that I was at the right place in the syllabus for the trip. While this was a bit of a last-minute thing, I was happy to fly to Naval Air Station Miramar, and I excitedly spent the next couple of days doing flight planning and preparing for the multiple flights, or "legs" that the trip would take.

The first leg of our trip would take us to Cannon Air Force Base, New Mexico. This was about a five-hundred-and-fifty-mile trip, a distance that was well within the range of the T-2C. This event was in the middle of June, so one of the primary issues we faced would be the weather. While students like myself were easily capable of plotting a course and doing fuel calculations, one of the primary issues that all aviators constantly face is changing weather. Students just didn't have enough experience to judge the nuances of a forecast. In this case, there was a chance of afternoon thunderstorms at

Cannon, but the weather for the rest of the trip was forecast to be clear.

The first part of the flight was uneventful. We met in the Ready Room, briefed, and then took off for New Mexico. While you might think this would be a good opportunity to enjoy flying a jet with a huge canopy and a great view of the surrounding countryside, these were all "Air Navigation" events that required the student to fly "under the bag." The bag was a vinyl cover that a student pulled up from the back of the cockpit and buttoned around the canopy rim so that we could not see outside. Our focus was supposed to be entirely on the instruments. This was a form of torture, but as I came to see in the years that followed, this stress was intentional; good instrument flying was truly the backbone of operations around the aircraft carrier.

After two and a half hours of uneventful flying, we finished this first leg and landed at Cannon Air Force Base. The objective was to get fuel, look at the weather, file a new flight plan, and take off for Miramar. The unique thing about getting fuel at an Air Force base was that they used JP-4, a slightly different type of jet fuel than the JP-5 used by the Navy. After our jet was full of Air Force fuel, we crawled underneath it and Vinny showed me how to change the fuel control on the engines to account for this difference. We then got in and attempted to start the aircraft. Now, there were two important things taking place at this time that I was very aware of. The first one was there was a monstrous thunderstorm now approaching from the southwest of the field. The second one was that we could not keep our jet engines running; they each would just flame out after a few seconds. I went through the three starts on each engine that we were allowed by NATOPS (the book of procedures and limitations) and then stopped, waiting to get out of the airplane and call home. At a minimum, "the book" said that we needed to wait for thirty or so minutes before we tried again, in order to keep the batteries from overheating. Vinny, however, was in a hurry to beat the storm. So, he continued to try to start the aircraft until he fried the batteries, which, in retrospect, was probably not a bad thing, as the massive thunderstorm was now almost right on top of us. When it finally became clear that we were done for the day, Vinny reluctantly got out of the airplane. However, instead of phoning back to base, he found an Air Force maintenance crew that had the capability of rebuilding our batteries, and he worked some kind of deal so that they would repair them overnight.

When we arrived at the jet the next morning, we had fresh batteries and were again ready to go. After one additional unsuccessful start, we discovered that if we moved the throttle up to nearly 85%, the engines would not subsequently flame out. This discovery resulted in Vinny deciding that we would get both engines going, keep them at high RPM, and just use the brakes to keep the jet from getting away from us. Surely, the engines would be fine in flight. This procedure was definitely not in accordance with our NATOPS standards, but I was not courageous enough to intervene. So when we taxied for takeoff, I had to stand on the brakes in order to keep the jet from running away because of the high power setting required to keep from flaming out. As we taxied, Vinny explained that his risk mitigation decision for this challenge was that we would never bring the throttles below 85%. He was sure that after we landed at Miramar and got JP-5 from the Navy, the jet would be OK again. Fortunately, this plan worked, and we arrived in San Diego without further incident a few hours later. While I was expecting a debrief and discussion about our flight, after we arrived in California, Vinny said something like, "Enjoy Miramar, see you the day after tomorrow," and quickly disappeared.

The next time I saw Vinny was in Miramar Base Operations two days later, where we were briefed for the first leg of our trip home. This time we paid close attention to the instrument departure from Miramar. The procedure was somewhat tricky for a flight student, and I had been told that it was easy to get in trouble in San Diego's airspace. Filling the jet with JP-5 had seemingly "cured" our engine challenge, and our start and taxi were unremarkable. After we arrived at the hold-short of the runway, we were given an amendment to our clearance. Instead of the standard departure that I had planned for, we were to fly on runway heading and wait for radar vectors. I repeated this change back word for word over the radio. We were then cleared for takeoff, and away we went. After takeoff, we flew for a surprisingly long time on the runway heading until air traffic control gave us vectors on course, sounding a bit peeved. We turned to the east, climbed to our cruising altitude, and were just about over the California-Nevada border when we got a dreaded message "Please contact the San Diego Air Traffic Control Center at this phone number when you land." I nearly melted. Even as a student, I knew we were in trouble, and although Vinny didn't seem terribly concerned, I saw a "walk of shame" heading my way.

Despite my fear that we had busted our clearance, Vinny was remarkably quiet. During the first two legs on the way out to Miramar, he had frequently questioned me about my wind and fuel calculations. I was surprised that he was not doing the same on the way home. Instead, at some point, he came up on the Inter-cockpit Communication System (ICS) and asked, "How do you feel?" I thought he was worried about our departure and decided to play it as coolly as possible, "I feel fine." Ten minutes later, he asked again, "Are you feeling OK?" At this point, I had begun to notice a few things. One of which was that I was a little dizzy. The other was that Air Traffic Control was trying to talk to us, and we were constantly missing radio calls. I then took off one of my gloves and saw that my fingernails were all blueish, just like they had been in training. This was a clear sign of hypoxia, and I said, "I think I have hypoxia." He said, "Yeah, me too. Take the bag down and pull your green ring."

Wow, this situation was now very real. The "green ring" was the actuator of an emergency oxygen bottle that was in our ejection seats. I pulled the ring and then told him that I had brought the bag down. He then said, "I want you to declare an emergency. What is the closest divert field?" I looked at my chart and saw one of the best things ever. We were right over the top of Luke Air Force Base. In fact, now that the bag was down, I could clearly see the field. At this point, I was very surprised that I hadn't heard Vinny say, "I have the jet" and take the controls. Instead, I was still the one talking to air traffic control and flying the aircraft from the back seat. So, I got on the radio and declared an emergency. These are the "magic" words in aviation, and we were instantly a priority. Since I could see our destination, I declined any further help and essentially dove the aircraft down from twenty-five thousand feet and flew the airplane to a "straight-in" approach. The entire time we were descending I had been waiting for Vinny to take the controls from me, but as he still hadn't said anything, I continued to fly the jet until we were only a couple of feet from touchdown. At that point, he completed the landing and then gave control of the jet right back to me. Very non-standard.

One of the things about declaring an emergency is that when you land on a military base, you will generally be met by a few fire trucks and assorted emergency equipment. As I taxied the jet to Base Operations from the back seat, we were escorted to a parking spot by a parade of emergency vehicles that astonished me. Once these crews understood we didn't need their support, all but a single blue Air Force crew van departed the scene. After we shut down the jet and got out, an Air Force duty officer came over and listened to our story. Despite Vinny's reluctance, we were essentially ordered to go to the hospital on base. I'll say this for the Air Force, when it comes to things like this, they are efficient. Upon hearing about our symptoms, an Air Force flight surgeon gave us "Arterial Blood Gas" tests (which hurt like hell, by the way) and told us he'd be back in a while.

After waiting for about an hour, we were called into his office to hear the results. "You guys had carbon monoxide poisoning." Apparently, the levels of carbon monoxide in my blood were very high but were nothing when compared to Vinny's. He was a smoker and had a cigarette before the flight. As a result, his blood was already loaded with carbon monoxide, and he was close to being in a coma. It was at this point that Vinny admitted that he didn't take the controls after declaring an emergency because his vision was blurry and he couldn't see. The doctor then told us we were "med down" for at least forty-eight hours to clear our bodies of carbon monoxide. With the diagnosis complete, the next most important phone call of the day was made to the San Diego Air Traffic Control office. By the time Vinny called, they had "played the tape" and acknowledged that I had done what I was told and that it wasn't our fault that we flew right over La Jolla at a low altitude. I was off the hook. Not only was I not going to be in trouble for busting flight regulations, but I had also essentially saved the day from the back seat of the jet.

In the end, this single cross-country trip probably brought me closer to disaster more times than any mission in my next decade of flying. Not only did we never find the source of the carbon monoxide poisoning, but we continued to try to fly this obviously broken airplane home to South Texas. A three-day trip to San Diego and back eventually took twelve days, with a lengthy stop in El Paso, Texas, after it was discovered that our Liquid Oxygen Tanks in the jet had been damaged. To add insult to injury, the last leg of this trip was supposed to be a very important check ride that was a real milestone of that stage of training. This was part of the original bargain that Vinny made with me, and the check ride was supposed to be completed on the way home. However, I flew much of the last leg home in formation, dodging thunderstorms with another T-2C. Because I didn't do it under the "bag," Vinny graded the flight "incomplete," and the training department made me fly it again.

As I look back at my log book, I am astonished at how quickly the entire Intermediate Jet training experience went by. My first flight in the T-2C took place in March, and my last flight occurred in July. Five months. In those five months, we all went from students who could barely be trusted to talk on the radio to solo jet pilots who were expected to take off, complete a mission, and return by ourselves (with some oversight, of course). We still did not have an instrument rating, but weather gradually became less of an issue. We had soloed enough that we all felt comfortable in an aircraft by ourselves. Life was good. It was at this point that we were now facing the most important hurdle of the Intermediate Phase, our first Carrier Qualifications (also known as CQ).

Well, this was true for everyone else in my class. Unfortunately, I was still running a bit behind schedule as a result of my earlier extended cross-country flight with Vinny and had not yet flown the very dynamic Air-to-Air Gunnery syllabus (known as "Guns"). Despite being behind the class, the squadron training officer wanted me to continue to CQ with the rest of my shipmates. He knew that if I didn't go to the boat with the rest of my class, I'd have to wait until sometime in the fall before there was another opportunity. This would mean that I would sit without flying for a considerable period, losing the skills that I had attained but not yet made permanent. Fortunately for me, my grades were good, and my air work was solid, so the decision was made to allow me to proceed with CQ and complete the air-to-air gun syllabus after going "to the boat."

Carrier qualification is exactly what it sounds like, the art of safely conducting an arrested landing on an aircraft carrier (known as a "trap"). If successful, this was one of those skills that would immediately mark a new Naval Aviator as unique in the world of aviation. Lots of people around the world were flying jets, and very few did so from the deck of an aircraft carrier. As I look back, I think it is remarkable how quickly the CQ phase went. It was eleven days from the first time I climbed into a T-2C to fly my first Field Carrier Landing Practice (FCLP) to the day that I flew from Beeville out into the Gulf of Mexico to land on the USS John F. Kennedy (CV-67). Over those eleven days, I flew fifteen solo events and logged seventy touch-and-goes. The speed of this phase was partially intentional; the instructors didn't want students to think too much about the upcoming task. Much of CQ at that stage of training was just developing the right muscle memory, the ability to respond immediately to radio calls, and memorizing carrier procedures; like many hazardous tasks in the military, overthinking was sometimes dangerous. The pace of the process was also a symptom of how carrier qualifications were managed; these events were almost always on compressed timelines. Carrier availability, or "deck time," was at a real premium, and the weather was a huge issue. It wasn't just the training command that needed qualification traps, but every fleet squadron in the Navy needed to maintain some level of currency. So, when the training command got a block of time on a carrier to get students done, they pushed them hard.

Being in the CQ phase granted a student a certain amount of

status in the squadron. First of all, it made you a priority for scheduling, which was a bonus that meant that you were never canceled for lack of an aircraft. Of course, since it was typically the last task of the Intermediate Phase, it also meant that the squadron had deemed you to be professional and capable enough to move to the next step of Advanced Jet training. One of the ways this professionalism manifested was with our new relationships with the squadron Landing Signal Officers, or LSOs. Also known as "Paddles," LSOs were a separate breed from the rest of the instructors. LSOs were the advisors, trainers, and mentors who taught us the art of landing on an aircraft carrier. For me, while I looked up to and respected all the instructors, LSOs were the coolest of the bunch. When it came to the CQ phase, we could talk to the LSOs with a sense of equality that we couldn't talk to the other instructors. During this eleven-day endeavor, it felt like we were almost teammates (of course we were…to a degree, anyway).

On a carrier, the LSOs are positioned on what is known as the LSO Platform at the rear of the ship on the left (or port) side. From this exposed position to the side of the flight deck, they can watch every aircraft as it comes aboard. As they stand on the LSO platform, "Paddles" manages the safety of landing operations through the combination of a radio handset with which they can talk to the pilots and another handset that is connected to a set of lights that are mounted on a visual landing aid. This landing aid is on the left side of the ship and is known as the "Lens" or "Meatball." When you are flying real missions in the fleet, the objective is for there to be as few radio communications with aircraft as possible. In the training environment, there are no such restrictions. The radio commands that the LSOs use are standardized and are expected to be responded to immediately. There are several commands that might be made, but "Come left," "Right for lineup," "Power," or "Wave-off" are the calls that a pilot will hear on a normal day. As students, we were taught to react to these calls without question; anyone who ignored them would be immediately disqualified. We learned that we might not see the same thing that the LSOs did, but, much like our instruments, we needed to disregard our own perceptions and trust paddles.

As we began this new training process, one of the most fundamental things that the LSOs taught us was the grading scheme that would be part of our professional lives for as long as we flew aircraft off of a carrier. Every arrested landing by every fixed-wing pilot on an aircraft carrier, no matter how senior, is graded. This is a central part of Naval Aviation's safety processes and is strictly adhered to. Each "pass" is described in an arcane type of shorthand that is transcribed in a little blue book with a pencil by another LSO. The comments that the LSO makes about this pass, along with the grade, were used to debrief and track every landing a pilot made. The best grade possible is an "underlined OK," which is worth 5 points. This grade is usually only applied in case of emergencies, foul weather, or other exceptional circumstances (I think I only saw three or four underlined OK passes in my decades of flying). An "OK" pass is essentially perfect; it is worth 4 points. An "(OK)" pass is known as "fair," it is an average pass and is worth 3 points. A "Bolter" is a pass where the jet's hook skips the wires and the jet takes back off again; it is worth 2.5 points, and a "No Grade" is an ugly but essentially safe landing worth 2 points. If a pilot is waved off because of their technique, this is a 1.0 grade. The worst grade is a "cut pass," which is exceptionally unsafe. If you have a cut pass, you won't be flying around the carrier again until after you get more training and have a visit with some very senior people at a minimum, and if it was bad enough you may never get another chance. There are also colors associated with these grades, underlined OK was blue, an OK pass was green, an (OK) pass was yellow, and a No Grade was brown. These colors didn't matter in the training command but would be a huge part of my life in the fleet.

It was during my first FCLPs in the T-2C that I was introduced to the magnitude of the risk that was involved in our flights. During our preparations for the boat, an LTJG from one of the other squadrons was flying a TA-4J from Beeville to an outlying field called OLF Goliad in order to practice carrier landings. As I would later learn, the twenty-five-mile flights from NAS Beeville to OLF

Goliad were a lot of fun for solo TA-4J students. At the beginning of the FCLP period, four or five students would take off from Beeville at about the same time and race toward Goliad in order to make it to the outlying field first. The incentive to take the lead was that you would be the first one to get into the landing pattern at Goliad and could attempt something known as a "shit hot break." The landing pattern for carrier operations is flown at six hundred feet above the ground, and it is entered by a maneuver called a "break." A break is a one-hundred-and-eighty-degree turn that begins at eight hundred feet above the surface and gradually descends. As this turn progresses, the aircraft slows down, and the pilot gradually puts the jet into a landing configuration, lowering the flaps and landing gear. The objective was to come into the break quickly, pull four or so "Gs," and decelerate to a perfect landing approach.

However, the thing about flying at these speeds and altitudes is that there is not much margin for error. We were in the middle of a busy day of flying at Beeville when we all heard the news that an aircraft had gone down at Goliad. As we watched, a range of official steps were taken to manage the crash scene, and as with almost everything in the military, there is a process. The story that later made the rounds was that this young aviator had been low and fast as he approached Goliad. The investigation concluded that as he maneuvered the jet to align it with the runway heading, he had looked down in the cockpit to change the frequency on his radio. In the few moments that he was distracted by this task, he lost awareness of his altitude and inadvertently flew into the ground at high speed, perishing instantly. This was certainly not the last mishap that I would be in close proximity to, but as I later looked at the shattered parts of his aircraft that had been brought back from the crash scene and placed in boxes in an empty hangar on base, it was the first time that I realized that the "risk" our instructors talked about meant that there was a real chance that I might take off in a jet and not come home.

After almost two weeks of "bouncing," the time came to go to the ship. In order to become carrier qualified, T-2C students were required to get two touch-and-goes and four arrested landings. It is difficult to describe how little I specifically remember of this event. I do recall that the first curveball of the day was that I didn't get to fly out to the carrier myself. We had more students than aircraft, and I was the odd man out. So, I rode out to the boat in the back seat of a jet that was flown by an LSO who was acting as a "Lead Safe." His job was to lead the students out to the carrier and then orbit overhead while they got their arrested landings and catapults. At the end of this time, he would then land on the carrier himself. I would come to recognize that the LSOs were always looking to collect as many traps as they could themselves, and they lived with the hope that there would be extra fuel and time for a few "bonus" arrested landings. Unfortunately for my instructor, after the first batch of students was done, we were out of fuel, and the boat needed to adjust its location, so we got a single trap, shut down, and got out. As the ship was preparing for the next student event, I got the chance to wander around for a few moments in the hangar bay, but it wasn't long before I climbed into a T-2C that was parked on the flight deck. At the signal of a Yellow Shirt (flight deck director) and with a radio call from the Air Boss, I started my engines and prepared to get my traps.

I am now pretty glad that I didn't have time to think about the situation too much. Starting on the flight deck and launching right into the landing pattern after three hours of sitting in the back seat of a jet was not an ideal setup for a student. This transition demanded that my brain literally go from zero to one hundred and twenty knots in just a few minutes in a very dynamic environment. The good news was that once I was launched, I was directed into a holding pattern overhead the boat to settle down. Once all the aircraft were airborne, the Air Boss called us into the landing pattern by side number with the time-honored call of "Charlie." As is sometimes the case, my event did not move very quickly. After my two touch-and-goes and first two traps, I sat on the deck and waited to be refueled. In the end, the entire event took almost three and a half hours. Despite my fatigue, I was totally energized as I taxied out of the wires from the last trap, and the LSOs told me that I was a "qual" over the radio. After I was taxied over to the bow of the carrier, my aircraft was parked on the flight deck for the third time. Now totally drained, I didn't have to go far. I moved into the back seat of the jet and was flown home to Beeville by one of the LSOs.

With carrier qualifications finished, one of the last and most fun parts of the CQ phase were the LSO bets and the CQ party. Alcohol was a key part of the CQ process. Each student made a series of bets on their performance. We could bet on almost anything; the overall grade average at the end of our CQ period, the fact that we would not bolter or be waved off, or the average wire that we would catch (a ship typically had four arresting wires). The bets were not financial, they were alcohol-based, and the wages of each bet involved a bottle of liquor of the LSO or student's choice. Not being much of a betting man, I wagered on three of the "recommended" items; my overall grade average, no one-wires, and no bolters. This meant that three bottles of booze were on the line. As I recall, I lost two bets and won one, meaning I only owed a single bottle of booze, a bottle that was happily delivered to the head LSO. The CQ party itself is a very hazy event, but I understand that it did result in a visit by the Beeville police after I had gone home. Three days after going to the carrier, I was back in the jet, trying to finish up the syllabus so that I could move to the next phase of training.

Now that I had mastered the biggest challenge of the T-2C syllabus, the next mission was to complete the aerial gun phase. While the CQ phase was the most emblematic of the unique nature of Naval Aviation, the "Guns" phase probably required the most dynamic flying. To be clear, the T-2C did not have a gun, but it did have a very basic gunsight, so the goal was not to put holes in things. Instead, the objective was to demonstrate that a solo student could operate the aircraft in three dimensions and in close coordination with at least three other students. The gun pattern was flown around a T-2C that was pulling an actual gun banner. A gun banner was a forty-foot-long orange and white nylon flag that was physically connected to the aircraft that was towing it by several hundred feet of steel cable.

In the guns pattern, we learned to start a gun run from "high perch," a location where we were a few thousand feet above and to the side of the banner. We would then pull into what amounted to an "S" shaped maneuver that gave us a few seconds of simulated gun time on the banner before we pulled up and had to fly a similar pattern back into the same perch. When you had three or four aircraft in this pattern, it was exhilarating. It was also nerve-wracking because you had to maintain sight of all the other aircraft and be able to sort out the required distance from each other when managing the mild (hopefully) variations in the pattern. The guns syllabus consisted of several flights, more than half of which were solo; as a result, this phase gave us all a real feeling of professional accomplishment.

The guns syllabus also gave me my most severe emergency in the T-2C. On one of my last flights, before I moved to the advanced phase, I was selected to be the banner escort. There wasn't much to the job; as I recall, you were there to watch to see if the banner cable broke and identify where the nylon flag came down if it did. While I was flying the jet from the front seat, I had an instructor in the rear seat, and it was his job to keep an eye on things. We started and taxied together with the tow aircraft. We then watched the lead jet get hooked to the banner, and after the maintenance guys got out of the way, saw him take off. From our position next to the runway, we could see the tow wire snake back and forth across the runway, and then the banner leaped into the air behind the jet. As soon as the banner was airborne, we rapidly pulled onto the runway and, after completing our takeoff checks, were soon airborne and trying to catch the lead so that we could take a position above and to the side of the banner.

Now, at this point, I was very busy. I was essentially executing a "running rendezvous" and was joining the tow aircraft at a low altitude. This was a bit advanced for a T-2C student, so I was concentrating on my stick and throttle skills, trying to impress my instructor. I am not sure he had time to be impressed, because not long after takeoff he asked, "What are you doing?" in a very alarmed tone. I don't think I managed to get an answer out before I heard an odd sound and realized both our engines had flamed out and were winding down. The instructor quickly said, "I have the airplane," followed by, "Do the air start procedures!" An air start is exactly what it sounds like; you have a few quick actions that you must take in order to attempt to restart your engines in flight. As I ran through the memorized steps, the next call was one that I thought I'd never hear. The instructor got on the radio and broadcast to the jet that was in front of us, "Huck, we are going down!" After this call, there wasn't much to do, but to hope that at least one of the engines re-started. We were not very far above a mandatory ejection altitude, and if the engines didn't restart, it was going to be a bad day. However, happily, no drastic action was required. The left engine came back to full power quickly, and the right engine took a bit longer, but it gradually came back as well. We declared an emergency and quickly returned to the field. Today, I find it astonishing how little excitement there was about that event when we got home, and I still wonder what happened to those engines, but never heard a thing.

With the completion of the aerial gun events, I was now officially done with the Intermediate Jet Syllabus. The T-2C, which had initially looked somewhat imposing to me as a new student, was now a familiar friend that we called the "Tubby Two." The next challenge for me was the sleek TA-4J, a two-seat version of the A-4 strike aircraft affectionately known as the "Scooter." So, I walked through VT-26, got my log book and my NATOPS jacket, collected all my flight gear, and walked to the hangar next door, where I became a new member of the VT-24 "Bobcats."

4

ADVANCED JET TRAINING

TA-4J "Skyhawk"

As I arrived at my new squadron, my move to the TA-4J was typical of almost every transition in my Navy career. I had just come from T-2Cs, where, as an above-average student, I had achieved a certain level of status during my five months of training. Despite my pride in this accomplishment, the short walk across the parking lot from the T-2C hangar to the TA-4J hangar instantly dissolved any "social capital" that I believed I had earned and sent me right back to the bottom of the pile. There was nothing personal about this demotion; it was just how the system worked and was probably a good way to keep growing egos in check. Despite this temporary setback, it was now time to learn how to fly a "real" jet.

Known as "the Scooter," the TA-4J was an awesome aircraft to fly. It was fast, simple, and reliable. If it had any shortcomings, it was the fact that it was not very representative of the modern aircraft that some of the students would be moving to in the Fleet. The Navy and Marine Corps had used A-4s in combat in Vietnam, and despite their age, there were still a few dozen that were used as adversary aircraft in places like Top Gun or in dedicated adversary squadrons like the one I had done my temporary duty in. Every once in a while, one or two of these Fleet jets made it to the Training Command flight line at Beeville. Most of the aircraft in the Navy Aviation Training Command were painted in a highly visible orange and white paint scheme. Now, for the first time in our experience, we might get the opportunity to fly one of a few aircraft that were painted in gray camouflage. This was progress!

As we began our first classroom training events, the inherent attrition rate of flight school became very clear. My TA-4J class now included only about a dozen aviators. These were guys whom I would occasionally run into for the next couple of decades. One of the more notable students who started the syllabus with us was Lieutenant Dave "Doc" Brown. Doc was a Navy Flight Surgeon. He had been selected for an elite program that allowed him to earn his wings of gold and even become qualified in a fleet aircraft. As an MD, Dave had a "real job" in addition to learning to fly jets. He worked at the base clinic while also spending full time learning to operate the A-4. Although Doc was on a separate training track (aviators always take care of their flight surgeons) and had soon accelerated ahead of us. Doc did hang out with our group for quite a while, he wasn't a big drinker but generously volunteered to be the designated driver for a couple of boozy trips down to Corpus Christi. Along the way, we all told him that he was certainly heading to NASA. He would never admit this, but it was clear that it was in the back of his mind. He got his wings several months ahead of me and went to Whidbey Island, Washington, to learn to fly the A-6E Intruder. From there, the Navy sent him out to the carrier in Japan, where he flew operationally for several months. The last time I ran into him was at NAS Fallon, where he had become part of the staff of the Naval Aviation Strike Warfare Center. I was not surprised, however, when I heard that he had made it to NASA. He was a great guy, and his death in STS-107 had a significant impact on me, even though I hadn't seen him for years.

Starting the new syllabus in the TA-4J meant that it was time to buckle down and study. Despite how cool it was to be flying an aircraft that was derived from a combat-proven model, my first memories of this phase of training involved sitting in the back seat, under the bag again, doing instrument work. The cockpit was our office, and there wasn't much to it. The TA-4J was entirely analog, with "steam gages" (dials and tapes) to provide engine information, a three-dimensional attitude reference instrument that was known as the "ABAJABA," a TACAN, two UHF radios, and a very tiny backup gyro. A TACAN is a 1950's 1950s-era radio navigation aid upon which I would depend for the next fifteen years until GPS took its place. Essentially, a TACAN receiver gives the pilot a bearing and distance from one of many stations that are on the ground (even today, there are TACAN stations all over the globe). As a pilot, you tuned your TACAN to a particular ground station, and it was up to you to translate your bearing and distance into an understanding of your physical location (and to do this in your head). This is not as easy as it sounds, and knowing which way the TACAN needle would move as you traveled from station to station was the heart of the first year or more of our navigation training.

The first objective of the Advanced Jet Syllabus was to get students instrument-qualified. An instrument qualification would allow the students to fly solo missions through the weather and enable them to complete all the other phases of training without any unnecessary delay. The preparation for the instrument check-ride was very demanding. While being able to navigate to and from an airfield and fly instrument approaches was clearly a necessity, we also spent hours in both the simulator and the aircraft completing timed turns, climbs, and descents under the bag. Sometimes these maneuvers included simulated emergencies or failed flight attitude references. We also learned to execute a full set of aerobatics "under the bag" with only our instruments and a clock for reference. By the time I got to my Air Navigation 10X check-ride, that flight that served as the last step in my instrument qualification, I was certainly tired of the torture. It is probably telling that I don't remember the fight itself, but I do remember the endless preparation, studying all of the Navy's instrument flying policies and regulations, and preparing for the preflight briefing that had more of a fearsome reputation than the flight itself.

With most of my instrument syllabus behind me, one of the most satisfying flights of my early career took place at the end of the formation phase. As a recently instrument-qualified pilot, I was now able to take a jet into inclement weather by myself. The training in this particular case was known as a "Division Formation" flight. When two aircraft fly together in formation, it is known as a "section." For three or more aircraft, the formation is known as a "division." On this particular day, I arrived at the base on an overcast and rainy morning. Over the previous eighteen months of flying, a rainy day like this generally meant that my flight would be delayed or canceled. While there were several events in the syllabus where we could rely on the instructor's instrument qualification to go flying when the weather was bad, most of the time, clouds or rain meant a day off. Today, however, was different; bad weather now meant inconvenience, not a cancellation.

I remember how professional it felt to sit in a briefing room with the instructor and the other student. The ready room was essentially empty; it was just us. We sat in a small briefing space and talked our way through the event. After the instructor described the maneuvers that we would conduct and quizzed us on emergency procedures and weather minimums, he spent a fair amount of time talking about the weather forecast at the field and the potential divert fields that we would use if the weather got so bad that we couldn't land at home. The feeling of professionalism merged with a strong sense of the surreal as we put our flight gear on, walked out to our aircraft, did a preflight, and started the aircraft up. In the back of my mind, I was still waiting for someone to say, "No, the weather is too bad; go home."

After I had the aircraft running, I asked for and received my instrument clearance for the working area. When all three aircraft were ready, we taxied out to the runway and then took off into the clouds individually. As was the case many times in my early flying years, I instantly became too busy in the cockpit to get a real sense of how awesome it was to fly by myself in the clouds. However, when I broke out of the weather and found myself in a huge hole that just so happened to be where we were supposed to do the mission, a little lightbulb of awareness started to flicker. After a few moments of delay to see if we had enough space to complete our mission, our instructor picked a clear point in the area and established what was known as a "TACAN rendezvous." I quickly assessed the location of the point he identified, and I headed in the appropriate direction. The resulting rendezvous felt almost like magic. I found the instructor's aircraft and joined on his wing, just like it said in the textbook. Within moments, my friend also joined up. We were now flying in a division and had gotten there through the weather ourselves; this was what we were there to do!

For the next forty-five minutes or so, we ran through the syllabus events of division formation in the midst of an impressive ring of towering cumulous clouds. We did a few "break up and rendezvous" drills and practiced an "under-run." We also did as much division aerobatics as the weather allowed. When all the training objectives were complete, we took a moment to check the weather. It still wasn't good; in fact, it had gotten a bit worse. So, without any further delay, the instructor detached us from the flight, and we all picked up individual instrument clearances from Air Traffic Control. Within moments, I was back into the clouds by myself, conscious of the weather, my fuel state, and the distance to my divert field. Despite the stress, this is what we were training to do, and I had enough "spare" situational awareness to realize this. So, I navigated back to the field, shot an actual instrument approach, and landed. Walking from the jet into the hangar that day was one of the best feelings I can remember. Although it was still early in the program, I felt like I had arrived as a Naval Aviator. I had put all the pieces of our training together into a one-point-seven-hour flight and executed the mission without any drama. If there was a single moment when I felt sure I would make it to the Fleet, it was in the short debrief after the flight. The instructor brought us into the small room, told us that we had done a good job, gave us each a grade sheet with a couple "aboves," and dismissed us. Just another day in the office. What a cool friggin' job!

Once we had mastered how to reliably get an aircraft to and from an objective, it was time to learn the basics of fighting the jet. We started with the basic building blocks, the most important of which was learning how to coordinate with another aircraft in a tactical environment. The first task was to learn how to fly tactical formation (or TACFORM), a set of aggressive formation flying skills that provided the basis of the weapons and air combat maneuvering that we would conduct later in the syllabus. TACFORM taught us how to maneuver in combat spread, a type of formation flying intended to provide maximum mutual support for two or more aircraft. In this type of formation flying, we would fly about a mile apart at a set speed and maintain relative position with altitude adjustment instead of our throttles. Once we could stay in position, we learned how to maneuver the formation, with and without radio communications. This involved making 90 and 180-degree turns and using big "wing flashes" to indicate intent. As simple as it was in concept, this was demanding flying. It was difficult just to maneuver with a friendly aircraft, and it was hard to imagine how difficult it would be when an adversary was added to the mix.

When TACFORM was complete, students would move into whatever advanced phase had an opening. For me, this meant preparing for the "Weapons Detachment." This was probably one of the most fun phases of the A-4 syllabus. While not particularly long or comprehensive, during this period, we were taught about the basics of low-level flying and air-to-ground weapons employment. In "O-Navs," we practiced tactical navigation. This meant we flew at five-hundred feet above the ground, at either 360 or 420 knots, using paper strip charts that we had made to help us maintain our route. There was no GPS at the time, so in order not to get lost, we flew the way most aviators had since WWI. We used compass headings, known airspeeds, and timing to navigate between points on the barren South Texas landscape. Once familiar with the basics of low-level navigation, the level of difficulty was increased by adding imaginary weapons employment to these low-level flights, picking out trains or trucks that were driving on the rural roads of South Texas, doing "pop-up" climbs, and conducting imaginary strafing runs on these unknowing victims.

The final section of the phase involved flying out to Naval Air Station El Centro for about a week. This austere base is in the desert along the California – Mexico border and serves as the winter training ground for the Blue Angels. For the weapons detachment, the base provided consistently great weather and easy access to several gunnery and bombing ranges. While today's students generally don't get to fire any ordnance until they are assigned to their fleet aircraft, at this point, we were still allowed to shoot and bomb the desert. During this detachment, we were going to employ three weapon systems; we got to strafe a ground target with the 20mm cannon that was in the wing root of the jet, fire 2.75" Zuni rockets from a rocket pod, and rain "blue death" from the sky. "Blue Death" were the small, blue training bombs that replicated the trajectory of real bombs and which had smoke cartridges in their nose to show impact points.

The weapons flights were a blast, but they were over far too quickly. We would take off, fly out to the "Shade Tree" bombing range that was just a few miles outside of El Centro, and get into the "wheel of death." Much like the old aerial gun pattern, when we arrived at the target, the four students in the flight would gain the spacing required to safely and sequentially attack the target. During these events, we learned the communications that helped us know who was where in the pattern and executed our practice strafing, rocket, and bombing runs. As was the case in previous tactical experiences, much of the challenge was centered around keeping the proper distance from the other aircraft in the pattern.

On the days when we would launch with real ordnance, we briefed, climbed into our aircraft, started, and taxied to the end of the runway, where we were "armed." This was the first big difference between practice and real events. Since we had actual weapons at this point, we had to taxi to an area where the jet's "safety" could be removed. This meant that the gun was charged, the umbilical for the rockets was attached, or the pins were pulled from the bomb racks. Once that was complete, we took off and flew the ten minutes into the bomb range, where we set up our wheel and, when cleared by the Range Safety Officer, commenced to attack.

For me, these flights all seemed anti-climactic. We had all been warned that the 20mm cannon in the jet was troublesome and that many of us wouldn't even manage to fire a single round, especially if we pulled zero or negative "g's" at any time before our strafing run. This was fine from the training perspective, as the point wasn't necessarily to see how accurate we were, but it would be a bummer as a student. I got lucky with the cannon on my jet. As I circled for my first actual attempt to shoot, I armed the gun, called "in hot," and dived on the target. With the "pipper" of the basic gunsight on the target, I pulled the trigger and got most of my rounds off. I then pulled up out of the dive, safed the gun, called "off safe," and continued in the pattern. I remember how cool that experience was. The cannon had a slow cyclic rate, and the thump of the rounds going off was awesome. With only a few rounds remaining, I circled for my second attempt, established my dive, armed the gun, called "in hot," and pulled the trigger when the pipper was on the target. Click. Nothing. Crap. I pulled out of the dive, safed the gun, and continued the rest of the flight with a jammed or non-functioning weapon. As it turns out, I seem to recall that I was one of the few students who got any rounds off at all. The word on the flight line was that none of the weapons had been very thoroughly cleaned.

The next flight was rockets. We got the opportunity to fly with a single pod that contained four Zuni rockets. Again, we taxied, armed, and took off into the range. The rocket pattern was flown at a higher altitude than the gun pattern but was fundamentally similar. Get into the circle, get the range cleared, and then begin to attack. The Zunis had no warhead but were literally a blast. Pull the trigger and get an immediate response with a "whoosh" of a missile speeding down range. While there was no warhead, the feedback was pretty immediate because you could generally see a puff of dirt where you hit. Of course, you weren't supposed to watch for the hit. The danger with all of these events was something called "target fixation," and it was repeatedly hammered into us that once we had pulled the trigger or "pickled" the bomb, we needed to begin climbing off target. Many an aviator had focused for too long on the ground in order to see how close their ordnance was to the target and inadvertently become a part of the desert themselves when they flew too low to safely recover.

My final weapons flight was the bombing mission. We started the event with four blue bombs, and as before, we taxied, armed, and took off into the bombing range. For this mission, I had an instructor in the back seat of my aircraft who was tasked to act as range safety. This meant that the flight was still "mine," and theoretically, the instructor wouldn't do more than talk on the radio and keep an eye on all the students. After a normal launch and transit, we arrived, circled the target, and each began to drop our bombs, one by one. Such a blast. All of my bombs hit somewhere near the target, a result that was not as bad as it sounds, as there were lots of humorous stories of bombs being flung all over the desert. Ideally, each blue bomb would issue a smoke cloud when it struck; sometimes, this didn't work. In this case, a worker at the range graded the event and phoned it back to the base. After we all had completed our last attack, we declared that we were all "safe" and began the quick flight back home. After landing, I got a "good job" from the instructor, who had honored his role of an observer and who hadn't touched the controls once.

When we were all complete, there was some kind of Weapons Detachment party at the El Centro officer's club. I don't recall it being too crazy, but it is where I earned my first temporary call sign of "Mr. Green Jeans" as I somehow tracked mud into one of the instructor's rooms after taking a shortcut across an area where an irrigation line had busted. All of the students with above-average weapons grades were recognized at the event. As I recall, I had higher than average marks in the rockets and my gun run, but was only one bomb away from making it into the top group. Even though it didn't matter, I was totally bummed by this failure. Now that I had seen how it all worked, I knew that with one more chance to try bombing, I'd "shack" every one of my bombs. But there would be no second chances, and aside from the HARM missiles that I would later fire from an EA-6B, this was the last opportunity I would have to employ ordnance from an aircraft.

When I arrived back in Beeville from the weapons detachment, I was mentally prepared to move to the next big combat-related section of the syllabus, Air Combat Maneuvering (ACM). However, much like had happened in T-2s, a Carrier Qualification (CQ) event was approaching. As the Training office looked for students who were ready to go to the boat, they found that I would just barely have the minimum number of hours required, and my grades were good. As a result, I was pulled into the upcoming CQ event. This was fine with me. Thanks to my initial experience in T-2s, FCLPs, also known as "bouncing," was a reasonably familiar pattern, and I enjoyed the repetitive nature of the events. My first CQ flight took place with an instructor, and the rest of the fifteen flights were all solo.

The TA-4J was a much different jet to fly in the landing pattern than the T-2. With the big delta wing and single engine, it was much easier to find the right angle of attack and fly smooth passes. The biggest danger in the jet was that you didn't want to get slow because the J52 engine did not "spool up" very quickly, and the drag of the delta wing increased rapidly at higher angles of attack. As the training progressed, I logged 78 landings over those two weeks of bouncing. My fellow CQ students and I raced from the base in Beeville to the outlying field in Goliad in our jets, much in the same way as the guy who had crashed the previous summer. It is difficult to describe, but the combined feeling of independence and responsibility was intoxicating. Not for the last time, I could understand where the risk of such a seemingly benign event came from. Of course, the LSOs were happy to bring us down to earth by telling us that our landings just weren't that good, but we only half believed them (which is about normal for LSOs). As our TA-4J FCLPs concluded, we were anxious and ready to go to the boat. However, this time CQ would be different. Unlike my T-2C experience, where we flew from Beeville to the USS John F. Kennedy just off the coast of Corpus Christi, when FCLPs were complete this time, we all got into a Navy C-9B transport and were flown to Naval Air Station Key West, where we would CQ aboard the USS Lexington, (CVT-16).

It was an amazing honor to become carrier-qualified on this ship. In 1990, the old carrier was definitely an artifact of the past. The ship was built in 1942, saw combat in World War II, and remained in the Fleet through the next forty-eight years, ending up as a training carrier. While the USS John F. Kennedy that I had qualified on in T-2s was an early example of a "supercarrier," the USS Lexington was small and narrow. Not all of it was old-fashioned, it had been modernized to the extent that it had steam-powered catapults and arresting gear, but amazingly it still had a wooden flight deck. The rumor among the students was that it had pumps running all the time to ensure that it didn't sink. None of this mattered to me at the time, but I now reflect on this small but direct connection between the beginning of my flying career and the heroes of the war in the Pacific; it is amazing.

As was always the case on such a detachment, there were more students than available aircraft. So, as we arrived in Key West, we were divided into two groups. The first group would do their qualification events the next day, and the second group would fly the day after. I was in the second group. These assignments were immediately followed by a strict lecture from the LSOs for those of us who now had thirty-six hours to kill. We were told that it was okay to go out into town that night but that it would be prudent to consider ourselves confined to the base BOQ after that. The Navy had invested two weeks of time and effort in FCLPs, and nobody wanted a student to be unable to fly because of some unfortunate incident in Key West.

Now, I will say that in my recollection, the direction to stay in the BOQ wasn't exactly an order but only a strong suggestion. Anyway, that night, we walked from the BOQ and into town for a beer and some food. Key West was known as "Key Weird" by the LSOs, and it had quite a reputation. As we walked into town, I was expecting to be shocked by the behavior that I had heard about, but it seemed like a cool beach town with lots of bars. Despite the buildup, nothing remarkable happened that night, aside from sharing a couple of beers with the LSOs out at Sloppy Joe's bar and listening to their stories of the Fleet. There was no doubt that we drank a fair amount of beer, but I walked home to the BOQ early, with the warnings from our instructors still ringing in my head.

In the bright light of the next morning, the urgency of the warnings from the LSOs had significantly decreased. The first group of students had gotten up early, been driven to the airfield, and were preparing to fly out to the USS Lexington for their CQ events. The rest of us met in the lobby of the BOQ and wondered what to do. Now, I am not a rebel, so when one of the guys picked up a pamphlet out of the rack near the door and said, "We should charter a boat and go snorkeling," it didn't ring any alarm bells. The options were to sit around and do nothing, or go out and enjoy the water for a few hours and come home. The consensus was that this was not the kind of thing that the instructors would be concerned about. After a quick phone call from the payphone at the front desk and a discussion of how much it would cost, four or five of us got a cab and went down to the dock to meet the charter crew. Along the way, we bought a case of beer but deliberately didn't go crazy with alcohol. We had all agreed that this was to be a subdued event, not a typical beer bust. When we arrived at the pier, we found that the boat was a large catamaran that was run by a man and his wife, chartering people like us to make ends meet. They were pleasant enough, and when we loaded up, they put our beer on ice and drove us out to a set of reefs to begin our snorkeling adventure.

As I recall, the slow trip out to the reef took an hour or so. We dropped anchor, got a briefing that suggested that we should watch out for moray eels, and then distributed rented gear; everyone got a mask, but only a few got fins. We had been snorkeling for about thirty minutes or so when one of the guys near me started thrashing around in the water. The skipper of the boat saw this and yelled that a couple of guys should help our friend back onto the boat. There was no sense of urgency at this point; after a few minutes the guy stopped yelling, and when he made it to the boat we helped him back aboard. It was at about this time that we noticed that it looked like he had been whipped. There were large red streaks all over his upper torso, and he was in immense pain. The skipper immediately called everyone back onboard, started the boat, and began to head back to Key West. As he did so, the situation became much more urgent; the young aviator went into shock, passed out, and stopped breathing. "Holy shit!" As a couple of guys started CPR, the skipper called for help from the Coast Guard on the radio. Unfortunately, there were no Coast Guard ships in the vicinity. Instead, the captain of a large cigarette-style motor boat heard the emergency call, said he was close by, and offered to help.

Fortunately, after a few minutes of rescue breathing, the stricken young aviator was breathing on his own again, but he was still unconscious and was moaning in pain. So, we waited and watched as this large motorboat pulled alongside us. Now, there was a decision to be made. Which of us was going to take this guy to the hospital? After some hesitation, two of us climbed aboard the boat with our friend, both of us in our swimming gear. The ride back to the pier was much faster in this huge motorboat. The trip that took the catamaran about an hour only took the motor boat fifteen or so minutes. The captain of the boat had called ahead, and as we pulled up to the pier, we saw that there was an ambulance waiting, along with a crowd. Within a few moments, our shipmate was transferred from the boat, and the ambulance rapidly disappeared with our friend. It was at this point that the two of us found ourselves standing on the pier with no real idea what to do next. Thankfully, I had my wallet and knew which hospital they were taking our shipmate to. So, we managed to find a cab, got to the hospital, and found that our friend was in stable condition. Great news!

The bad news was that it was now time for somebody in our little adventure to notify the chain of command – and this job ended up being mine. Fortunately, I had a little slip of paper in my wallet with the phone number of the duty officer. There were no cell phones at the time, so I asked to use a phone at the nurse's station and made one of the most unforgettable phone calls of my early career.

"Hi Sir, this is Ensign Springett. I am here in the emergency room of the Key West Hospital. A group of us went snorkeling, and one of the guys had an encounter with a jellyfish. He stopped breathing, but he is in stable condition now."

As you might imagine, there was a long pause at the other end, followed by, "We will get the flight surgeon and be right there."

Within about thirty minutes, two anxious-looking men in flight suits arrived at the hospital; the first was the Executive Officer (XO) of my squadron, a Marine Lieutenant Colonel who was in charge of the CQ detachment, and a Navy flight surgeon. The flight surgeon briefly listened to the story and went off to find the injured student. I was pulled aside and directed into an empty room with an angry senior Marine. After relaying the details of our adventure, I experienced what I remember as one of the more brilliant but subdued ass-chewings of my young life. There was no yelling, but much shame was generated. Summary – we were idiots. With ass-chewing complete, the flight surgeon returned after a few minutes with good news; the student would be ok and, surprisingly, would be released within an hour or so. With this news in hand, my friend and I got the "ride of shame" back to the BOQ with the XO, where the story about our mishap was already circulating among the rest of the students and instructors. Needless to say, I didn't go out for beers that night. The next morning the last group of students collected in the lobby waiting for a van to take us to the base. As we sat there I was shocked to find our jellyfish-inflicted friend coming down the stairs. The unlucky swimmer was still in pain, experiencing something like a bad sunburn, but had been judged sufficiently recovered to fly by the flight surgeon.

My TA-4J carrier qualifications were much more compressed than my day-long adventure in the T-2. We were taken out to the airfield in a van, briefed, and launched out into the Gulf of Mexico, where we soon found ourselves circling overhead the carrier. We spent some time in the overhead pattern but were rather quickly told to "Charlie" by the Air Boss. Within minutes, I was in the break, slowing down for my first touch-and-go. While T-2C students needed two touch-and-goes and four arrested landings, in the TA-4J, we were required to get two touch-and-goes and six traps. I don't remember what order they occurred in, but I ended up with two touch-and-goes, six traps, and two bolters (landings where the hook did not catch a wire). At one point, I was sidelined for fuel and got out of the aircraft long enough to wander through Lexington's hangar deck, but I was quickly back in the aircraft. Now topped off, I completed my required landings and was released to fly back to NAS Key West by myself, a newly carrier-qualified TA-4J pilot; total flight time of the event, was 2.5 hours. I was a "qual!"

While I still had a few low-level and instrument flights that needed to be completed, with my carrier qualification done, the remainder of my Advanced Jet syllabus was dominated by the Air Combat Maneuvering (ACM) phase. I remember ACM as fun but stressful. ACM involved a new emphasis on managing the energy state of an aircraft that was a really good fighter, with the fastest roll rate of any jet in the Navy, but which didn't like to "depart" or stall. In preparation for this phase, all the students got a refresher flight in a T-2C, reinforcing our procedures for Out-of-Control-Flight. The truth was that the TA-4J was a reasonably forgiving platform at slow speeds, but there were situations that you didn't want to find yourself, and most of them involved being more than 60 degrees nose up while you were running out of airspeed.

As we began the ACM phase, we initially learned to "fight" against a single aircraft. Everything was done with basic building blocks. We started one of several set-ups with our jet behind an instructor's aircraft, immediately giving us an advantage. Starting with an advantage taught us how quickly a fight could be lost if we fought the jet inefficiently or misjudged our energy state. Next, we started a number of set-ups with an instructor behind us, teaching us how to start a fight from a defensive position. After we satisfactorily demonstrated an understanding of offensive and defensive maneuvering, we moved on to "neutral" set-ups, where we would start an engagement heading straight at each other at around 400 knots, passing no closer than five-hundred feet laterally. These are the kinds of air combat maneuvering scenes you see in the movies, and they always began with the call "fight's on" over the radio, and ended with the call "knock it off." As we progressed, we were taught to differentiate the difference between a one or two-circle fight, the appropriate responses for our initial maneuvers, and that there were occasions it was just smart to "extend" and run away.

The ACM phase included the worst flight in the TA-4J for me. At this point in the syllabus, I could see the end of the training pipeline, and my wings of gold were only weeks away. My grades were good, and I felt like I might be getting the hang of the mission. Well, as things happened, I was scheduled for two events in a single day. The first event of the day was an ACM 4 flight with an instructor with whom I was pretty comfortable. The flight went well but had what was nearly a catastrophic end.

During my preflight walk around the aircraft, I noticed that the right main landing gear strut was more compressed than the left one (they look like big shock absorbers). I mentioned this to my plane captain, and the contract maintenance support dutifully brought out the equipment to charge the strut with some additional nitrogen. With this small bit of maintenance complete, I manned up the aircraft, started, and went out to fly what turned out to be a decent flight. ACM was a true challenge, and pulling the jet around and attempting to gain an advantage on another aircraft was definitely a lot of fun.

When we returned from the mission, I led the section from the working area back to the field. I brought my instructor back into the break and entered the landing pattern. As the lead aircraft, it was my job to land on the downwind side of the runway so that I would not drift across the path of the second aircraft that would land just behind me. On this day, there was a reasonably strong right-to-left crosswind at the field. This meant that the downwind side of the runway was the left side. As a result, I would land on the left half of the runway, and my instructor would land just behind me on the right half.

At this point, the details of the following incident require just a little more discussion of the TA-4J. The A-4 series of aircraft had long landing gear relative to the size of the aircraft; they almost looked like stilts. When the jet was designed in the early 1950s by Ed Heinemann, the longer length of the landing gear was required for the A-4 to carry large weapons on the centerline store station, as the inboard stations on the wings would almost always have external fuel tanks attached. The long landing gear occasionally made the Scooter unpredictable on landing, especially in a crosswind. In some circumstances, the wind was very likely to tilt the jet and send it careening off the runway. As a result, the aircraft had been fitted with "pop-up" spoilers on the trailing edge of the wing that would kill lift as soon as the jet landed and a weight-on-wheels switch was compressed; of course, this switch was on the right main landing gear.

When I landed, it instantly became apparent that my right main landing gear had been over-serviced. The extended strut kept the oleo from compressing as much as was required to pop up the spoilers. As a result, the crosswind picked up my wing as advertised, and I was now leaning somewhere near ten degrees to the left while going more than a hundred and twenty miles an hour. I immediately began to skid across the runway on what now felt like a bicycle instead of a tricycle. This might have been a little easier to manage had I landed on the centerline of the runway, but since we were landing as a section, I had landed in the center of the left half of the runway, giving me half of the space I would normally have.

In a fraction of a second, I knew that I had three choices. The first was to abort the landing and try to take off. Unfortunately, I quickly judged that if I tried to take off again, I would continue drifting left while I did so and might leave the paved surface before I got airborne. The second choice was to eject. I knew the aircraft was very likely to flip over if it left the runway, and I understood that if it did, I would probably be crushed. However, I also knew that as a big guy, ejecting with any kind of angle of bank would result in me impacting the ground without getting a parachute. There was not much margin in those old ejection seats, and the aircraft needed to be wings-level to be safe at that speed. The third choice was just to ride it out - and so I did. I skidded at an angle across the runway while I slowed down, trying to stay on the pavement with a combination of brakes and rudder. After several seconds of intensive concentration, the aircraft came to a stop at the very edge of the runway, having left a long set of dark skid marks from where my struggle began. After I came to a halt, I just sat there in the aircraft for several seconds, breathing hard. Within a couple of moments, my instructor, who had landed just behind me on the right half of the runway, pulled next to me in his jet and came up on the radio, "We can go now."

After we taxied back to our line and got out of our aircraft, I expected that my crazy and dangerous landing would be discussed at length. However, the instructor either didn't find it that remarkable, or he hadn't seen it. Instead, he gave me a net-above grade sheet and sent me on my way. As a result, I returned to the ready room after a short break to prepare for my next flight, ACM 5. Well, this flight happened to be scheduled with the Commanding Officer (CO) of VT-24. It is at this point in this book that I considered breaking my own rules about not using names because the CO was a jackass. Now, to be clear, this was more than three decades ago, and in the intervening time, I have also been known to be a jackass in a jet. I also have been the CO of a couple of squadrons at this point, so I know that the CO has a lot on his mind when he is taking a student out to fly. In this case, it was quickly apparent that the CO had not read the briefing guide for the flight.

Normally, the early flights in each new phase "demonstrated" or "introduced" one or two new maneuvers. These demo maneuvers were flown by the instructor first, and then the student got a chance to fly them and be critiqued, but not graded. In this case, the CO made me attempt to demo the new maneuvers that were on the grade sheet without ever having seen them. Even worse, he was what we knew as a "screamer" and was very vocal about my failure to execute these maneuvers correctly. At some point, I was tired of being yelled at for trying to read his mind, and essentially just did what I thought was right and let him stew. After we landed, the aircraft was silent. I got my flight gear off and found him in the briefing room, eyeballing the grade sheet. I was fairly certain I was going to get my first "unsat" of the program as I watched the CO consider what he was going to do. As he publicly relayed his disappointment with my performance to a couple of instructors who were in the room, I remember the moment that he realized that the procedures that he wanted to grade as unsatisfactory were, in fact, ungraded demos. As this realization hit, his tone instantly became less aggrieved. There was no apology, but instead of giving me a "down," he left me with a "ruler job" of an average flight and walked away. Am I still carrying a grudge? I guess so. Is there anything that will change this? Of course not.

As things happened, my unhappy flight occurred the day before one of my two roommates also had a bad day of flying. It was now Friday, and I was not scheduled, so I went to the bowling alley for lunch. When I arrived, I found my buddy at a table looking pretty depressed. We ate lunch, and I listened to him discuss a fairly bad flight that was going to derail his aspirations to be a pilot. We shared stories of our misfortune, and after a while, we decided to head home. Not surprisingly, an ad-hoc competition was established; the last one back into the garage would have to drive for the rest of the evening. I had a Chevy S-10 Blazer at the time, and he had a Trans Am, so it quickly became clear that my speed would not win this race. As we headed down the road, he began repeatedly passing me, taunting me with his superior speed. I knew that there was no way I could beat him with my truck, but much of the route home involved sharp corners and narrow roads, and this kept our distance pretty tight. As we entered the development where our rental house was, the route to access our garage required two right 90-degree turns and then a left 90 into the building. Seeing that I could not gain the lead at this point, I just turned and drove right across a neighbor's yard at a high rate of speed, cutting across the front of my friend's car to take the lead. While the geometry of this maneuver put me in the lead, at this point I was going very quickly. When I realized how rapidly I was approaching my destination, I slammed on my brakes. All four wheels of my Blazer were locked up as I slid across the driveway and into the garage, where I miraculously came to a halt within an inch or so of the garage wall. The manner of this victory seemed like some kind of sign and started a chain of events that found us at Pinky's (a bar in Beeville with pool tables and dirt floors), a friend's house (until the booze ran out), and then another buddy's place that was miles outside of town. Along the way, the Trans Am ended up stuck in a gravel ditch, and one of the Jeeps that had become part of this experience hit a deer. To say that this night was epic is to understate just how much it felt like it was reaching some kind of a crescendo. Fortunately, the night died with a whimper rather than a bang, but it is one of my favorite memories from flight school.

Most of my ACM flights took place in the airspace around Beeville, but at some point, the weather in South Texas turned bad, and the Training office realized that they had a couple of students who would not be ready for their scheduled winging unless they tried something different. This resulted in a quick three-day trip to NAS El Centro, where we finished the last two ACM check flights. These flights were notable because there were now two students fighting one instructor, and they were a blast. ACM sorties complete, we flew back home to Beeville, where I landed, taxied up to the hangar, and received the ritual "dunking" of a last flight. When an aviator has their last flight in a squadron, they are doused in water. The water could come from a firehose, it could come from a fire extinguisher, or it might even come from a bucket. I don't know why this ritual exists, but in this case, two buckets of VERY cold ice water were poured over my head. This took place right before what was known as my "soft winging," where a leather patch with my first Naval Aviation wings was placed on my flight suit by the very same Marine Lieutenant Colonel who had chewed me out only a couple of months before in Key West. There would be a formal winging ceremony in the weeks to come, but soft wings allowed us to wear wings on our flight suits until the "real" ones were presented later.

Surprisingly, this was not to be my last TA-4J flight. When I arrived back at Beeville, I was expecting my soft wings and to be told what aircraft I was going to fly in the Fleet. The good news was that I did get my soft wings; the bad news was the squadron didn't have an answer for where I was headed next. Instead, the XO pulled me aside and told me that the Navy Personnel Command now thought that I was too tall for most of the Navy's jets. Now at six foot two, I was hardly a giant, and I had just spent seven months flying the jet with the smallest cockpit in the Fleet. However, bureaucracy is nothing if not pedantic. What I was told was that I would be assigned to fly the F/A-18C Hornet if I could get an Aviation Physiologist to sign off on the fact that I fit in the ejection seat. Since there were no F/A-18Cs in Beeville, I needed to fly to somewhere where there was one.

This is how I ended up flying to Naval Air Station Jacksonville, Florida, with a Commander (CDR) who was going to be the next squadron XO. NAS Jacksonville was where the Hornet training squadron, VFA-106, was based. If all went as planned when we got there, I'd sit in a F/A-18C, the physiologist would say that I "fit fine," and all would be good. So, early one morning, we took off from Beeville in a TA-4J and headed to Florida. This flight was awesome because, for the first time in years, it was not a graded event. In fact, I was amazed that the CDR offered to let me have the front seat for the flight home. We arrived at the base in Florida without incident, walked into the hangar, and were met by the Aviation Physiologist. After days of consternation and an unexpected trip to Florida, it took all of five minutes for me to sit in a F/A-18C and be given a "thumbs up." Within another minute, the paperwork was appropriately signed off. I was ecstatic; I was going to be a Hornet pilot. Forty-five minutes later, our TA-4J was full of fuel, and all we had to do was return home. The CDR then made one of the most fateful calls of my career. He dialed the squadron to let them know that I had been signed off and that we were heading back. As he was talking to the squadron, he turned to look at me, said, "Ok, got it," and hung up. The next thing he said changed my life, "Now they want you to sit in everything."

In a moment, I went from a prospective Hornet pilot to "Oh shit." So, we walked down the flight line at Jacksonville, and I sat in an S-3B; I fit. Then we got back into our jet, and I flew us north to NAS Oceana, where we got lunch. After the meal, we went to the flightline and I sat in an A-6 and an F-14, and unsurprisingly, I fit. This adventure had now turned into a very long day. The CDR decided we'd fly to Pensacola and spend the night and then head home in the morning. So, he took the front seat and flew us down to Pensacola. When we arrived at the airfield, it was getting dark. As we came into the break and entered the landing pattern, we quickly noted that our left landing gear indicated "unsafe." This was not good; we were low on fuel, and it was nearly dark - not much time to troubleshoot. I broke out the emergency checklist, and the CDR did all the emergency procedures, including applying positive and negative G's. We flew by the tower, and as they looked at us with binoculars, they told us that it appeared as if the gear was hanging partially down. This was the worst circumstance possible for us. If we couldn't get the gear all the way up, we might have to go out over the Gulf of Mexico and eject. Fortunately, there was a T-2C returning to the field, and they offered to help. The T-2C pilot joined in formation, took a look underneath us, and said that it appeared that the gear would not come fully down, but it would go fully up. This was great news as it meant that we could safely land on the runway with our wheels up.

Within minutes, the helpful T-2C landed, and firetrucks lined the runway. It was nearly dark, and as I later learned from more than one person, word quickly got out about our emergency. The squadrons whose Ready Room windows overlooked the runway were soon packed with people watching the drama. One of the unique things about the TA-4J was that the jet was almost always flown with two external fuel tanks hanging from the wings. We were far from the first TA-4J that this had occurred to, and the last-ditch answer to a landing gear issue was to bring the gear up and land on the drop tanks. After deciding that this was the right answer, the CDR lined the jet up on the runway and brought us down onto the concrete very smoothly. At first, the sensation was not much different than using the landing gear; there was just a rumble. The CDR maintained us on the runway centerline until the rudder stopped being effective, and then we slid a bit sideways and came to a halt. There had been sparks trailing out from under the wings the entire time, and as the jet slowed, the residual JP-5 fuel that had been trapped inside the drop tanks spilled out and caught fire. As a result, when we finally came to rest, the cockpit was surrounded by flames. After what seemed to be a long time, I could feel the radiant heat through the Plexiglas and decided I didn't want to burn. I gave the firefighters about three seconds to put the fire out, and then I pulled the emergency canopy jettison handle, a cartridge-activated system that blew the canopy off the jet. Unfortunately, I then remained in my seat as I struggled to get out of my parachute harness. As I fought to unlatch the last buckle, I watched the CDR sprint from the airplane. Within a few more seconds, I found myself entirely covered in fire-fighting foam and then was helped away from the aircraft by the fire department.

The rest of that evening was spent in the hospital, where they did a post-accident physical, took chest X-rays for no apparent reason and, as always, collected lots of blood. Much later that evening, I collapsed into bed at the BOQ, totally drained from a day that started with me believing that I was going to get orders to fly Hornets and ended with me being in a TA-4J mishap in Pensacola. As the next day dawned, the emotional roller coaster wasn't quite over yet. Later that morning, a couple of instructors from Beeville ferried a new aircraft to Pensacola so that we could get home. The CDR and I got in the jet and headed back to Texas without much conversation. We arrived in the break that afternoon, landed, and went into the hangar to take off our gear. Given all that happened, I wasn't entirely surprised that the CO and XO met us in the Ready Room. What I was surprised by was the next thing the CO said as he reached out to shake my hand, "Congratulations, you got Prowlers!"

5

"WELCOME TO THE FLEET!"

EA-6B On Flight Deck, U.S. Navy Photo

Although it sounds like an exaggeration, I honestly had no idea what an EA-6B was. I suppose I had seen a few of them while I was on my Midshipman training cruise when I spent a couple of days hanging out on the USS America (CV-66), but the thought that I would eventually fly Prowlers had never crossed my mind. As I was standing there in the Ready Room with my brain spinning and jaw agape, one of the senior Marine instructors in the squadron grabbed me and pulled me into his office. He pointed to a picture of a Prowler on his desk and let me look at an EA-6B NATOPS manual. As I paged through the thick book of systems descriptions, aircraft limitations, and emergency procedures, he helpfully pointed out that there "were lots of nitrogen bottles" in the jet, a comment that didn't make any sense to me at the time. At least he tried.

Prowlers. For those who are not familiar, the EA-6B Prowler was a carrier-based, four-seat variant of the venerable A-6 Intruder, the tough all-weather bomber that gained its reputation in Vietnam but which served in combat through the late 1990s. The Prowler was essentially the "extra cab" version of the Intruder and had two seats added in a three-foot fuselage extension. The EA-6B was introduced in 1970 and flew until its retirement in 2019, a remarkable length of time for a carrier-based aircraft – and amazingly, a period that covered almost half of the entire history of naval aviation itself. The EA-6B was designed to carry the ALQ-99 airborne electronic warfare system. This system consisted of several sensitive radio-frequency receivers primarily located in the tail of the aircraft, a signal-processing system operated by two weapon systems operators in the two rear crew seats, and the ALQ-99 jamming pods that were carried under the wing. While the aircraft could employ HARM missiles, the truly critical capability that the jet provided were the smart electronic warfare experts in the back two seats who could sort out ambiguous signals, correlate them with the correct adversary radar systems, and with the flip of a switch, send thousands of watts of power into their receivers.

The fact that an EA-6B could cause chaos across the radio frequency spectrum was one of the primary reasons that most of our peacetime missions were flown alone. As an EA-6B crew member, our common fate was to launch from a carrier or airfield, go on a mission by ourselves, and do "those Prowler things." This mission was sometimes described as "Prowler go long." No self-respecting fighter or attack crew wanted to be seen anywhere near the big, ugly four-seater, especially if we were jamming. Unfounded rumors of impotence, cancer, or other health-related effects of our high-powered transmitters were also common (these things seemed funny at the time, not so much now, as cancer has afflicted many of my shipmates). As "Prowler guys," we made much of the thin gold film on our canopy that supposedly kept us safe from our own radiation and told the fighter guys to cover their genitals when they flew near us, lest they only produce female children. Anyway, despite our lonely life during peacetime, during wartime, the calculus was dramatically different; there were lots of fighters out there, but not so many jammers. No fighter or bomber was allowed to go anywhere in a combat zone without jamming support.

A typical EA-6B crew consisted of one pilot (me) in the left front seat and three Electronic Counter-Measures Officers, or ECMOs. The ECMO in the right front seat handled navigation and communications, and the ECMOs in the rear two seats operated the majority of the electronic warfare systems. While pilots clearly always flew the aircraft, the ECMOs routinely rotated through the other three seats. The EA-6B was a big aircraft for the flight deck, at about fifty-six thousand pounds on a normal launch, and it could be tricky to fly. The fuselage extension that provided room for the two additional seats substantially altered the flight characteristics of the aircraft when compared to the A-6, and as a result, it was capable of surprising pilots in unhappy ways. Soon after its development, several aviators, including its first test pilot, discovered that the aircraft was unforgiving in a stall or spin, and the first test aircraft was lost in a crash when the test pilot intentionally put the aircraft into a spin and could not recover. In fact, of the 170 aircraft built, more than 40 crashed or were lost to mishaps. The jet was capable of pulling 5.5Gs, and was fully aerobatic, although many maneuvers had been administratively restricted due to the risk of accidents.

One of the strengths of the EA-6B was its two J-52 P-408A engines, which each had a little over ten thousand pounds of thrust at max power. While a total of twenty thousand pounds of thrust doesn't sound like much when compared to today's fighters, the aircraft was capable of maintaining over five-hundred knots until it ran out of gas and technically could break the speed of sound when diving from its service altitude of forty-thousand feet. At low altitudes, there weren't many aircraft that could keep up with us, at least not without running out of fuel very quickly. Up high, however, the aircraft was a bit of a pig, especially when carrying the normal loadout of three pods and two external fuel tanks. In general, the EA-6B was a wonderful aircraft to fly, and even though the EA-18G that eventually replaced it is much, much more capable, I think it is missing a bit of the character that the earlier aircraft developed over the years. I am sure this will change.

Not only did the assignment to Prowlers define the aircraft that I would fly, but it established the location where I would live (or at least keep my stuff) for the better part of the next two decades. While all the other carrier-based aircraft in the Navy's inventory had east and west coast bases (primarily in Virginia, Florida, or California), the EA-6B community was stationed in only one place, Naval Air Station Whidbey Island, Washington.

NAS Whidbey provides the basis of a book all by itself. The island sits at the eastern end of the Strait of Juan de Fuca. It is farther north than anywhere in the eastern U.S., with a latitude similar to Newfoundland, Canada. Among other things, this means that the summer days are long, and the winter days are short. The island is covered with tall pine trees and is surrounded by the always-cold waters of Puget Sound. With the exception of about a month during the summer or winter, the weather can generally be summarized as 50 degrees and overcast. At 58 miles, it is the longest island in the continental United States. The Naval Air Station sits near the north end of the island and is about a two-and-a-half hour drive north of Seattle if you take I-5 and follow your GPS across the amazingly scenic Deception Pass bridge.

The local area itself is very rural, and there are dozens of beautiful farms in the mountain valleys. With the rugged Cascade mountains to the east and the Olympic mountains across the sound to the west, the island's skyline was always defined by the ragged outline of those snowy peaks. Despite the high likelihood of being "50 degrees and overcast," Whidbey was noted to have more "basic Visual Flight Rules" days than any other Naval air station in the continental U.S. What this meant from a practical perspective was that the weather was generally better than 1000 feet of ceiling and 3 miles of visibility. Honestly, I think these statistics somehow left out all the foggy mornings (and there were many.) Whidbey Island has been home to the Naval Air Station since WWII and had initially hosted flying boats. While the infrastructure has gradually changed and vastly improved, half of the air station was still known as "the Seaplane Base." In general, it was a great place to fly and a good place to live.

So, I was headed to fly Prowlers on Whidbey Island. While I was a bit dismayed at first, I quickly got over my disappointment. I had gotten my wings and was going to go fly jets from an aircraft carrier. I packed my truck and headed…well, I went straight west first. As is normal with the Navy, I had a school to attend along the way, and it was a notorious one, Survival, Escape, Resistance, and Evasion (SERE). This school was based in NAS North Island, California, a scenic base in the heart of San Diego Bay. The SERE course had a dire reputation among many flight students, mostly because we didn't know anything about it, other than we had heard that you better make sure you keep your graduation certificate so that you wouldn't have to take it again. At its most basic, part of the course covered the survival skills we had seen in our initial Land Survival course, but the balance of the training was designed to give us a sense of what we could expect if we had to eject from our aircraft over enemy territory and were captured. We learned to survive, escape, resist, and evade.

Not long after I arrived at NAS North Island, I ran into an acquaintance from flight school. I don't remember knowing this beforehand, but when we caught up with each other's news, it turned out that he was heading to Whidbey to fly Prowlers as well. As Monday arrived and we started SERE, it quickly became clear there was no homework and the classroom material wasn't that difficult, so we took it upon ourselves to enjoy San Diego in the evenings. The primary target for two young Naval Aviators with brand new Wings of Gold was Wednesday night at the NAS Miramar Officers Club.

Now, this topic requires a quick sidebar. Wednesday night at the Miramar Officer's Club was definitely as good as its reputation. This is the place that some of the most famous scenes in the first Top Gun movie were modeled on, only in real life, there was no singing. Everyone in carrier aviation knew that Wednesday night at Miramar was "Ladies Night." These were the days when gate guards were ordered to allow civilian women on base without an escort so they could come to the club. The social scene in the bar and the patio deck out behind the building were legendary. Music was loud, the beer ran freely, and there were lots of beautiful southern California girls looking to catch their own Top Gun. It was, as the fighter guys say, a "target-rich environment." This lifestyle was not limited to Miramar, by the way. While we could not manage to connect the dots on this trip, it is worth noting that Friday nights at the Naval Air Station Oceana in Virginia Beach were just as good as Miramar on Wednesday, and it was a notable achievement to take a jet across the country and attend both in a single week. The East Coast culture was slightly different, there were generally as many attack pilots as there were fighter pilots at Oceana, but the gates to the base were open to any women who wanted to attend, and the weekly party was just as rowdy and outrageous on the east coast as it was on the west coast. To get a sense of just how libertine these nights were, at the time both clubs hosted strippers in back rooms, although in Oceana they were billed as "lingerie models."

Despite all the fun that was had, the downside of this particular Wednesday night for my friend and I was that we had to get up very early the next morning, shuffle onto a government bus, and be driven up to Warner Springs, an austere Navy training facility at 3200 feet up in the high desert. Anticipating that some of the students may be inclined to enjoy themselves while on liberty, we had been strongly warned to get a good night's sleep and make sure that we were very well-hydrated before the heart of the course began. The physical and mental challenges we faced at this camp were very stressful. Despite this warning, it is at this point that I can assure you that when we arrived back at our rooms somewhere after midnight, we were definitely "well hydrated," but when my alarm went off at five a.m., I certainly was not rested. Three or so hours later, when we finally unloaded from the bus, I did not feel very well. While I am not going to discuss the specific events that took place at this training, I can tell you that it was one of the best courses I ever attended (and I never, ever want to do it again). I will also suggest that if you ever find yourself on the way to SERE, I can absolutely guarantee that you do not want to begin this part of the course dehydrated and with a huge hangover.

With SERE in the rear-view mirror (and multiple copies of my certificate in hand), I headed north to Whidbey Island and arrived in late May of 1990. Arriving at my first command as a Naval Aviator was exciting at first, and then, not so much. The EA-6B training squadron is VAQ-129, known as the "Vikings." This squadron is where all EA-6B flight training was conducted and was known as the Fleet Replacement Squadron or FRS. Older language from previous generations had known this unit as the Replacement Air Group, or "RAG," and we used these terms interchangeably. My first impression of VAQ-129 was a little bit underwhelming. The squadron felt like a bit of a backwater. My friends who had selected other aircraft spent their first summer with wings learning to fly their new aircraft; I had entered the longest student pool of my career. The only job I needed to learn at that point was to stand Squadron Duty Officer (SDO), a twenty-four-hour job that was quite significant, especially in the days before cell phones. As the SDO, you were the communications focus for the squadron after normal working hours. If there was an issue or an emergency with a squadron sailor, officer, or aircraft, the outside world contacted you, and you were responsible for getting the information to the right senior leader. However, aside from SDO, those of us who were waiting in the pool didn't have much else to do. Not only was this boring, but it was a horribly inefficient use of our time, (but nobody cared what we thought.)

Despite not flying, that summer in Whidbey was pleasant. I had a decent paycheck and no real job. I rented a townhouse with two of my classmates, wandered around in the Cascade mountains with the Toyota pickup that had replaced my Blazer, and occasionally studied my new jet. On weekends, several of the students would either head down to Seattle or up to Vancouver, searching for a good time. But no flying. At least no jet flying. I did get volunteered for one mission, and it turned out to be eye-opening, but not in a good way.

Dozens of Military Low-Level Routes crisscross the nation. These routes are reserved for military aircraft only and allow pilots to fly at low altitudes and high speeds in order to practice evading enemy air defenses. During that summer, I was ordered to join four of my fellow pool members and go flying with five Civil Air Patrol pilots who were flying Cessna 172, 182, or 210 aircraft in order to conduct an aerial survey of several low-level routes in the region. Several routes were the responsibility of the Commanding Officer of NAS Whidbey Island spread out over Washington, Oregon, Idaho, and Nevada, and they needed to be surveyed every five years. Anyway, back when the government had the resources to do so, the Navy would pay for the Civil Air Patrol to fly along all of these low-altitude routes looking for new obstacles, buildings, wires, and even tall trees that might be of interest to an aviator flying below five-hundred feet, at more than four-hundred and twenty knots. Most of the routes were five miles wide, and we had five aircraft so that we could fly each a Cessna a mile apart and cover the entire area.

The five students from VAQ-129 were tasked to serve as representatives of the Navy. We had a basic familiarization with low-altitude flying and were supposedly there to help maintain flight safety for civilian pilots who didn't have much experience flying in formation. I remember that the pilot I flew with was a train conductor and that at least one of the civilian pilots only had one eye. Honestly, after weeks of nothing but watch-standing, flying anything sounded good. While the trip seemed interesting at first, the truth was that I had zero experience in such low-performance aircraft, and despite what you may think, this does matter. As I took off for our first leg, I quickly learned that it is one thing to fly at five hundred feet and four hundred and twenty knots and entirely another to fly the same route at seventy or eighty knots, especially in aircraft that was subject to turbulence and which had no air conditioning.

In retrospect, this was an event that deserved a lot more risk management than the Navy applied. Some of the low-level routes that we surveyed were flat, monotonous, and hot. While uncomfortable, they were safe for a Cessna. However, the final route that we flew is known as the VR 1355. This route starts south of Mount Adams, near the Washington/Oregon border, and winds its way north up the spine of the Cascade mountains. In fact, the gorgeous scenes among the jagged mountain peaks in the second Top Gun movie were flown on the VR 1355. As I would come to know over the years that followed, this route was exhilarating to fly in a jet, but was a bit terrifying to fly in a Cessna.

While nobody died on this trip, it wasn't for lack of trying. Formation flying was a bit more challenging in what amounted to powered kites, and we were quite fortunate that we did not run into each other. In addition, the lack of power and speed resulted in some miscalculations when avoiding obstacles. One crew ended up flying beneath a set of high-tension power lines that they didn't see until the last minute. Another aircraft brought back some grass and branches in the landing gear as they tried to tie the Cessna "low altitude record." For my part, I felt no desire to push the limits of the aircraft that I was in and agreed with my Civil Air Patrol pilot that we stay above the five-hundred-foot altitude that we were theoretically cleared to fly at. During that last leg, as we flew up the Cascades, there were at least two locations where we could not make it over a ridge line and had to circle and gain altitude. Thankfully, we didn't have any weather issues while doing so, or life would have become much more sporting. When we arrived back at NAS Whidbey, we brought our five Cessnas into "the break" five-abreast, going as fast as we could. It was not, however, very impressive. Once on the ground, I told the guy in charge that this was a disaster waiting to happen and that I'd never do it again.

The months of boredom rolled by. Every Friday evening was spent at the Whidbey Island Officer's Club. This was the period before Officer's Clubs started disappearing from military bases across the nation. Upcoming defense budget cuts began with what our politicians and senior leaders deemed to be "extraneous" expenditures. Officer and Enlisted Clubs were essentially shut down or privatized. Those who stayed open were required to pay rent to the government and operate at a profit. Dozens of additional quality-of-life facilities began disappearing; Morale, Welfare, and Recreation were slowly strangled, and car repair, rental equipment, and other support were all eliminated. For many bases, these closures were not a huge deal; there were alternatives out in the civilian world nearby. In Whidbey, there were no real options. This made it important to keep Officer's Club membership numbers high and encourage participation. The conundrum was that the primary money-maker at the club was the bar, and we were also entering a period when alcohol-related incidents were starting to become an issue.

Despite the impending change, in those early years, the club rocked. As squadrons wrapped up work on Friday afternoon, they would drive up to the top of the hill and have a beer. The club would be packed and overflowing, and hundreds of officers, spouses, and significant others would be in attendance. Every month or so, the FRS would hold a graduation ceremony. The CO of the FRS would stand up and try to get the crowd to be silent. They would welcome everyone and then be handed a set of 3x5 cards with the names and vital information of the new graduates. One at a time, the newly qualified EA-6B aviator would be called to the front of the room, and the CO would attempt to read the card and introduce them. When the name of the squadron that was receiving the new aviator was called, there would be a roar from somewhere in the room. Several members of the fleet squadron would rush up on the stage, rip the VAQ-129 patch off of the flight suit of the "FNG," and replace it with their squadron patch. At this point, they would generally hoist the new aviator into the air and take them outside onto the deck, where they would be drenched with champagne, beer, or whatever was available. It was always fun and sometimes dangerous, as more than one new guy had his head smashed on a door frame as they were ceremoniously carried from the room.

On nice days, the wide deck attached to the back of the club was filled with aviators enjoying a fantastic view of the Puget Sound and the San Juan Islands. Every once in a while, an A-6E or EA-6B would conduct an "attack" on the field and fly by the club at low altitude. The general scene at Whidbey was not nearly as licentious as the ones in Oceana and Miramar, primarily because of the isolation of the base. There were always several single women from the local area in the club, but they tended to be the same visitors every weekend, mostly because at least one person from the group had to have a military ID card to get through the front gate. Usually, this meant at least one of the women in the group was the dependent of a service member stationed at the base (not a good thing).

As the afternoon faded into evening, the temperature would quickly drop, and only the cigar smokers would find themselves on the deck. At this point, a third or more of the crowd would have gone home, and the remaining group was moving into second gear. This inevitably meant that a couple of tables in front of the bar were cleared, and a dice game would start. This was a contest of wills that would begin with a competition between participants to see who would buy the next round of beer. However, as it got later in the evening, the casual drinkers would bow out, and money would show up at the center of the table. I was never interested in playing, but there were a couple of years that I regularly saw hundreds of dollars, an occasional set of car keys, or other promissory wagers from desperate gamblers that had been placed on the center of the table.

As Friday night progressed, the mid-evening crowd would subdivide yet again. Those who were not inclined to go anywhere else would stay at the bar. The rest of us would go home, change, and head to wherever the house party was, and there was almost always a party. These parties were always related to the FRS in one way or another. Sometimes the party was hosted by the most recent CQ class, sometimes, it was just a squadron party, and frequently it was located at one of three or four bachelor pads that regularly would buy a keg or two and invite the crowd. None of these events were particularly outrageous, think "post-college crowd with paychecks" but there was always lots of beer, and the conversation was always about flying. A few of the "regular" locations had hot tubs, and since Whidbey Island's weather was almost always conducive to their use, many of these parties ended up in or around the keg and the hot tub. Like any such tight-knit social circle, there were occasional scandals, but I don't remember too many arguments and very few actual fights.

In October 1990, the log jam in the pilot pool began to break. I started to fly the simulator component of the syllabus, took all my required tests, and prepared to start flying the mighty Prowler. Unfortunately for me, Saddam Hussein had a desire for some Kuwaiti territory; in fact, he desired all of it. I had finished the first set of simulators and got my initial flight in the right front seat of the EA-6B in November, and then the FRS essentially shut down. The nation was going to war in the Middle East, and all resources were devoted to that effort. This was disappointing and was made especially so by the fact that I had a younger brother who was an Army officer leading a scout-sniper platoon in the 101st Airborne Division. He had been deployed as part of the deterrence effort ("speed bump") in the fall and was in Saudi Arabia stationed on the Iraqi border, preparing for the invasion. I desperately wanted to get out to the fleet and join the fight and was quietly unhappy about the slow pace of the squadron.

For me, this was a time of watching the news and getting fitful information back from my brother in the form of letters and an occasional update from my parents. As the Allied invasion began in January, my attention was pulled in two directions, I was concerned about my brother, but I had also been notified that the syllabus would begin again. Now, despite its sophistication as a radar jammer, the basics of flying the EA-6B are not that demanding for a new pilot. While fighter pilots directly employ the weapon systems of their aircraft, as an EA-6B pilot, we refreshed our formation flying skills, did some low-level flying, and learned the basics of "what was going on in the back." There was one peculiarity of the EA-6B community that was immediately clear to new students; we were unbelievably fixated on the details of the airframe. While Naval Aviation definitely believes that a deep understanding of engineering information, aerodynamics, and construction of the jet is useful, the Prowler community is obsessed over these issues to an extent not relevant to the operation of the aircraft. In retrospect, there were many decades of man-years wasted on knowing how many batteries were in the jet, the number of ridges on the trim button, or pieces of wood that could be found in the airframe. Generations of Prowler crewmembers were tortured by such trivia for no worthwhile reason, especially when there was an ocean of Electronic Warfare-related intelligence that was much more relevant to the mission. Despite this slight lack of focus on the mission, the truth was that nighttime CQ was the primary obstacle that every new EA-6B pilot faced before they graduated.

Although not terribly dramatic in this particular case, my run of "interesting" cross-country adventures continued with the Prowler. As in the training command, one of the key objectives of the program is to get the students enough hours in the jet to meet the minimums required to take it to the aircraft carrier, usually about 50 hours. In April, I was approached by three ECMO instructors who wanted to take an EA-6B to NAS Norfolk, Virginia, for an airshow. One of the guys had family there (his father was an Admiral), and we all agreed that any day away from Whidbey was a good day. This opportunity sounded great to me; it got me to Virginia for a weekend and was a good way to build flight hours. So, I did the flight planning, and we headed across the country on a Friday morning. One of the first things that I learned from that flight was that the EA-6B could go a long way on a single load of fuel as long as you were very careful with how you managed the aircraft (and had a good tailwind). The first leg of this trip was nearly 1400 miles from Whidbey to Offutt Air Force Base in Omaha, Nebraska. When we arrived, we were pretty low on fuel, and there was a monstrous crosswind that was technically out of limits on the single runway. With no other options, I landed the aircraft without incident and breathed a sigh of relief when we safely turned off onto the taxiway. I then learned the procedures of cross-country stops that I would repeat many, many times through the coming years. Get out of the aircraft, put the safety pins in the ejection seat, take off flight gear and leave it in the seat of the jet, do a walk-around of the aircraft to ensure you haven't lost anything, set up the ground refueling panel and leave the gas card stuck in the little door, and then go inside to Base Operations to hit the bathroom, get a candy bar and a Coke, and check the weather.

With an experienced bunch of instructors, the turn-around at Offutt went smoothly. The Air Force came and fueled the jet, the weather at our destination was ok, and we filed a flight plan for NAS Norfolk. Within an hour, we were back in the aircraft, started, and ready to take off. By now, the winds had decreased a bit, and I took the runway and got us airborne. However, as we climbed to about twenty-thousand feet, I got a generator light. Now, the EA-6B has two primary generators, one on each engine. Either generator can carry the entire load for the aircraft, but without them, life gets very interesting. The aircraft did have an emergency Ram Air Turbine that I could deploy, and we would get enough power to make it to a safe landing, but it was not something you really wanted to do. That said, it was not particularly uncommon for generator lights to come on, and they usually reset on the first try. However, as a brand-new student, this was not how I was taught to handle it. Instead, we broke out our checklists, and we went through all the procedures until I got to the point where I attempted to reset the generator. I lifted the switch and reset it, expecting the light to go out, but unfortunately, the generator didn't come back online. At this point, we were probably less than a hundred miles from Offutt. By the book, we needed to turn around and land as soon as practical. However, the three instructors definitely did not want to spend the weekend in Omaha; they wanted to be in Virginia Beach.

Now, the delicate part of the following discussion for my instructors was that they could not recommend that we contravene NATOPS operating procedures. Even though I was a student, I was still the Pilot in Command, and if I decided that we needed to head back to Omaha, nobody could complain (out loud). As I talked it over with them, I quickly discovered which way the "wind was blowing." The logic went something like this...the rest of the jet was ok, we had some good emergency diverts along the way, and we would be closer to Navy maintenance facilities when we arrived in Norfolk. If we went back to Offutt, we would need to wait for maintenance to fly out from Whidbey. So, I allowed them to convince me to fly with one generator for the rest of the trip, nervously watching that light for the next two and a half hours. After we landed in Norfolk, I tried to reset the generator one more time. Lo and behold, the light went out. Great news! So, we "put the jet to bed," got rooms at the BOQ, and walked across the street to the Breezy Point Officers Club to have a few beers.

It was at this point that we probably should have called back to maintenance and gotten some help with the generator. Instead, we sat in the club and drank a lot of beer. Breezy Point was a bit of an old-school club, and it didn't get as much use as the more popular facilities in the Virginia Beach area. While the crowd was good, it was not very lively. I vaguely recall that we were visited by a three-star Admiral who was interested in why we were at Norfolk instead of Oceana. Once we left the bar, I also recall physically pulling one of the guys out of the huge boxwood hedges that were next to the Officer's Club, where he had somehow gotten stuck. For me, this trip was awesome. While I initially had envisioned a flight with three instructors as having the potential for three times the torture, this was my first exposure to what I would later learn to be just a normal cross-country flight. I was now "part of the team." The next day we visited the Admiral's house and had a beer. A day after that, it was time to go home.

After a long weekend, we went to Base Operations and prepared to head back to Whidbey. While the trip from west to east was an easy two-leg trip, going back home against the jet stream usually required at least three legs. I don't remember where our first leg was supposed to land because we never got airborne. As soon as I pushed the starter button on the left engine, the light came on briefly and then went out. This was the classic indicator of a broken starter shaft. Thus began a multi-day effort to get the jet airborne. Despite the brave words about having more Navy maintenance support available, there was nobody to help us there at Norfolk. We eventually found somebody to put a new starter shaft in, and it too broke, and then another. We were stranded. It was at this point that the Training department began to get involved because I was supposed to start bouncing for the CQ detachment the next week.

After another day passed, they had enough. I was given a commercial ticket to fly home and returned to a lecture about taking a jet all the way across the country right before a CQ detachment. This wire brushing didn't seem particularly fair, but I suppose that since the other guys were still stuck in Norfolk, I was the only available target. In another unpopular move, I was also the genesis of a new rule for student pilots, who were now limited to West Coast cross-country trips before their CQ events so that this wouldn't happen again.

Carrier Qualification for the EA-6B was a much different experience than my previous two trips to the carrier in the Training Command. While I had gotten four traps in the T-2C and six in the TA-4J, all of them were in the daytime. The basic fleet qualification in the EA-6B was "ten and six." This meant that I would get ten-day traps and six-night traps. The bigger change for me was that I would not be alone in the aircraft. For the rest of my EA-6B career, I would have someone sitting next to me in the aircraft, and at least one crewmember in the back. All of flight school had been designed to prepare the students to fly single-piloted aircraft. As a young Prowler pilot the entire concept of "crew coordination" took a while to get used to, but eventually, it just became part of my life. With the preparation complete, it was time to take the next step in my professional career and land on the carrier in the dark.

FCLPs for my first CQ in the EA-6B were extensive. Every event that I flew in the months of April and May included at least five or six landings back at Whidbey. In addition, I began to fly numerous instrument approaches per flight, usually getting two or three back-to-back. Then, on the last day of May, I flew from NAS North Island out to the USS Abraham Lincoln (CVN-72). This was awesome. The truth is that landing on the carrier in the daytime is fun. While there may be those who think I am exaggerating, once you get "the hang of it," day traps on the carrier are not as difficult as they are sometimes made out to be. Sure, lots of things can go wrong, and it is a hazardous task, but it is a blast. With this in mind, the one important caveat to this is probably the weather. I have had quite a few uncomfortable and even downright scary daytime traps in bad weather. I occasionally miss flying around the boat, but I definitely don't miss the days when you'd launch into the clouds and then not see the ship again until the last twenty seconds before landing.

The best that one can say about a nighttime arrested landing is that it is a relief. While they are not necessarily always scary, a night carrier landing definitely requires intense concentration from the holding pattern all the way to the flight deck. Preparation for nighttime carrier operations is essentially all instrument training. There is generally not a well-defined horizon at night out at sea. You don't realize how much you reference your geographic surroundings until you find yourself flying an aircraft inside what seems like a black bag, heading deliberately toward the ocean's invisible surface at about a hundred and fifty knots. It is almost worse when the night is clear, and you can see a tiny collection of lights far, far out on the dark ocean, and realize that is where you will be landing. All those hours of instrument work in the training command were preparation for nighttime at the carrier, where you would find yourself in what was known as the "Case III" holding pattern high above the ship, waiting for your turn, listening to the radio as some folks had a good landing pass, and others did not.

As with all CQ events, in my experience, the following period was a blur. One of the things that I learned about on that trip was the Southern California "marine layer." This was a persistent layer of fog that formed over the cold water near San Diego and which sometimes lasted for days. This layer was usually pretty thin, maybe only two-hundred or so feet, but it played with your mind when it was clear as day right up until the last few seconds before you landed. The other big difference for this detachment was that I spent a couple of nights living aboard the carrier. Without anything to do, life on the carrier in between flights was boring. Nothing to do but eat, sleep, and watch bad television. The CQ process was not efficient; it took almost five days to get my ten and six. While I remember some stress, I ended up doing fine. Night time traps were ok as long as you flew good instrument approaches, and my performance was pretty solid. In the end, I got my EA-6B carrier qual and flew home in the back seat of a Prowler. This was something that no pilot liked to do, but I accepted the ride in the back because it got me off of the carrier and back to Whidbey. Upon arrival home, I learned that I was heading to my first fleet squadron, the VAQ-137 Rooks, and that I'd be going back to a carrier to get my first traps as a real fleet aviator in just three weeks, this time on the USS America (CV-66).

6
"ROOKS, ROOKS, ROOKS"

EA-6B Carrier Landing, Author's Collection

Joining the VAQ-137 "Rooks" started a very busy phase of my life that would find me flying off of an aircraft carrier or preparing to do so, from July 1991, until November 2001 in sequential squadrons, with only one short shore tour in the middle. This was not the normal tempo for an aviator's first decade, but this intensive period shaped me as an officer, Naval Aviator, and a person. While there was a two-year break in the middle, the majority of my most compelling, stressful, and interesting stories come from this period. These squadrons are where I met my best friends and lived a life of intensive flying that many would covet.

The VAQ-137 Rooks returned from participating in Operation Desert Storm in April 1991. They had been rushed into a last-minute deployment in December of 1990, fought the war to liberate

Kuwait, and then were sent home. Because the Department of Defense had surged all the Navy's available aircraft carriers into the fight in the Middle East, somebody had to return from the war, execute an abbreviated training effort, and go right back on deployment. The carrier and air wing that drew the short straw were the USS America (CV-66) and Carrier Air Wing ONE (CVW-1).

As a result of this compressed schedule, the USS America was scheduled to depart in August 1991 for a six-week exercise in the North Atlantic, return home in October, and then depart again for a full six-month deployment in December. As a new pilot, there was no better time to join VAQ-137. I had many friends who met their squadrons after the unit had just returned from a deployment and they would not end up going to sea for another eighteen months or two years. This was not a bad thing from the Navy's perspective. If a new guy arrived at the beginning of a training period it gave this pilot, known as a "nugget," time to adapt to their new environment and gain experience before they deployed. In reality, it meant that they were not flying very much and certainly were not getting any traps.

Reporting to a squadron as a "new guy" is always awkward. Squadrons are much like families. They certainly spend as much time together as families and sometimes bond just as tightly. When I showed up at the Rooks as a brand-new nugget, fresh from my FRS CQ detachment, the guys were pretty tight and were proud of their status as war heroes. I distinctly remember my first social event. I was invited to one of the guy's houses for a 4th of July barbecue. The home was in NAS Whidbey base housing, among the single-story, government-owned Ranch-style houses that were built in the 1950s to house military families. As we stood around the backyard in our jackets, watching a friend grill while having a beer, Whidbey Island weather was its typical self, cool and drizzly, perhaps in the upper forties, definitely not what one would consider a good day for celebrating the nation's independence outdoors. However, when I went home after the event, I had a great impression of the junior pilots and was excited about what they told me about the upcoming schedule; and that schedule was brutal.

Within the next two weeks, I would conduct my first Fleet FCLPS at Whidbey, fly across the country, and prepare to get my first traps on the USS America. As briefly mentioned, most naval aviation communities had East and West Coast squadrons to support East and West Coast carriers. Since the EA-6B community was so small, we were all stationed at Whidbey. This was great for the squadrons that supported West Coast carriers, but VAQ-137 was attached to CVW-1 and deployed on the USS America, a carrier that was home-based in Norfolk, Virginia. This meant that any time we had an event scheduled on the carrier, we needed to fly all the way across the country, complete the training, and then fly all the way home. While this may not seem particularly remarkable, the EA-6B is not an airliner, and each transit across the country meant managing the risk of an aircraft breaking down at some Air Force base along the way. In retrospect, it also meant that we got lots of extra flight hours and a great deal of useful experience dealing with fuel management challenges and adverse weather.

The cross country trip to the USS America in July of 1991 gave me a chance to record my first fleet traps and have an opportunity to see the ship where I'd be living for most of the next year. I can say that my first impression of the ship was not particularly favorable. The carrier had been commissioned in 1965 and was one of three Kitty Hawk-class carriers that the nation built; this list included the USS Kitty Hawk, the USS Constellation, and the USS America. The USS America was built as the Navy transitioned to nuclear power, and as such, it was one of the last remaining conventionally powered supercarriers that was afloat. As with many parts of this narrative, there could be a lot written about the USS America and its "peculiarities." There were many power outages, jet fuel in the drinking water, steam leaks that exposed us to asbestos fibers, and a variety of plumbing challenges that always seemed to result in raw sewage rolling around on the bathroom floors. There were many days when the ship seemed to earn its nickname of "CV-666." On the bright side, the bathroom nearest to my six-man bunk room had "Hollywood" showers. You will know them as normal showers, the kind that runs until you turn them off. The Navy alternative, and what was eventually installed in the months to come, were water-saving spray nozzles known to us as "push to talk." These were hand-held nozzles that projected needles of water that didn't so much get you wet as much as they stripped the dirt from your skin like a power washer. On the bright side, there was no shortage of hot water. It was not uncommon for nothing but scalding water and steam to sputter from the showers and sinks. This meant that you sometimes had to spray the water onto the ceiling so that it would cool down enough that when it touched your body it wouldn't burn your skin off. Showers weren't short on the USS America because we wanted to save water; they were short because we didn't want to be boiled alive.

After the brief CQ detachment on the USS America was complete, instead of flying home to Whidbey, we flew back across the country to Naval Air Station Fallon, Nevada. Fallon is a base that is roughly seventy miles east of Reno and is smack dab in the middle of nowhere.

Understanding why we were in Fallon requires a very brief outline of our normal training sequence. Carriers and Air Wings deploy in cycles, the length of which depends on the resourcing that the Navy gets, the demand for forces from Geographic Combatant Commanders, and the scheduling of regular ship maintenance. In 1991, these deployment cycles were generally two years long. A "regular" deployment was considered to be six months in duration and was followed by eighteen months of preparation before the next deployment; the total cycle length was twenty-four months. Each eighteen-month training period started with a month or so of downtime, and then all the components of the battle group proceeded into a deliberate training regimen known as "workups." Ideally, workups followed a "crawl, walk, run" method of training. You would conduct unit-level training for several months, then get together with the air wing to train as a group at NAS Fallon, and then go out to sea on the carrier for a month or so of training as an air wing/carrier team, come home, take a short break, and then deploy. Since the USS America and CVW-1 were on an abbreviated schedule, we were essentially fitting eighteen months of training into six.

In 1991 NAS Fallon was still an isolated Naval Air Station with great air space and bombing ranges. While today it is the home of tremendously sophisticated training capabilities and well-appointed living quarters for officers and troops that compare well to good civilian hotels, at the time it was not so luxurious or well-equipped. The barracks were very old, the water was so full of minerals that it felt slimy, and the training for EA-6B crews, in particular, was not very advanced. When we arrived at Fallon I was housed in a building known as "Sierra Hotel" with the rest of the Junior Officers. This was the oldest officers' quarters on base. Each room had two beds, and two rooms shared one bathroom. The air conditioning was fitful, and it always felt best to minimize contact with any of the building's exposed surfaces. On the bright side, it was just a dozen yards from the Officer's Club, which was one of only two places to eat while you were staying on the base.

It is worth pausing here to discuss just how big the air wing was. In 1991, CVW-1 was comprised of two F-14A squadrons. One A-6E squadron. Two F/A-18C squadrons. One EA-6B squadron. One S-3B squadron. One E-2C squadron. And last, but not least, the helicopter squadron that was flying the trusty SH-3H Sea King. This gave us about ninety aircraft. The amount of capability in this old air wing was astonishing. The F-14A Tomcat provided long-range fighter coverage that was designed to keep Soviet bombers and their anti-ship missiles as far away from the carrier as possible. With the AWG-9 radar and the Phoenix missile, they extended the carrier's anti-air coverage for a thousand miles. The A-6E was the last version of the A-6. A two-seat bomber, the A-6 could carry a truckload of bombs and drop them with precision at night or in bad weather. The F/A-18C was the newest fighter-attack jet in the Navy. Although it was always challenged by the amount of fuel that it carried, it had the best radar in the Fleet and could conduct both air-to-air and air-to-ground missions very effectively. The S-3B was a carrier-based anti-submarine aircraft. With straight wings and high-bypass turbofans, it was slow, but it could stay on station for a long time to locate enemy subs. The E-2C was our airborne radar platform. A two-engine turbo-prop with a huge radar dome mounted above the aircraft, the E-2C could see air and surface contacts for a long way and served as the center of our airborne network. Finally, the SH-3H Sea King was our lifesaving search and recovery helicopter. Not only were these helicopters dedicated to saving pilots who had to jump out of their aircraft, but they delivered parts and people around the battle group, flying more often than any other aviators on the carrier. Altogether there were almost ninety aircraft on the USS America when it deployed, a huge team that had to work together not only to be safe but to effectively project power.

My first impression of "Air Wing Fallon" was that flying in the Fleet was rewarding but that the mission planning was torture. Much like the rest of training, the concept for an air wing detachment was to start slow and then finish the detachment with a couple of days of high-intensity "war." As a result, the training detachment began by conducting unit-level training against some representative targets sprinkled around the vast government training complex. For the Prowler guys, there were some emitters that we could see with our onboard system and a few that we could jam and get feedback. There were also several good low-level routes and an entertaining valley that could be flown at very low altitudes against representative air defense systems. While many of the initial flights took place in the daytime, the schedule gradually shifted into night-time operations, as that is when we anticipated operating in real life. The training was conducted by experts in each squadron, and the integration was supervised by the squadron Commanding and Executive Officers, CAG, and the Deputy Air Wing Commander. While in Fallon, the staff of what was then known as the Naval Strike and Air Warfare Center (NSAWC) guided us through this two-week training event. NSAWC maintained an exclusive cadre of subject matter experts from every naval aviation community who had a very strict and professional training style (and it would later become the home of Top Gun). These experts would brief the air wing on a variety of tactical information as we trained and evaluate us in flight.

What the training in Fallon will emphasize is that when a fighter fires a missile or drops a bomb, they are not doing so on their own; they are at the pointy-end of what is now known as a "kill chain." (Or, in actuality, a "kill web"). As air wing training progressed and each mission became more complex, so did the mission planning. As a new guy, however, my experience with mission planning was underwhelming. The air wing was divided up into several teams. The teams contained one or more representatives from each aviation community in the wing. Each planning team was assigned a room inside the NSAWC building. When the team was assigned a target, the junior officers in the group grabbed some high-quality paper charts of the area, and the intelligence guys placed the known adversary defenses in the approximate locations. Then the strikers plotted a route, and everybody else planned their support missions around them. A lot of what we called "planning" was essentially arts and crafts. Much effort was spent to make the charts look good and have the right symbols in the right places. When the strike lead was happy with the plan, he briefed it to CAG. If CAG gave his blessing, the rest of the minions would start making the kneeboard cards with which the mission would be briefed and executed. The problem, from my perspective, was that while it took about an hour for the strike lead to get a concept blessed by CAG, it was uncommon for the rest of the work to be completed without twelve or more hours of additional effort. We spent a lot more time on building briefing materials than we did thinking about the tactics that would be required to defeat an adversary. This has since changed, and technology has eliminated much of the grunt work, but I am sure there are still JOs wrestling with kneeboard cards even today.

Flying a mission at Fallon was usually predictable for the Prowler. The entire strike would all launch and head out to the working area. For the EA-6B, this usually meant flying to a spot that was in the northeast corner of the airspace. Once everyone was airborne, the E-2 would start calling out radar contacts as the adversary or "Red Air" fighters launched into the area and set up their defensive positions. With all the pieces in place, the strike lead would set everything in motion. The sequence was largely the same every time. Fighters would press forward and attempt to sweep the adversaries from the sky. Strikers would head toward the target. The SEAD package would move on-axis with the strikers and start jamming and firing simulated HARM missiles. In these early days, while we all tried to get the "switchology" correct in the cockpit, the most important thing was that we called out our HARM shots on time over the radio. As the fighters completed their sweep, there would inevitably be one or two "leakers," which is to say, adversary fighters that would get behind our strike package and start to attack the strikers or the SEAD package. I was part of countless training strikes where I would be directed to run away in these cases. What this inevitably did was rob the strikers of effective jamming and increase the effectiveness of the enemy SAM systems in the target area. After the strike was complete, we would all return to Fallon in reverse order, with the Prowler in the rear, only to be followed by the E-2.

With the mission complete, we would land and head back to our parking spot in the ramp area, debrief any maintenance issues, and then head to the NSAWC headquarters. The first thing we would do was grab a Coke and prepare ourselves to sit through a mass debrief. The mass debrief was a presentation that included everyone in the mission, all of the instructors, observers, and senior leadership. It was held in an auditorium with a huge screen in the front of the room. All of the aircraft in the strike, including the adversaries, were equipped with something called a "TACTS" pod. This pod reported the location, altitude, speed, and some of the other parameters of the aircraft. As Prowler guys, we always carried a TACTS pod, but as soon as our jammers were turned on, they would interfere with the pod, and our jet would drop from the display. This huge screen in the front of the room would display the individual movements of every aircraft (other than ours) with fascinating, three-dimensional detail. In addition, since the TACTS pods communicated with the weapon systems, we could also see any simulated ordnance that was fired.

There was a certain formula to these debriefs. We would all have spent many hours preparing for the mission and would know how the event was supposed to be executed. So, as the replay progressed, there would be visible reactions among the crowd when things didn't go as planned. The icons representing aircraft on the screen were synchronized with the recorded radio calls, and as each engagement occurred, we could now actually see and hear what had only been an imaginary "picture" in our head during the event itself. As the replay continued, we would see all the various engagements with the adversary defenders. The fighter guys would call all their missile shots, and as each impact occurred, the staff would "stop the tape" and judge if they were good kills.

For the Prowler crews, our participation in the mass debrief was limited to hearing the radio calls that indicated when we shot our HARM, or shaking our heads when an adversary would manage to shoot us down. Occasionally, the brief would include video from fake adversary radar scopes and would demonstrate the fact that we had an actual effect on "bad guy" systems. Even better was when our jamming would be credited with a "save" of one of our fighter friends. In the end, however, most of the time spent would be on which fighters shot down which bad guys; everything else always seemed to be an afterthought. After we left the big auditorium and split up into our mission specialties, the SEAD-specific debrief would often take about thirty seconds. "Any questions? Any problems? See you at the club." It was not uncommon to note that we could have spent the whole event on the ground, and nobody would have known as long as we could call our HARM shots on the radio.

While the best parts of a Fallon detachment were the flying, the evenings in the officer's club and the occasional weekend road trips to Reno or Lake Tahoe were also a blast. My first trip to Fallon was fairly compressed, so I don't think we made it to Reno. However, what we did do was drink a lot of beer in the officer's club and spent a fair amount of time at local places in Fallon like Stockman's Casino, gambling away our paychecks at the old blackjack tables and eating massive steak dinners.

The Fallon Officer's Club is one of my favorite places on earth.

This club was reminiscent of all the stories I had read of the early days of aviation. I often felt I was living in a scene from "The Right Stuff." The Fallon Officer's Club bar was a place where aviators could walk to after a flight, grab a burger, and drink cheap beer while they told stories about their heroic actions, the crappy weather, or discussed someone else's fuck ups. There were a couple of pool tables behind the bar, an open patio, and a nice pool (that I never swam in). Inside, the walls of the place were covered by plaques from every squadron that came through, and the ceiling around the bar was hung with mementos dedicated by each Top Gun class. While the Officer's Clubs in places like Oceana and Miramar were well known for their social scenes, the bar in Fallon was really the crossroads of the professional side of Naval Aviation Strike Warfare. Although there was some overlap between the activities at these clubs, Fallon was more about combat flying, and much of Naval Aviation's modern future has been shaped by post-flight discussions over a beer in the Fallon club.

The other unforgettable part of the Fallon Officer's Club during this period was Ruthie. Ruth Heim had started working at the base as a waitress a couple of decades earlier, but by 1991 she was running the Officer's Club bar. She was an older lady who had seen it all. Inside that bar, her word was God. It didn't often get rowdy enough that Ruth would step in, but when Ruthie had seen enough - she would holler - and everyone from Ensign to Admiral would listen. While I never had the chance to do more than order a beer from Ruthie, I now wish I had gotten the opportunity to hear some of her stories - I am sure they would be epic.

In August, we flew back across the country again and went to sea. After leaving the Virginia Capes, the USS America and the battle group headed north toward the Arctic Circle. While the Navy doesn't do this much anymore, at the time, our primary adversary was still the Soviet Union, and the Navy's role in any potential conflict was to head far into the North Atlantic and keep Soviet subs and bombers from interdicting all the men and equipment that would need to be sent across the ocean to help defend Europe. For us, heading north meant flying around Nova Scotia, Greenland, and

Iceland along the way. Despite the fact that it was summer, the water was cold, and the weather was temperamental. I quickly learned how uncomfortable it was to wear a dry suit under my flight gear and what it meant to land on a pitching deck or in rain squalls that made it very difficult to see (or both). Despite these challenges, my landing grades were good, and this kept me from being benched in the same way as some of the other air wing nuggets were. In fact, my grades ended up being decent enough to find myself pretty consistently as a "Top Five Nugget" and the second or third best among the seven pilots in our squadron, a great place for a brand-new guy to be.

As we headed north towards Norway, we stopped for a few days to operate in the vicinity of the Shetland Islands. This allowed us to do some low-level flying, something we had heard great things about since most of Scotland was wide open for low-level flight. Up until this point, my fleet experience had been everything I thought it could be, and life was great, so I was ecstatic when I got the opportunity not only to fly a low-level with two F-14A aircraft but to lead the division of three aircraft. This was a huge win for a Prowler nugget, and my sense that this was unusual was reinforced when my CO decided to jump into a back seat. My crew and I prepared for the flight and with no real restriction, designed a route that crossed Scotland and ended up with an "attack" on an airfield near Inverness. Once the attack was complete, we would return down Loch Ness and out over the ocean, back to the ship.

On the day of the mission, the weather was decent. There were scattered clouds that we could avoid and a few rain showers that didn't cause any issues. After getting airborne, we checked in with UK Air Traffic Control and got cleared for our low-level strike. Before we launched, we had been told that there was a chance that we would be intercepted by British fighters, but as we crossed the coast, the flight remained uneventful. As we went further inland, I wanted to look around and do a bit of sightseeing, but it was clearly necessary to concentrate on flying at a low altitude and not getting lost. I was also very conscious of the two Tomcats that were flying combat spread on either wing and definitely did not want to screw things up.

When we eventually approached the target airfield from the west, we were prepared to peel away from the base several miles early and proceed with our trip down Loch Ness. Before leaving our low-level route, we got in touch with the airfield and, to our surprise, were asked to do a low-flyby. If there is one thing the first Top Gun movie got right, it is the fact that there is no Naval Aviator born who can resist the opportunity to do a low-flyby. At this point in the mission, I was at five-hundred feet or less, flying fast with two Tomcats on my wing. When I heard that we were cleared for a flyby of the field, I looked down at my Horizontal Situation Indicator (essentially my compass card) and realized that I was already lined up with the runway heading. Beautiful! As we got a few miles closer to the field, my CO in the back seat said, "Do you know where you are, Tater?" I said yes. I should have taken the hint because about two seconds later, I realized that I had reversed the headings in my brain and was about to do a low-flyby from the opposite heading that we had been cleared. We were seconds out from this airfield, now doing about five-hundred knots at about two hundred feet. Even as a new guy, I knew that some things couldn't be corrected. The two Tomcats had swept their wings back and were tucked up so close to my jet that it felt like I had to keep forward pressure on the stick. We zoomed past the tower going the opposite direction - very low and very fast - and instead of glory, I felt ridiculous.

As we departed the area after the flyby, the only saving grace was that the field asked us for another pass, so they must not have thought the first one was too bad. We declined "for lack of gas." With the simulated attack complete, I detached the fighters and then followed them down Loch Ness at a very low altitude. The Tomcats were so low, and the water so still, that I could see wakes created by their exhaust. Flying down the center of Loch Ness was an experience that I will never forget, but I had a hard time appreciating it. It had become very quiet in my airplane since the flyby, and I was sure that silence was not a good thing. Despite the quiet, it wasn't long before we made it back overhead the ship, recovered, and debriefed in our Ready Room. While the CO didn't do anything but shake his head, I deservedly caught some shit from the guys in my jet. What I feared the most, however, was that the story would travel across the airwing, forging my reputation as a "wrong-way Prowler guy." When I made it down to their Ready Room and grabbed the Tomcat guys for a quick debrief, it was clear that they had fun. They told me I had done a good job, thought the flyby was cool, and had no idea we flew it in the wrong direction. Bullet dodged!

The carrier and our associated battle group continued heading north until we crossed the Arctic Circle and then headed into Vestfjord, Norway. In theory, the carrier would operate in the fjord as a way to avoid Soviet submarines. In practice, this meant that the ship was constantly maneuvering in a restricted space, and recoveries were very challenging. Despite the difficulty, this week of flying was the closest I would get to the Cold War. One day I flew north along the mountains of Norway, following two A-6s. We got so far north that we turned east towards Soviet territory before we were out of time and fuel and needed to head home. On another day, I was in the daytime recovery pattern when a Soviet TU-95 Bear bomber did a flyby of the carrier. The F-14A crews that were assigned to intercept the bomber took pictures of the bomber with the carrier in the background. Unfortunately, they failed to get a Tomcat in the frame as well, making the Admiral unhappy enough that even the Prowler guys heard about it. Altogether, however, it was great flying. We did get a vivid reminder of the risks of naval aviation during the trip. While we were operating in the fjord, an A-6 from VA-85 crashed. The heavy aircraft lost an engine during a catapult shot and struggled to stay in the air. The crew safely ejected just before the jet stalled and both were recovered within a few moments. After a few days, the mission was declared to be complete and the USS America sailed south toward England without much flying, heading to a well-earned break.

My first port visit to the fleet was in Portsmouth, England. While I am sure I stood duty at some point, I don't remember being trapped on the ship. I do recall the first night in the town of Portsmouth, where I was drunk under the table by a bunch of female British sailors with great personalities and bad teeth. I then got on a train with several of my squadron mates and ended up in London. This was the first place that I saw the concept of an "admin" in action. In naval aviation terms, an "admin" is the unofficial hub of a port visit for the officers of the squadron. Since all port visits are actually work days, and there were several kinds of watch-standing jobs that needed to be covered, not everyone could get off the ship every day. As a result, we'd pool our cash, and one or two of the guys would go ashore, rent a hotel room or two, and stock it with beer and snacks. The bargain made with the rest of the group was that they could stay ashore for the entire visit as long as the beer was cold and the snacks were sufficient. Having an admin established gave us a place to meet before going out and adventuring, a "headquarters" of sorts to help to communicate issues on, and from the ship, and a cheap place to recover from the big nights on shore. For this visit, someone decided that our admin should be in London, not understanding that the train ride from Portsmouth was a couple of hours long.

When we eventually got to London, we found that our trusty "admin queen" (a term of endearment) had gotten a room at the Grosvenor House hotel, a five-star place that was ridiculously expensive but perfectly located in the center of the city. It was not the best place for a bunch of guys to sleep on the floor of a hotel room, but they didn't throw us out. My fondest memory of that visit was getting to the Tower of London for a tour and realizing that we had gotten there near closing time. Somehow one of the Beefeaters took pity on us (I didn't know they were all retired military until later), and he gave us the most wonderful living history tour of the tower that I could have asked for. The tour was fantastic; there wasn't a square inch of the place that didn't have a story associated with it. We visited the ravens, saw the crown jewels, and heard gruesome or tragic stories related to the various gates and walls. Visit complete, I traveled back to Portsmouth, and the USS America pulled back out to sea, headed back to Norfolk.

On our return trip across the Atlantic, we conducted an exercise known as a "FLEETEX," a training operation that was essentially the event that certified us as "ready to deploy." For the air wing, this meant we got to conduct a pretend war at sea and, as a result, conducted round-the-clock flight ops. The schedule was brutal, and we flew for several days despite some very crappy weather. This was one of a few periods during this entire trip that we also flew true "blue water ops," meaning that we had no divert available; you either landed on the ship or ejected. As a new guy, this was all a bit stressful, and the exercise culminated, as it usually did in those days, with an accident. In the middle of the night, an HS-11 helicopter disappeared from the radar without a sound. Four men died that night, two officers and two enlisted sailors. The best guess at the time was that they got disoriented in the dark and flew into the water. This might have been technically true, but the real issue was that they were tired. This was not the way we wanted to end what had been a very successful trip, but this accident and the time spent searching for wreckage brought the exercise to a halt, and eventually, we flew off the ship and returned across the country to Whidbey. It was October.

We returned to the USS America on the 4th of December. Every time we went to sea, each pilot in the air wing needed to get a certain number of arrested landings during the day and at night in order to be deemed "current." This usually meant that the first three or four days of deployment were spent right off the coast of Virginia doing flight ops before heading across the ocean. During this time, everyone was also settling in for the long haul. Bags were being unpacked, offices were getting set up, and the carrier was gradually turned into the giant seaborne airfield that it was meant to be. During the day on the 5th of December, an A-6E from VA-85 was approaching the ship for a landing when the left engine disintegrated. In a move that saved the lives of dozens aboard the carrier, the pilot brought up the landing gear as the jet veered away to the port side of the ship, just barely clearing the LSO platform. The crew ejected at the very last second and were quickly rescued from the cold waters of the Atlantic. It was a scary accident, but the crew was recovered without major injury. With the two aviators back aboard and safely in medical, the air wing continued flight operations, got everyone re-qualified, and then we headed across the Atlantic.

The deployment that followed was the only "peacetime" cruise of my career, which is to say, it is the only one where I did not fly a single combat mission. While Desert Storm had been over for months, we hadn't yet started the mission that would be known as Operation Southern Watch. What this meant for us was that the USS America would do flight operations for two or so weeks and then pull into port for a couple of days, pull back out, and then repeat the cycle with a different port. Essentially, we were going to be on a flying tour of the Mediterranean, the Red Sea, and the Arabian Gulf. This was known as a "Hollywood Cruise," and I could not have asked for a better schedule. However, despite this initially rosy outlook, our first port visit to Palma de Majorca almost caused this to change.

7

LIFE ON THE BOAT - A THUMBNAIL

EA-6B in Hangar Deck, U.S. Navy Photo

As I worked on some of these sea stories, it occurred to me that I am not sure what people know about day-to-day life on an aircraft carrier. A carrier is partly a large metal office building, partially an aviation maintenance space, and part airfield. If you are an aviator, flying is more than just a job; it is an escape from the office. The day-to-day existence of the five thousand sailors who run the ship and operate the air wing is challenging. I won't go into much depth here; there are lots of great videos of life aboard a ship that can be found online. However, for most of the officers and sailors on the ship, life is just a blur of working, eating, and sleeping – in an endlessly repeating cycle.

It is worth understanding that the carrier's inhabitants are essentially living in their office or maintenance shop. The good news is that the office occasionally moves to interesting destinations, but the bad news is that it never shuts down. While you may get a day or two to explore whatever new port you end up visiting, in all likelihood, those two days will be all you can afford, and then you resume your life within the steel walls of the ship. There are no days off on a carrier. You may not fly, but there is always work to be done. An aircraft carrier is emphatically not a cruise ship, and it probably needs to be understood that most of the people who work on the ship do not get outdoors regularly. The flight deck is an exceedingly dangerous place, and casual visits are not allowed. There are places like some catwalks and the hangar deck where you can go and view the ocean, but you can never forget that it is one big maintenance space, and anywhere you go can be hazardous. My point is only that life on a carrier is a real sacrifice, and it takes an amazing amount of teamwork to make everything happen.

Life in a squadron revolves around getting the mission done, and when we were at sea, this was a twenty-four-hour-a-day pursuit. A typical aviation squadron is run by the Commanding Officer and the Executive Officer, both of whom are Commanders or O-5. The unit is then divided up into several departments, each run by a Lieutenant Commander, or O-4. A Lieutenant Commander is sometimes known as a "hinge" (because of their predilection to always nod 'yes' to the CO). The majority of the officers are usually Lieutenants, or O-3s, or Lieutenant Junior Grade, O-2. Finally, depending on the size of the squadron, you may have two or three professional Aviation Maintenance officers (known to us as "ground pounders"), who might be any rank from a Warrant officer up to a Lieutenant Commander.

In a typical carrier-based Prowler squadron, we had five departments: Operations, Maintenance, Administration, Electronic Warfare, and Safety. The squadron had around twenty-five officers and about a hundred and fifty sailors. Most of our enlisted personnel worked in the Maintenance Department repairing aircraft, but there were several enlisted sailors in Administration and one or two in each of the other departments. In the Navy, not only are the officers responsible for flying and staying tactically competent, but they also have "ground jobs" where they run parts of the squadron in one of many supervisory and management roles. The longer you were in a squadron, the more responsibility you would get. There was a definite "ladder" of jobs that you wanted to be assigned to and succeed at so that you would be promoted (and get paid more).

The living quarters on an aircraft carrier are unique. As always, seniority rules. The squadron CO and XO generally had individual staterooms that shared a bathroom with another senior officer. Lieutenant Commanders generally had one roommate, and Lieutenants generally lived with several officers. The squadron's enlisted sailors lived in much larger rooms, with some berthing spaces containing as many as eighty or more racks.

For the aviators, the rooming situation was a bit different on each carrier. For example, some of the calculus depended on how "good" a room was perceived to be. If a room was noisy, hot, or in a place where nobody wanted to live, a Lieutenant might have a two-man space. On the USS America, I lived in a six-man stateroom. The room had three bunk beds. Along the walls, each of us had a fold-down desk, chair, a tall locker, and some drawers. Our room had two sinks for some reason, which was good because one sink served as an auxiliary urinal during the ship's drills when we were in "deep shelter." Everything was gray and smelled old and metallic. Our room had one phone, which was on a "party line," with another six-man room that shared a wall. This meant that the phone was likely to ring at all hours of the day or night, at least until one angry aviator in our room finally cut the cord. There was a constant battle over ventilation. There was a single air conditioning duct that ran through several staterooms in a row. You didn't want to be at the end of the line because if someone in one of the rooms before you pulled open one of the inspection vents (as occasionally happened), no air pressure would go any farther, making things very uncomfortable in rooms down the line. In the winter, this wasn't such a big deal. However, in the summer, this mattered - especially in the Arabian Gulf, because the air conditioning was already crappy, and most of the air wing rooms were right below the flight deck. For example, I had an upper bunk, and the roof above my head was the steel flight deck itself, a surface conveniently covered with a black substance known as "non-skid" that soaked up sunlight and transmitted radiant heat downward through the steel.

The fact that we slept below the steel flight deck also meant that we heard everything that happened up above. During flight operations, our rooms were always tremendously loud. An aircraft might literally be running a few feet above your head as you tried to sleep. When we weren't flying, the flight deck crews constantly moved aircraft around. The sound of tie-down chains and aircraft chocks banging on the deck was known as the "flight deck Olympics," and there were many nights when it seemed the deck crew was deliberately standing over your bed making noise. The worst sound we were exposed to was the screech from the hydraulic rams that raised and lowered the Jet Blast Deflectors or JBD. As each jet was launched from the catapult, a large water-cooled panel was raised behind the aircraft to deflect the full-power exhaust. When the JBD dropped, the hydraulic fluid squeezed through a restrictive valve that caused a screeching noise that was loud enough to cause hearing loss in some of our rooms. I slept with earplugs, but that only partially helped. As my tinnitus rings in my ears these days, much of the damage that was inflicted didn't come from the jet I flew, but from the noise below decks.

Our six-man room was almost always dark, and there was strict etiquette about turning on the overhead fluorescent lights. In essence, they pretty much stayed off all the time. We all learned to operate in the dark. If you needed to see, each desk had a little lamp that would give you a bit of visibility. Each bunk bed had a set of curtains and a reading lamp over the front of the bed (that I hit my head on thousands of times). These rooms were our home. In our six-man room, we had convinced the CO to allow five of the JO pilots to bunk together. Despite his obvious handicap, our only NFO roommate fit right in and only received occasional harassment, usually when he attempted to participate in the wrestling series that occurred between myself and the pilot who slept in the rack below mine. As we were both pretty big guys, these matches probably began as a way to stake out our territory but gradually became epic, round-the-room grappling matches that broke things and sometimes resulted in bruises or other contusions. Despite the intensity with which they were pursued, these events never transitioned to anger and always ended with a handshake.

Eating on the carrier was very institutional. The enlisted sailors on the carrier eat on what is known as the mess decks. Every meal is buffet style. There are three main meals a day (breakfast, lunch, and dinner), and there is a late-night half-meal known as mid-rats for those who are standing watch overnight. While it may not be anything to write home about, the Navy generally served good chow. The U.S. government goes to great lengths to make sure the troops are well taken care of. The officers, well, we were kind of on our own. One of the primary differences between the two meal systems was that while the enlisted sailors ate for free, the officers had to chip into a mess fund and pay monthly dues for their own meals. I still don't understand this, as the Navy is the only service that runs this way. Anyway, as most officers were cheap smacks, we ate well enough, but we did not eat steak and lobster (except for one unique case where we ate like kings for a couple of glorious weeks until it was discovered that the supply officer was kiting checks, resulting in a huge bill that had to be divvied up among us all).

While the USS America only had a single wardroom, on most carriers there were two wardrooms on the ship for the officers to eat. The most popular wardroom for the aviators was known as the "dirty shirt." The dirty-shirt wardroom was usually on the same deck as most of the air wing Ready Rooms. The thing that made them a "dirty-shirt" wardroom was that we could eat there in our flight suits. The "clean shirt" wardrooms were generally found a few levels down on the mess deck. They served the same food as the dirty shirt, but in order to eat there, you had to be in your working khaki uniform, something that aviators never wanted to do.

The wardroom was the location where I demonstrated the eating habits that ended up giving me my call sign. While there was usually salad and other healthy options available, the wardroom had a grill that ran whenever it was open. If you didn't like the main course that was being served, you could always get a grilled cheese sandwich, fried egg and cheese sandwich, hamburger, cheeseburger, or some combination thereof, and there were usually always fries. In the lexicon of the wardroom, a cheeseburger was a "slider," and a "Barney Clark" was a cheeseburger with a fried egg on top, named in honor of the world's first artificial heart recipient. Anyway, my simple eating habits gained the attention of the most prolific call sign creator in the squadron. My diet of "meat and taters" ended up being affixed to me as "Tater," and it is a label that sticks to this day.

When it came to food on the carrier, there was nothing better on earth than flying a night pass, debriefing the flight, and then shooting the breeze for an hour or so over a slider in the wardroom. This meal was always washed down with a glass or two of "bug juice" (a variant of cool aide that is apparently only sold to the Navy). The final and most important culinary pleasure of any wardroom was known as "auto dog." Named for its visual similarity to something that you would normally pick up from behind your pet dog with a plastic bag, this was the soft ice cream made by a machine that was always running. It didn't matter what time of day it was, you could almost always get a cone or bowl full of soft-serve ice cream with a flavor that admittedly was a bit peculiar, but it was one of life's little pleasures on the ship.

A brief digression about callsigns. Yes, every naval aviator has a callsign, and no, you don't get to pick your own. If someone has a "cool" call sign it is almost certainly ironic. Callsigns are used to such an extent that there are many officers who I had no idea what their real name was. Callsigns were (and are) used for tactical communications between aircraft, but they gradually become part of everyday life. They are generated in lots of ways. Sometimes a callsign was just a natural extension of an aviator's last name. Some names were earned by something that an aviator did, "Boom Boom," was a common callsign for a pilot who had blown their tires. Sometimes callsigns could be derivative, "Wedge" was the callsign for an aviator who was noted to be "mankind's simplest tool," or "Glanz" which was related to a body part. "Plugs" started as one thing and then became related to an officer's proclivity to have his nose "up the CO's ass." There could be secondary and tertiary derivatives; the callsign "Mullet" often turned to "Fish," which sometimes turned to "Fishman." They could also be rather complex, "MOLGOCMOV" was the abbreviation for "Master of Leisure, Genius of Comfort, Master of Vulgarity." Occasionally we'd get a couple of midshipmen to visit the squadron for a few weeks, they weren't flying but were targeted for outrageous temporary callsigns. I still feel bad for the kid who was temporarily saddled with "Crack Whore." There were lazy callsigns that were just a person's name, like "Chip" or "Pete." Anything could generate a callsign, and the aviator who received such a name could not refuse it, the harder you tried to change it, the more it stuck. One of the funniest things I remember seeing was some of the mission briefing cards from VA-85, the A-6E squadron that had a large variety of graphic callsigns. When you have aviators with callsigns like "Lick" or "Suck," the combinations of crews can quickly become entertainingly vulgar. Over time, the Navy's sense of humor about these callsigns gradually diminished to the extent that we eventually needed to employ "callsign police" to ensure that we didn't offend anyone, but they are still a key part of the culture that I remember fondly.

The Ready Room was our office (and our living room). The first thing that you would probably notice when you walked into a squadron's Ready Room were the lines of chairs. These chairs are legendary. These heavy metal chairs recline slightly, and have a desktop that can be pulled up, a drawer underneath the seat, and are fairly well padded. The design of these chairs has remained the same since at least WWII. These chairs are hard to find anywhere other than a carrier. When one of my squadrons did research to see if we could buy a few to outfit our squadron spaces at Whidbey, we discovered they cost thousands of dollars apiece. Each officer in the squadron had a dedicated Ready Room chair, and we all sat with some semblance of seniority. The CO, XO, and the senior department heads were in the first row, and the rest of us were logically assembled in the rows behind. The chairs all faced a whiteboard and a roll-down movie screen. Mounted in the corner of the room was a television that had two or three channels that always ran a selection of movies, and one channel that ran the Plat Camera, an external view of the flight deck that was on at all times. It is hard to overstate the importance of this simple room. On the USS America, VAQ-137 had Ready Room 1. Our Ready Room was the farthest forward of all ten, and it was ours because it had a special accommodation for some of our more technical mission planning equipment. The best part of Ready One was that it was only a few steps from safe access to the flight deck and was only about a hundred feet from my room.

The hub of the administrative life of the squadron was the "mailbox," where each officer received or delivered all their paperwork. This was the heyday of the official blue folder and the routing slip. Paperwork traveled from box to box. Documents were signed off by whoever was responsible and forwarded to the next in line, either "up" or "down" the chain. There was a delicate art to keeping your box appropriately full. You didn't necessarily want it to be empty, but heaven help you if you were a Lieutenant and the Department Heads noticed that your box was always full, the implication being that you weren't getting your job done.

The next most important administrative item was probably the message board. In the days before email, the entire military ran on "message traffic." Messages were delivered by highly encrypted radio-telecom equipment that lived deep in the bowels of the ship. Each day the messages for your squadron were printed out and picked up by the SDO. These messages were posted on a clipboard that hung on the wall or a desk. There were two message boards in each squadron, one for "Unclassified" material and one for "Classified" information. Much like the mailboxes, there was an entire game that surrounded the message board. The messages were stamped with a grid "CO/XO/OPS/Maint/Admin/Safety, etc." so that each officer could indicate with an initial that they had read the material. Sometimes the CO or XO would write notes on the messages, the CO in red ink or the XO in green ink, and assign an action to a particular officer. Many times, these notes asked a question or voiced concern, and prompt feedback was always desired. Occasionally, these notes were a test. Heaven help the JO that didn't read the message board. It became very obvious that they were failing to accomplish this important task when red or green question marks or a terse "status?" would be added to the initial request.

Another critically important component of general interest that could be found in every Ready Room was the "Greenie Board." This board was managed by the squadron's Landing Signal Officers and provided a visual accounting of the squadron's landing performance, and every pilot's name was posted. As previously described, "OK" landings were identified by a green sticker, "(OK)" landings were in yellow, "No Grade" in brown, and a white sticker with a "B" was used for a bolter. The grades didn't stay up there forever; a deployment or training period was divided up into "line periods." At the end of a line period, an average was calculated, and the board was reset (which allowed a streak of bad grades to "disappear"). Landing grades are very competitive, and while the objective is to have safe landings every time, each pilot generally would try to maintain a high enough average that they could compete to be among the top ten pilots in the air wing. While being in the top ten was largely a ceremonial accomplishment, it demonstrated a lot of skill. The physical reward for this achievement was a patch that said "Top Ten," which was proudly affixed to the pilot's green nylon flight jacket. While the Greenie Board was ultimately about safety, an aviator's professional reputation was built on their performance in the landing pattern. I guarantee that when we would go visit other Ready Rooms or when visitors came to ours, the first thing they looked at was the Greenie Board.

The 1990s were a time of vast technological transition, and it was nowhere more apparent than in our lives on the carrier. For a long time, I was one of the only JOs in the squadron with a personal computer, meaning I didn't have to wait in line for one of the few Navy machines to do my paperwork. In addition, during previous generations "movie night" in the Ready Room meant breaking out an old reel-to-reel projector. By the time I served, we were using expensive ceiling-mounted projectors and VHS tapes. Most evenings in the Ready Room had a movie playing, and it was the SDO's responsibility to find one that was worth watching. Since there were almost always night flights in process, the Plat Camera was on in the corner of the room. During night-time recoveries, everyone kept one eye on the movie and one on the flight deck. We watched a LOT of movies during a typical deployment. One of the results of watching so many films, (many on a repeated basis) is that most naval aviators can sustain an entire conversation with just movie quotes.

While food was not allowed to be taken out of the wardroom, the ship did sell snacks that were an important part of movie watching. You could wander down to the small ship's store and buy almost anything you might see at any normal 7-11. At some point, our squadron bought a popcorn machine. Most squadrons raised money in one way or another to support their "coffee mess" and help defray the costs of their admin. Usually, they sold t-shirts or patches. We decided that selling popcorn would be a good thing, and it was. Every evening we'd get a few dozen of our fellow aviators to come by for a fifty-cent bag of popcorn, and they'd take them back to their own Ready Room and watch whatever movie was on.

There was another form of old-school recreation that could be found in almost every Ready Room, the Acey-Ducey board. Acey-Ducey was one of those games that never appealed to me, and as a result, I can't tell you how it is played. It is similar to Backgammon and has a naval history that goes back to the turn of the twentieth century. Supposedly, the game became a fixture on the ship because the dice and board needed to play the game could be easily packed and stored while aboard. My impression, however, was that it was mostly played by "Hinges" and the CO or XO. I very rarely saw any JOs playing, and that fact alone was enough to keep me from learning.

The most important occupant of the Ready Room was the junior aviator operating as the SDO. On the days that we flew, the SDO was responsible for "running" the flight schedule. They notified the operations department if missions or times changed, coordinated with the maintenance department to assign jets, managed individual crews (if someone was sick or couldn't fly), sometimes got weather briefs, coordinated low-level times, and many of the little tasks required for the Administration of the schedule. Only Lieutenants (and below) stood duty. The LCDRs of the squadron were deemed too busy to manage such a mundane task (and they were). The Ready Room was the SDO's place of work on the ship or back at home in the hangar. During days when we were not flying, the SDO stayed in the Ready Room during normal work hours and was available and near a phone at any other time.

One of the unique things about our squadron spaces on the USS America was that we had a lockable room where we could put a real washer and dryer. This space was right next to the CO's stateroom and was the cause of some angst and some entertainment. Normal laundry was done by the ship. Each of us had a laundry bag; it was stenciled with our name and the last four digits of our social security numbers. The bag was closed with a huge laundry pin. The laundry was collected a couple of times a week and took a day or two to return. The thing about laundry on an aircraft carrier is that it is all washed together, it is washed in a bag, and it is apparently done without much soap. As a result, all our clothes would gradually turn grey. While the items that were returned from the laundry didn't smell horrible, everything ended up smelling like the ship. I still have a few T-shirts from that era stored in cardboard boxes. The second I open them up, the unmistakable smell immediately transports me back to the boat. Flight suits were never at risk of damage, but the laundry always seemed to use a device that crushed or removed buttons from our khaki uniforms. When it came to our civilian clothes, the risk of loss, or theft was not a good thing for the limited inventory that we brought with us. All of these issues meant that having access to a real washer and dryer was fantastic. So, while most of our official laundry was still done by the ship, we washed our civilian clothes in these machines.

Using our own laundry facility occasionally generated some friction. One of the most important challenges was the fact that our laundry room was right next to the CO's stateroom. This meant that if a machine started making noise, he would hear it through the thin metal walls. The final straw for him was when someone put some sneakers in the dryer, turning it into a reverberating drum. At this point, he stood up in front of the Ready Room, declared the machines off-limits, and took the keys to the laundry room. First of all, whoever dried the shoes was an idiot, and it was understandable that the CO was pissed. However, placing the machines off limits was a big deal, and rebellion quickly began brewing. As soon as the CO relented and the keys reappeared, some stealthy JO crept into the room in the middle of the night, placed a handful of change in the dryer, locked the door, and hid the key. While the battle of the washing machines continued, this was one of the most humorous skirmishes.

Humor was an everyday part of our lives and was definitely a coping mechanism for life on the carrier. Humor could be found almost anywhere. New guys were always good targets for fun. It was common to tell a new aviator that they had to "pick a color" for the pen that they would use on the message board. We often told them the only color that was available was pink. Every day when the message board contained a pink initial was a thing of joy. Sometimes we'd send new guys down to the simulator, of course, the first thing that they had to do was to get the keys. The young aviator was sent from ready room to ready room in search of the simulator keys, generating mirth everywhere they went. Sometimes they persevered with their search to the point that they found themselves down in the bowels of the ship, usually in the engine spaces, when it finally dawned on them that there was no simulator.

On one occasion, we had several new guys show up in different squadrons at the same time of deployment. These young officers were convinced that they had to stand "mail bouy" watch, the concept being that this was how we received our mail while at sea. They were given an official life vest, and a pair of binoculars, and sent to the bridge of the ship, where a camera they didn't know about broadcast their diligent search to all hands. It was hysterical when one of the guys actually located a buoy and called out his contact. At some point, it just became embarrassing when our own new guy went up there. The concept being that we can make fun of our new guys, but not the rest of the air wing.

There were infrequent battles between squadrons. Sometimes squadron mascots were taken hostage and compromising photos were taken and released over time. One hard lesson was not to leave your coffee mug in another squadron's space. One guy from another squadron who was not well-liked did so. His cup was returned without incident after a few days. A few days after that, once we were sure he was using it again, pictures of his mug containing a lot of nasty things were delivered to his mailbox each day over the next week or so. I also remember a JO who was having a difficult time with one of our Department Heads. This young officer had a bit of a creative streak and generated multiple ways to gain revenge via the coffee mug. One of the easiest was just to place a piece of cellophane tape in the bottom of the mug. It would take a minute, but after hot coffee was poured in, the adhesive would weaken and the tape would float to the top. In a more time-consuming effort, he stole the same mug and took it down to a maintenance shop, where he drilled an almost invisible hole in the bottom, the leaky mug providing days of entertainment for those of us "in the know."

Finally, while there are many other details of everyday life at sea that may be interesting, the last one to discuss would probably be alcohol. Any military history buff could probably tell you that alcohol has been forbidden on U.S. Navy ships since it was banned by Navy Secretary Josephus Daniels in 1914. Whether the connection is true or not, this is apparently why sailors call coffee "a cup of Joe."

Anyway, while alcohol is banned on ships, as with any bureaucracy, there are exceptions. If a ship is at sea for longer than forty-five days without a port visit, the Commanding Officer can request a "beer day." If permission is granted, each sailor can have two government-funded beers. Having earned this privilege a couple of times, it is generally underwhelming. The Flag mess, where the Admiral eats and entertains, can provide alcohol if deemed necessary for official functions. Finally, the most important exception for the air wing is known as a "booze locker." Since hard alcohol is expensive, while on deployment, a squadron is customarily granted permission to maintain a locked (and sometimes inventoried) footlocker for hard liquor so they don't have to buy it in a foreign port. This locker stayed in the CO's cabin and went ashore to the admin and back. Aside from a few other exceptions, booze is banned at sea. This, however, does not mean that there is no alcohol on the ship.

In CVW-1, a couple of staterooms were known to be locations where an aviator might imbibe a bit if the weather was bad or on evenings when there was a reason to celebrate. For example, a certain fighter squadron eight-man stateroom was known to throw parties with enough frequency that the Master at Arms repeatedly tried to catch them in the act. For quite a while, the Master at Arms believed they could catch drunk sailors going to the "head" (bathroom in Navy parlance). Since the stainless-steel sinks in the rooms made handy urinals, these young aviators repeatedly avoided being caught as a result of this physical necessity. Legend says that one of the eight-man rooms had a cut-off pipe that just barely fit an empty beer can or bottle. So, it became common to discard empties in this location. What these young officers didn't know was that the pipe dead-ended in another space. When beer cans started raining down, the Master at Arms knew it was time to pounce. Working with the engineers, the Master at Arms traced the pipe, and when cans started dropping, the party came to an end.

My squadron was not so bold. Aside from the guys who were invited to participate in other squadron's parties, there was not any real desire to break the rules. That said, we were the entrepreneurs of the wing. Before one deployment began, we took the opportunity to exploit a hole in the regulations so that we could load a few pallets of fake beer onboard with the intent of selling it along with our popcorn. At some point during the on-load process, one of the ship's supply officers objected to the multiple pallets of fake beer coming aboard that were not part of his manifest. Senior leadership was consulted, and we were eventually allowed to keep what had been lifted aboard; about half of our anticipated load was left on the pier. This was probably good as we all had to store this near-beer in our rooms, and since it was not the best stuff, it took a while to get rid of.

Finally, I do remember one enterprising squadron officer who had a "hanging beer bag" sent to him. All one had to do was pour warm water into this bag, and it would supposedly make "beer" over time. Water was poured, and the bag hung inside his dirty flight suit for a suitable duration. When the beer was declared "ready," a couple of hardy souls drank at least some of it, probably more out of a sense of rebellion than taste. From my perspective, I was happy not to drink at sea. In fact, it seemed clear to me that being on the ship was a good way to get a break from all the alcohol that we imbibed on shore.

8

USS AMERICA (CV-66) 1991-1992

USS America (CV-66), U.S. Navy Photo

Ten days after pulling out of Norfolk to head on deployment, the USS America was scheduled to make its first port call. Unlike my first trip to England, where duty didn't interfere with my visit, when we pulled into Palma de Majorca, I had been scheduled to be the SDO on the second day in port. Since SDO duty began at 0730 and ran for 24 hours, from a practical perspective, this meant that I could go ashore with the first group, get a few beers, and have something to eat before I returned to the ship. As long as I came back that night, I would be able to take the duty first thing in the morning. So, this was my plan.

When we got off the ship, the first thing we discovered was that the air wing admin queens had all set up operations in the same hotel. This was good news. However, the problem was that this hotel was nowhere near the port where the ship was docked. I can't remember exactly where the hotel was, but it was about thirty minutes down the coast somewhere. This meant that getting to the admin required a cab ride, something that was always an issue in a foreign port. Anyway, I got to the admin with a few of the other guys, sat down, and had my first official beer on my first real deployment. It was awesome. As the afternoon continued and we wandered around it became clear that the town and hotel were empty. It was December in Palma, and most of the restaurants and bars were closed. After returning from our brief survey of the local territory, I remember standing on the balcony of the hotel room. It was several floors up, and I looked out at a nice pool in a courtyard below. As the evening progressed, it was clear that there wasn't much to do. So, I found someone else who needed to get "back ship," drank one last beer, caught a cab back to the port, and went to bed.

At seven the next morning, I dutifully got up, put on my uniform, and walked down to the Ready Room. I signed the duty log, checked the notes, and saw that there had been nothing urgent to report the day before. There was no requirement for me to stay in the Ready Room at that point; in fact, it was a good opportunity to go get breakfast. However, I sat down to read for a bit before I went back to my room to do some work and then take a nap. I hadn't been there for more than twenty minutes when the Ready Room door opened. In walked CAG, the Navy Captain, who was the air wing commander. I jumped up and stood there, stunned; CAG never came to our Ready Room. As I stared at him like a moron, CAG looked at me and asked, "Where is your Skipper?" I was pretty sure that my CO was on the beach with the rest of the squadron, and I told him as much. "I want to see him as soon as possible." With that, he turned and walked out.

"Holy shit." To be clear, these were the days before cell phones. The only communication with the beach was the handheld radios that the ship's officers used. From a practical perspective, there was no way for me to contact the guys in the admin. Hell, I really had no idea what the hotel was even called. The only way to get in touch with the Skipper was to send one of the officers who was not on duty to the admin and pass the message verbally. And this is what I did.

At about nine o'clock, an obviously agitated CAG walked back into the Ready Room. "Where is your CO?" I told CAG that I had sent two messengers into Palma to find the Skipper and bring him back. For the second time, he looked at me like I was a drooling idiot, turned around, and walked out. At this point, it was clear that there would be no nap for me. As the morning progressed, a couple of my squadron mates returned to the ship and the picture began to get clearer. There had been some kind of liberty incident involving our squadron the night before, and police had been called. I asked if the guys had delivered the message to the Skipper that CAG was looking for him, and to my surprise, the answer was, "Yes, he knows."

At noon, a now very angry CAG came into the Ready Room. "Where is your Skipper?" It was at this point that it was probably a good thing that I was a brand-new guy. CAG was totally pissed, but he knew that yelling at me was pointless. "Have him come see me as soon as he comes aboard." I acknowledged the order and relaxed a bit. Clearly, the Skipper's delaying tactic was working. CAG still wanted to see him, but the timeline had changed to "as soon as he comes aboard." I waited around anxiously for the rest of the day, and it gradually became clear that something bad had happened in several locations. Bored and drunk sailors on a wintertime port visit is not a good thing. At some point very late in the evening one of the fighter squadrons that was staying in the same hotel as my squadron had looked out of their balcony and realized that the pool was within striking distance of the beer bottles that they were rapidly emptying. With nothing else to do, they began to throw bottles at the pool. This was bad enough, but it didn't help that they were quite inaccurate, and a number of the bottles broke and scattered on the patio. They were warned several times by the hotel but eventually wore out the owner's patience, and they got kicked out.

That would have been bad enough, but unfortunately, they also got every other English-speaking person in the hotel kicked out, whether they were part of the air wing or not. To add insult to injury, when asked what squadron they were, they said they were "VAQ-137."

This strategic misdirection was effective, CAG had heard that the misbehavior in the hotel was our squadron's fault, and this is why he had wanted to have words with my CO. What I didn't know at the time was that there had been a large number of alcohol-related incidents across the city that first night. As news of all of these issues trickled back to the carrier, my Skipper's intentional delay was the best thing that he could probably have done, especially since it turned out that he actually had his own run-in with the Carabinieri (Spanish Police) the night before. As it turned out, things were such a mess in port that the Admiral had attempted to cancel liberty and recall everyone back to the carrier. The problem was that getting that message to the thousand sailors who had gone ashore was impossible. There was only one way to deliver that order, but unfortunately, nobody was familiar with it, so we stayed.

With this port call complete, I can't say that I was very impressed. It seemed clear that our glorious trip around the Mediterranean was doomed because it was cold, the weather was bad, and there were no tourists in town other than ourselves. Despite the rough start, and after another uneventful week at sea, we pulled into Naples harbor, the port where we would spend the next ten days across both Christmas and New Year's Eve.

Naples was not Palma. While life in Palma revolves around the tourist trade, Naples is a port that has been exposed to the antics of visiting sailors for thousands of years. There was nothing that Naples hadn't seen, and our visit wouldn't make so much as a ripple in the busy city's holiday routine.

So, I was now a salty veteran of two port visits, one that was enjoyable and the other that was less so. For this third visit, I would try something new. As the carrier approached each port visit, the Morale Welfare and Recreation officer (often known as the "Fun Boss") would usually arrange a wide variety of tours and events for the ship and air wing. I had heard from the other guys that these trips could be hit-and-miss, but several of us signed up for a Christmas trip to Rome. As described, we would catch a bus to Rome, tour the city, go to midnight mass at the Vatican, and return.

After the ship pulled into port, those of us who had signed up for the trip disembarked and located the bus that would take us on our adventure. Upon boarding the bus it was immediately clear that the vehicle had seen better days. The primary challenge that I recall was that one or more windows in the rear of the bus would not close, and it was cold outside. The second issue was that our guide, a helpful gentleman whom I will call "George," clearly did not speak much (if any) English. Regardless of these issues, we found our seats on the bus and headed north.

The trip from Naples to Rome is about three hours by bus. Somewhere near the halfway point, we pulled off the road into a little restaurant to have lunch. This restaurant looked a little threadbare, but the owner was clearly happy to see us. Despite my initial reservations, the first and most important thing about the restaurant was that the room was warm - we were all freezing from the open windows on the bus. The second most important thing was that the meal was excellent country-Italian food. The final critical issue was that they had alcohol. After being seated, we asked for some red wine. Within moments we were delivered copious amounts of "vino de casa." The wine was a bit raw, and we guessed that the grapes might have been stomped during that fall harvest. However, it contained alcohol, so that made it good enough.

After lunch, we loaded back onto the bus, headed north, and finally arrived in Rome. True to the contract, we traveled to all the major sights in town, places like the Coliseum, the Forum, and the Pantheon. The funny part for me was the methodology by which George allotted the time required for us to visit each location. It seemed that he had about a three-cigarette limit. Get out, take some pictures, read a guidebook, and walk around for a bit. However, when George was done with his three cigs, it was time to get back on the bus. Very efficient and, at some point, kind of hysterical. At the end of our whirlwind tour, we were dropped off at our hotel, a huge building that was almost empty. The rooms were spare and cold. The owner reluctantly turned on the heat after some complaining, and then it was time to head to the Vatican for mass. It was at this point that our helpful guide disappeared. We were supposed to attend the service, but as midnight approached, we found ourselves wandering around St Peter's Square with thousands of people and no tickets.

With only about thirty minutes before the service remaining, we were approached by a guy who asked us if we were Americans. The truth was that anyone could tell that we were Americans. A bunch of short-haired guys in slacks and blue jeans wandering around looking lost. In later years, we might have been more concerned with a potential terrorist plot, but instead, we struck up a conversation with the gentleman. As it turned out, this guy said he was from the American Embassy, and he just so happened to have extra tickets to the service. Again, it seemed too good to be true. Perhaps these were the tickets we had signed up for, but I don't think that was the case. What I remember about this interaction was that it seemed exceptionally random.

Of course, we gladly accepted the tickets and then moved to get in line. Even more absurd than the circumstances around getting tickets was the fact that within twenty minutes, we found ourselves in seats that were literally three or four rows back from the giant, ornate altar in the center of the cathedral where the Pope was holding mass. It was awesome. I mean, I could hear the Pope speak with my own ears. Now, I am not Catholic, but that service was one of the most amazing events of my life. There was no planning that would have put us in that spot. It certainly felt as if something had led us to Rome, and into seats for a service that was certainly the highlight of the trip. Honestly, I don't remember the bus ride back to Naples, but that midnight mass is something that I will never forget.

My final memory from Naples is that I was unlucky enough to have SDO on New Year's Eve. For many of the guys being on duty for this evening would have been a disaster, but after a week of Naples, I was more than ready to get back to work. However, the thing about being in Naples Harbor for the New Year was that I got the opportunity to see the craziest fireworks display of my life. I think it was actually my CO who told me that I should plan to go up to the flight deck and watch. So, as midnight approached, I made it to the flight deck and was wondering what might happen when, at the stroke of midnight, the town erupted into fireworks. Fireworks came from every window in every building, every street, every courtyard, and all the rooftops. I have no idea how they didn't burn the city down. The display was amazing, and the chaos of that night made me happy that I was safely on the ship instead of dodging alcohol-fueled fireworks displays. It was an astonishing night, but I was ready to head back to sea.

Over the next couple of weeks, we actually didn't do a lot of flying. Ten days after leaving Naples, we found ourselves in Souda Bay, Crete. This was a nice visit, but nothing sticks in my memory from the trip, although I do think an aviator from one of the other squadrons ended up in a Greek jail for attacking a Coke machine that was supposedly owned by the town's Mayor. A week later, we were the first carrier to pull into Athens, Greece, in more than six years.

Athens was an interesting visit. The Greek port of Piraeus had a little bit of the flavor of Naples. Piraeus had also seen sailors for thousands of years and seemed to shrug about our arrival. The people of Athens, on the other hand, weren't fond of our visit. I think this was the only port during my entire career where I did not feel welcomed. I saw people spit at us as we passed by in town. The fact that they did not like us did not keep us from setting up an admin and having a good time. I remember a night in a little bar that we essentially took over. I think the occasion was a "wetting down," the celebration of a promotion. The owner of the small bar did not have very many choices for American music, and as I vaguely recall, Frank Sinatra's "New York, New York" must have played at least a hundred times.

I didn't do much sightseeing during that trip, but I did make it to the Acropolis. This was the middle of the winter and there were no regular tourists, so we had the place to ourselves. In addition, unlike today, there wasn't much of the ancient site that was roped off; we wandered everywhere we could. As I walked among those ancient stones, I really felt an unusual sense of history. It was awe-inspiring to imagine who had visited those ruins. I took more pictures here than almost any place during that cruise. Someday, I'd like to go back.

Despite the wonder of the Acropolis, I was not disappointed to pull out of Athens. After a few days of flying in the confines of the Eastern Mediterranean, it was not long before we pulled into Antalya, Turkey. By this point, I was already a little jaded about port visits. Antalya was nice. There were a lot of German tourists, and their influence on the area was clear. With little aside from good food and beer to be had, it wasn't a particularly noteworthy visit. Lots of guys went out in town to search for carpets, but I had no interest. The one thing I do remember was the beautiful leather jacket that one of our shipmates bought that smelled horribly of urine when it got slightly wet. After a few days, we pulled back out to sea and proceeded on our tour of the Mediterranean.

As an aside, occasionally someone will see today's headlines about Unidentified Flying Objects and ask if I have ever seen one. The answer is, "I'm not sure." As we headed from Turkey towards Israel, we did a bit of flying off the Israeli and Syrian coastline. One very, very dark night, we were doing orbits over the Mediterranean to the south of Cyprus and were looking at interesting radar signals from the region when one of the guys said, "Hey, I think we are being followed." As I looked around, it certainly seemed that there was something on my left wing that occluded the stars. There were no lights, but there was essentially a shadow in the dark that appeared to be flying formation with us (if that makes sense). So, I began to maneuver our jet, a little like a kid trying to find the location of a scary shadow in their room. My intent was to see if I could force whatever it was that was flying near us into the open. After a few minutes of trying, I couldn't shake whatever seemed to be following us. As my maneuvers became increasingly "energetic," my CO (who was in the backseat) said something like, "If it can stay with us like this in the dark, we probably shouldn't mess with it."

Disappointed, I agreed. I returned to level flight and never identified what I might have flown formation with.

Ten days after leaving Antalya, we pulled into Haifa, Israel. It is worth noting that there are two general kinds of port visits; during the first kind, the ship pulls "pier-side." Pier-side liberty is awesome; it makes trips into town much easier and cuts down the number of officers and sailors required for duty positions. In the second kind, the ship anchors in the bay somewhere near the port. Haifa was one of the ports where the carrier anchored out, and this had implications for all of the JOs in the air wing.

The biggest issue for us was that if the ship was anchored out, this meant that we were all eligible for a duty known as "Boat Officer" or "Boat-O." This was one of the worst duties in a long list of crappy jobs you could get assigned to do during a port visit. When the ship anchored outside the port, the supply officer would charter several ferries to run the ship's crew back and forth to the shore. These ferries could be of any size but usually were large enough to carry at least a few dozen sailors. A Boat-O was stationed aboard this commercial ferry as a safety officer; they would be wearing a dress uniform but had no real authority to override whoever was operating the ferry. This had real-world implications because the ferry operator was generally paid to keep running whether they had sailors on board or not - and no matter what the weather was. If the weather got bad or the ferry seemed like it was being operated in a less-than-ideal manner, a Boat-O was technically responsible for keeping the operator in line but in actuality, could do little more than complain (at least until you got to the ship or the shore and could relay the issue to someone with real authority).

For a Boat-O, keeping the peace among the drunk sailors returning from their visit was a more practical objective. This role was a necessity during the evening and night ferry trips when the crew was heading back to the ship. Many a sailor came back "three sheets to the wind," as has been the nature of sailors since the beginning of time. Most had calmed down by the time they got on the ferry, but occasionally the Boat-O needed to step in to stop an argument, intervene in a fight, or just manage a very "enthusiastic" sailor who may be singing, yelling, or somehow annoying everyone else. Monitoring who was coming aboard was important. Generally, the most inebriated sailors were kept on the pier until they were sober enough to not cause an issue. Those that were the worst off found themselves in a "clamshell." This practice has been discontinued, but when a sailor was stupid-drunk and violent or aggravated, they were occasionally sandwiched between two canvas stretchers that were then tied together (clamshell) and placed on their belly until they sobered up.

The more challenging variant of this duty put a Boat-O in a position of more authority, with equally increased professional risk. This occurred when the officer was assigned to one of the ship's own boats, known as a "motor whaleboat." These boats were carried on the hangar deck of the carrier and put in the water to augment the ferries. A motor-whaleboat could carry a couple of dozen sailors. It generally was open to the weather (sometimes they had canvas covers), had no heat, no navigational equipment, and the motors were likely to quit at any time. While the Boat-O was technically in charge, the motor whaleboat was run by a Coxswain (pronounced "Coxsun"). In my experience, this was a very grumpy sailor who usually had been awake for at least twenty-four hours and who was very much not interested in what some aviator thought about his seamanship. As the Boat-O on a whaleboat, it was not unlikely to find yourself slightly lost or adrift somewhere in a foreign port with a radio that didn't work. Usually, however, the worst case was confined to sailors puking on their shoes as the small boats bounced through the waves.

The visit to Haifa rounded out my personal journey to some exceptionally historic places of interest. I had a running joke with my parents about visiting all these "old rocks," but my sense of history had actually been energized by the trips to Rome and Athens. So, when we pulled into Haifa, I decided to sign up for another tour. As circumstances would have it, everyone on the ship decided to sign up for tours as well. As a result, when I went down to the mess decks to see what was available, there was only one tour left, a multi-day trip with the official Rabbi for Sixth Fleet. First of all, who knew that the Navy's Mediterranean Fleet had a Rabbi on the staff? Second, why was he giving tours? Anyway, I signed up for this tour with several guys from my squadron, including my CO. For the second time on this deployment, I was exceedingly lucky with my choice of tour.

It turns out that the Rabbi was an awesome guy who had put together a very thoughtful itinerary that took us from Roman ruins to lunch at a working Kibbutz and then finally to Jerusalem. At each location we stopped, he knew enough to explain the historical and religious issues of interest. The tour was awesome. However, Jerusalem was the highlight of the trip. First of all, I found that my attention in my Bible study classes was sorely deficient. We visited most of the stages of the Cross and the Wailing Wall and wandered through the wonderful, narrow, and terrifying streets of Old Jerusalem. At some point, we eventually found ourselves visiting the Church of the Holy Sepulcher. If you aren't familiar (and I wasn't), this church is recognized as the site of Jesus's crucifixion and the tomb where he was buried. The church entrance just looks like a door in a huge sandstone wall, and it is run by a few different denominations of monks who divide up the responsibility across the year. While I am no expert, the architecture was fascinating.

As we entered the church, there was a lengthy line to visit the tomb. Not excited to wait, I wandered off into the dimly lit building by myself, looking at the wonderful paintings and decorations, killing time until we were ready to leave. After aimlessly walking deeper into the church, I found myself in a dark room that was lit by candles. There were monks doing some liturgical chanting somewhere else in the building. Their chants echoed off the walls and, when added to the flickering sensation of the candles, became instantly alarming. With no warning, the hair on the back of my arms stood up and I felt what writers always call "a sudden chill in the air." In an instant, I had the strongest feeling that I had been launched sometime far into the past. I know it sounds crazy, but I really felt like I had been transported a thousand years in an instant. In a near panic, I retreated from the room as fast as I could, not entirely sure of where I was, but definitely wanting to see someone from my group. It took a few minutes to escape, but I eventually found the line and joined back up with the group as we moved on. To this day, however, I swear that if I had gone deeper into the building, the story might have ended up differently.

With Haifa in the rear-view mirror, it was time for the USS America to transit the Suez Canal and start a trip towards the Arabian Gulf. Today, a carrier's Suez transit is usually a high-security affair, with heavily armed helicopters, military guards, and everyone locked inside. On this occasion, there were some armed sailors around the exterior of the ship, but for most of us, it was just a no-fly day.

The trip through the Suez was my first opportunity to experience a flight-deck picnic. Initially, this sounded great. Much of the air wing had just been through the same transit less than a year prior, so they were prepared. There were folding chairs and small inflatable pools brought up to the flight deck. The mess decks were closed for lunch, and burgers were grilled in the open on the flight deck. The thing about the Suez Canal, however, is that you are surrounded by endless sand and lots of less-than-hygienic agricultural pursuits. This resulted in a picnic where you had to fight the flies for your burger and then pick the sand from the meal. Despite this, it was a very interesting trip, and we were heading to a place where there had just been a war. So, as we entered the Great Bitter Lake, I left the flight deck and prepared for the events to come.

Flying in the Red Sea was the closest I had come to getting a sense of what Desert Storm had looked like. However, unfortunately for the excited new guy, the initial indications were that there wasn't much to see. We couldn't fly into Saudi Arabia or Egypt and were confined to flying over international waters. As we exited through the Bab al-Mandab Straits (known to us as the "Barbara Mandrel" straits), we did some flying near Djibouti and then headed to the coast of Oman to participate in an exercise called "Beacon Flash." This exercise was notable because of a low-level route that was called "Star Wars Canyon." Every aviator in the air wing was ready for the canyon. I had heard about it several times and was looking forward to seeing if it matched all the hype.

On the day I was scheduled to fly, we carefully briefed the route, pointed out all the issues, and discussed the fact that we had to be careful leaving the canyon so that we didn't cross over some active Omani air defenses on the way back to the carrier. Then we flew out into the middle of the desert and found the river canyon that we were looking for. Yes, Star Wars Canyon is cool. Yes, the route is a bit like the movie. The issue that I discovered once I got down below the edge of the canyon was that the Prowler was not really the right jet to zoom around the sharp, blind corners that the route contained. At some point, I finally climbed towards the top of the canyon and skipped over some of the turns that I probably could have made but which I couldn't "read" from below the ridge line. Underwhelmed as I was, it was still better than most of our average missions, and I can say, "been there, done that." It was only a few years later that a young F/A-18C pilot didn't make one of those turns and hit the canyon wall.

If you have to be on a carrier in the Arabian Gulf, April and May are not bad times to be there. We pulled into the hazy and hot gulf with a bit of ceremony, as the USS America was the first carrier to return to the region since it had participated in the Gulf War. To our surprise, we only flew for a day or so and then headed to the water north of Bahrain and dropped anchor. I was now a member of the exclusive group of sailors who had the wonderful experience of sitting at the "Bahrain Bell." What this meant was that the carrier sat well off the coast of Bahrain, under the protective cover of our land-based Patriot missiles. This procedure was the Navy's solution for the fact that we running out of gas money and nobody had scheduled a port visit. So, we sat. This period introduced me to one of the least fun duty experiences of this cruise.

This was an era when cell phones were still huge, handheld devices that were about the size of a brick. The supply officer leased three or four of these things and set up an area at the top of the carrier's tower where we could get reception. We taped the phones into their chargers, and then allowed every sailor to come up and talk for five minutes - maximum. The officers charged to enforce this time limit were the air wing junior pilots. We had this watch in four-hour blocks. A sailor would make it to the deck after waiting in a line that snaked around the carrier. I would dial the number, give the sailor the phone, and they would start talking. No matter how many times they were warned that they were only getting five minutes to talk, the time would always catch them short. Inevitably, they would just be getting past the "How are you?" stage of a conversation and then discover their wife had left them, the washing machine had died, the car was broken, or their kid was sick, and then have to hang up. Horrible. The only consolation we could offer was to send the sailor back to the end of the hours-long line so that they could get more information in their next call.

When we finally got back into the air, we spent our time flying around in the Northern Arabian Gulf. While it may appear to be a large body of water, there is not much space for a carrier to maneuver, and they were restricted to specific areas or "boxes." There were similar restrictions for aircrew; we were always at risk of causing an international incident by flying too close to Iran, in particular. I specifically remember finding a radar contact on the surface somewhere up north. We circled overhead and then dove down to take a look. We were very low and at a pretty slow speed, only to find out that we were flying by an armed Iranian Osa missile boat. As the Iranians yelled at us on the radio, we hauled ass out of there. I am not sure we got pictures of that one. However, I was happy that we had the XO in the back seat, as he was the one who ended up explaining our actions to CAG.

The only other exciting event was flying the "Blue Two" low level that went around Kuwait in a clockwise direction. At about thirty minutes long, the low-level route gave guys like me who had missed Desert Storm ample opportunity to see the residue of combat. There were hundreds of blown-up tanks, bunkers, oil platforms, and other equipment. The gas flares were mesmerizing, and the destruction around Bubiyan Island emphasized how brutal the fight had been. Aside from the residue of combat, the route was flat and boring. It was also the first low-level where I discovered that camels don't run from jet noise, but sheep do.

The rest of our flying was routine. Aside from random warships, the primary hazard for us was the airspace over a place called Farsi Island. Literally a two-hundred-yard-wide sand pile, this island sits right in the middle of the gulf. Being the good guys, the U.S. honors this lump of sand with a twelve-mile standoff (although I am not sure the Iranians knew or cared). Since these were the days before GPS, it didn't take much of a navigation error to clip this twelve-mile standoff. If you were airborne and heard the term "Hotdog Red," you knew you were in trouble. It always seemed as if the ship's air traffic control was trying to put the air wing holding pattern right over the island, and then we'd get blamed.

After a week or so at sea, we began a series of port visits. We visited Dubai, then Abu Dhabi, and then Dubai again. Unlike the fabulous built-up cities that exist there today, in early 1992, these towns were just getting started with their huge construction booms. Before we pulled into port the first time, we were repeatedly warned about never being alone, watching for terrorists, and generally keeping a raised level of awareness. Everyone was jumpy when we went ashore. As is frequently the case, the hotel where we had our admin required us to take a cab or bus. I remember getting into a cab with a friend from another squadron, providing the destination, getting a nod from the driver, and off we went. After driving for a while, the driver turned to the back seat and began to speak very earnestly in Arabic to us. As neither of us had any idea what he was saying, we nodded. Within a few moments, the cab was pulling to the side of a vacant road. Now our "fight or flight" instincts were kicking in. When the driver went to the trunk of the car to open it up, we were moments from defending ourselves. You may imagine the relief we felt when the driver pulled out a prayer mat, stretched it out on the edge of the highway, and began his evening prayers.

I don't remember a ton of significance, however, I do recall that one of our first admins was in a hotel that looked kind of like a single-level Best Western. We had been warned that we could not get our usual multiple cases of beer to stock the admin in Dubai itself. We could find places to drink, but only in select hotels and clubs. In one of the better moves made by an admin queen, our guys found a beer distributor in Abu Dhabi (a neighboring emirate) who would send a truck loaded with beer to our hotel for the right price, but he would do so only as long as he delivered it to a parking lot that was not connected to the hotel. I remember that this success resulted in us humping multiple cases of beer over the tall hotel security fence to the amazement of the rest of the air wing.

In general, these were good visits. We saw the great Gold Souk, the spice and perfume sellers, and visited all the British bars that served alcohol. We learned from one experienced member of our squadron that we should be looking for good Filipino cover bands. I had one of the best gourmet buffets I have ever had in one of the large hotels downtown. Along the way, many of the guys had discovered that genuine Persian Rugs could be had for a relative pittance. There was a roaring trade in buying rugs and then shipping them home so that they could (supposedly) be sold for two or three times the cost. I had no interest in rugs, gold, or perfume. I remember getting "Bombed at Biggles" and listening to a British couple who entertained at an Italian restaurant by playing a "country song" that was just John Denver, over and over.

In May, it was time to leave, and we put the Arabian Gulf in the rear-view mirror, headed back up the Red Sea, did another flight deck picnic through the Suez, and turned for home. We arrived off the coast of Norfolk in June 1992. It was a wonderful first deployment for a "nugget" pilot and gave me a solid foundation for the more strenuous deployments that were to come.

Flying formation in the T-34C "Turbo Mentor" Somewhere over South Texas

Flying my TA-4J through the weather on a division formation flight

One of many cross-country stops made while transiting to or from the USS America (CV-66)

Being dunked after my last flight as a TA-4J student

Standing Squadron Duty Officer - Naples

All Photos from the Author's Personal Collection – All Rights Reserved

A snowy Christmas in the Alps

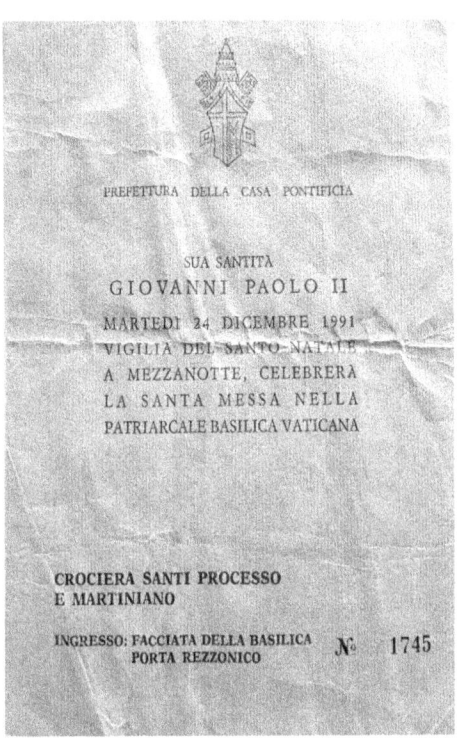

My Ticket for Midnight Mass at the Vatican

A Sign of Maintenance Department Frustration

The ticket for my Acropolis Tour

Loading the magazine of my trusty .45

View before engine starts, behind Cat Three

Preparing for a flight in the mighty EA-6B Prowler

Another "Hero Pic," with obligatory cruise mustache

A "Hero Pic" as I sat in an F-14A before my LSO Cross Training Flights

Time to disestablish a squadron

All Photos from the Author's Personal Collection – All Rights Reserved

First class travel, C-17 style

Camp McCool

The Amazingly Beautiful Hindu Kush

Camp McCool Front Gate

The Deadly Pech River Valley

Bagram Air Base Just Before a Combat Recovery

All Photos from the Author's Personal Collection – All Rights Reserved

Life as XO. Totally Not Stressed

The AN-12 that landed and burned in Bagram

One of a few visits I made to Kandahar Air Base

Airborne somewhere over Afghanistan

The Best VAQ Squadron ever and our Desert Camo EA-6B

All Photos from the Author's Personal Collection – All Rights Reserved

My office view as Commander, CVWP

Snow and a line of EA-18G aircraft at Whidbey

An evening tanking event with a KC-135 high over Western Washington in an EA-18G

Last flight in the Navy. Flew an EA-18G up the VR-1355 Low Level Route

My last Navy portrait while working for CNO

All Photos from the Author's Personal Collection – All Rights Reserved

9

PEACETIME FLYING AT SEA

EA-6B in Low Holding, Author's Collection

While there are several war stories in this book, it seems worth spending a little time and space describing normal peacetime flight operations. In the majority of my experience, a carrier would fly for twelve to fourteen hours a day. These flying days were divided into "cycles," each cycle being defined by a launch and recovery. Generally, a cycle was about an hour and a half long, and this meant that we'd fly eight or so cycles a day. It is important to note that this did not mean that your flight would only be an hour and a half long. The order of launch and recovery onboard a carrier is dictated by how the flight deck manages space as each jet takes off and lands, and by their general fuel states. For the F/A-18C, this meant that they launched later and recovered earlier. For an EA-6B, this usually meant that we launched earlier and landed later. As a result, most of the peacetime flights from the carrier in my logbook are somewhere between 1.7 and 2.3 hours long.

The first thing to learn as a Prowler pilot flying from the aircraft carrier was how to conserve fuel. While the FRS made us memorize a variety of speeds and angles of attack, flying around the boat made these performance metrics part of your muscle memory. We generally launched with a 56,000-pound aircraft. This loadout included three ALQ-99 pods, two 2,000-pound external fuel tanks, and internal fuel. This gave us 19,400 of fuel or just under ten tons. Of course, you can't use all this fuel, because need to have some left in the tank when you land. While we could land with as much as 8,800 pounds of fuel in the aircraft, it was typical to find yourself "in the wires" after an arrested landing with somewhere around 5,500 pounds. An EA-6B pilot who paid attention to the most efficient climb rates, descent rates, and airspeeds at altitude could make one tank of gas go a long way. A pilot who did not would inevitably put their aircraft and crew at risk, and create headaches for leadership.

To help us manage our gas, we created what was known as a "fuel ladder" for every hop. This simple chart counted back from the fuel state you wanted to have when landing. You almost always launched above the ladder, and this meant that you had some amount of "extra" fuel to do the core mission with. Once you burned enough fuel to intersect the burn profile outlined on the ladder, it was time to stop what you were doing and conserve fuel. If you went below your ladder, you were generally out of luck. There was no "extra" fuel around the aircraft carrier, and if you burned too much gas, there were no early landings. While the carrier almost always had a tanker airborne (in the early days it would be a KA-6D, after that, it would be an S-3B), the Prowler was rarely scheduled for any offload. This fuel was generally reserved for the strike fighter aircraft that were always short of gas. At best, as a Prowler crew, we occasionally visited the tanker and got day and night "dry plugs" to keep up our qualifications, but that was about it.

As I gained experience in the airplane, I learned just how slow I could fly to keep the transmitters in the ALQ-99 pods online. The pods were powered by an external Ram Air Turbine (RAT) that turned in the wind. If we didn't need to jam, I would keep the aircraft as close to the aircraft's maximum endurance speed as possible to save fuel. This was always tricky, as it was only a few knots faster than being in a stall, but as my time in the jet grew, I could fly the jet to its maximum efficiency in my sleep (or nearly so). If a pilot managed the jet correctly, you could save enough gas to allow about ten minutes of full-power cloud chasing, two or three descents to the water and back to altitude, or one or two fast runs at low altitude.

While the intent was always to come back to the carrier, most of the time there was a designated divert field. The divert field was required if an aircraft emergency dictated that you couldn't land on the carrier. As a result, it was a necessity to always be aware of how much gas it would take to fly to that field. This was known as a "bingo fuel." One of the hard and fast rules of carrier aviation was that if you reached this pre-designated emergency fuel state and were not very, very close to landing on the carrier, you automatically turned and climbed to the most efficient altitude and headed to the divert. I think I only "bingoed" two times in my career, and both times were during CQ. However, this doesn't mean that "bingos" were that unusual. In my experience, the carrier would send fighters that ran out of gas to the beach several times each deployment. Anyway, it is a bit difficult to explain how important this was - but fuel became the center of my flying life, and my stress level was managed by my fuel indicator (and it still is in my cars, where I never let the tank get below half).

There were a few common missions for an EA-6B to fly from the ship. One of the most common of the "Prowler go long" missions was called SSC. This mission was a surface search intended to help the Strike Group intelligence guys maintain a good "picture" of all the ships that were in the vicinity of the carrier. During an

SSC mission, we'd get assigned a specific sector of the ocean somewhere near the carrier and spend our allotted time finding and identifying ships, noting their type, heading, and speed, and bringing that information back to the intelligence spaces after the flight. Sometimes we would be looking for specific ships, sometimes we just were looking for unusual configurations, speeds, or locations.

In some cases, we'd "rig" the ship that we had seen from altitude. We always carried a government 35mm film camera in the jet. Sometimes the front seat ECMO would have it, sometimes it was in the back. If we decided to "rig" a ship it just meant that we would fly very low down one side, do a turn, cross the stern (so that we could see the name and flag), and then do another turn and fly up the other side. We were generally careful not to cross the bow, especially of warships, as this is technically a sign of disrespect (I don't think anyone else recognizes this rule). While it was easy to think of these as a "low flyby," I generally resisted the temptation to waste gas unless there was something unique or entertaining about a target. That said, there was nothing better than rigging a cruise ship, or warship at five-hundred knots, and then pulling four or five G's and climbing away into the clouds. This speed often made getting a good camera shot a bit trickier, but a seasoned crew could make it work.

Another common mission for us was a "JAMEX." It might not be surprising that a radar-jamming aircraft would do jamming missions, but while we were deployed, we were always very careful about doing any "real" jamming, because there might be someone out there recording our transmissions. Anyway, a JAMEX was typically flown against a friendly warship that wanted to get some training against an actual jammer. We'd coordinate with the ship in advance, go find it after we launched, and then do a variety of mission profiles. Our favorite was always the low-altitude strike. This required a Prowler to fly very low (often at two hundred feet or less) while jamming the target, with the intent of arriving overhead the ship without being engaged by their weapon system. These profiles almost always ended up in a fast flyby of the ship and a vertical pop-up back to altitude. As a veteran of thousands of such runs, I can say that the one deployment where we sent an ECMO to visit the ships in the battlegroup to describe our capabilities was very helpful. I can't count the times when we'd do a successful flyby, only to be told that the ship "couldn't see jamming." When asked if they ever saw the aircraft on the radar, they nearly always said "no." Drawing a line between these two facts was often a surprisingly difficult task.

We also did similar flights with our fighter brethren. A mission known as "AIC" was a common task, and boring. The fighter squadrons needed to maintain currency with their radars and fly known profiles against what was usually a non-maneuvering target. Sometimes the ship's radar operators needed to practice vectoring fighters around. In many cases, the target was a Prowler. We'd set up thirty or forty miles apart from each other and then turn in and fly toward the fighter until intercepted. We'd generally do this for three or four runs before we were all "on our ladder." Occasionally, we would be asked to jam the fighters, so that they could try to work through the issue. Much like their shipboard sensor operators, however, the fighter guys didn't like being jammed, because it made their life difficult. It was also embarrassing for them when they would fly right past us on a clear blue-sky day while looking down at their empty radar screen. It was always obvious when this happened, and if we saw them before they saw us, we'd turn onto their tail and then call a missile shot. Every once in a while, we'd get into a bit of more aggressive maneuvering with the fighters, but we rarely had the fuel to waste, and this always ended up with us being "shot down" in an embarrassingly short time.

Low levels were also a good option but were not scheduled very often because flying low and fast burned a lot of fuel very quickly, and the ship had to be close enough to shore that we could complete the entire route inside a single cycle. While all the tactical aircraft communities flew low levels, the Prowler community lived for them. During my first deployment, I learned that they were a bit more difficult to fly than just jumping down into the Cascade mountains at home. We flew a few low-level routes in France and Italy during this first cruise and then again in Oman and Kuwait. They were always an adventure and a bit stressful, as you didn't want to get lost at 500 feet in a foreign country (like our USMC friends).

One of my low levels on this cruise was essentially right down the bottom third of the boot of Italy, from the north to the south. It was a beautiful day for a low-level flight, with clear blue skies and good weather. These were still the days when we were following paper low-level charts and maintaining our location by using a fixed groundspeed and heading. We had a very good Inertial Navigation System in the EA-6B, but it would drift, and its accuracy depended on how good the ship's location was when we started. While most of the route was low risk, the only thing that I remember that was briefed as a hazard was that we needed to turn to the west before we went out into the Gulf of Taranto, the body of water inside the "boot heel" of Italy. There was some kind of Italian helicopter exercise going on. As we headed south at more than four-hundred-and-twenty miles an hour we eventually found ourselves flying over the top of a low layer of clouds or fog. We could occasionally see the ground but soon lost that as a reference. We turned to the west "on time" and flew for several minutes when the clouds broke up and we realized we were out over the water. Crap. The only good thing was that nobody was yelling at us, so we quickly changed our heading and got back over the coast. No harm, no foul.

One of the kinds of flights that I enjoyed once I had enough hours to become qualified were "Functional Check Flights," or FCFs. There were three common types of functional check flights, an FCF C was done when there had been maintenance on the flight controls, an FCF B was done when there was maintenance on an engine, and an FCF A checked out the entire aircraft. In each case, there was a strict checklist for what was being checked and in which order. The FCF C was easy and very common. For example, the Prowler frequently had issues with its leading-edge slats not coming completely up, or requiring a "bump" to get them to indicate up. Once maintenance had been done on the aircraft, an FCF was required. The FCF C required us to transition into landing configuration and ensure that the issue had been repaired.

The FCF B was less common. We tried to keep major maintenance to a minimum at sea, but inevitably there was an engine change because they reached "high time," or had some kind of blade damage. The most likely symptom of this damage was compressor stalls, or "chugs." Essentially, we knew that there might be a problem with the engine if a large fireball came out of the front when we rapidly brought the throttle back to idle. While this was okay if it happened occasionally, if it happened with some frequency and could not be mitigated by maintenance, the engine was swapped.

The FCF B profile was fun because it required you to take the jet to its service ceiling of 40,000 feet. While this might not be an issue for a commercial aircraft or a fighter, it was a challenge in a Prowler and it took quite a while to get up there. Coming down from 40,000 feet was the only time that a Prowler might potentially exceed the speed of sound. I remember initiating a steep descent on my first FCF at that altitude and then realizing that there was no way that I could bring the nose up because the air was too thin. We blew right through the airspeed limitation for our pods but the CO who was with me only laughed. The truth was that there was little risk and the jet was so bulbous that it quickly slowed as the air became thicker.

One of the most entertaining missions we could fly was simulated air combat. The EA-6B did not carry any air-to-air ordnance, so the entire reason for our air combat training was to enable us to survive by running away if we were jumped by an enemy aircraft. There were two kinds of Defensive Air Combat (DEFTAC) training flights for us; those where we fought against other Prowlers, and those where we had a mission that was supported by a real fighter. The ones where we fought against another Prowler were the most fun. While the intent was to neutralize our opponent and successfully escape, it was very difficult not to turn a fight against another EA-6B into a competitive event and see who could outmaneuver whom. Not wanting to "follow the rules" frequently made these events very frustrating for my instructors, but I could rarely resist trying to gain an advantage instead of turning tail and racing away.

When it came to maneuvers against a real fighter aircraft, the outcome of these DEFTAC "fights" was always kind of depressing. An F/A-18C or F-14 could easily turn and kill an EA-6B within twenty or so seconds. This didn't keep us from trying to get a simulated missile shot when we could, but there was no practical way to gain an offensive position against a knowledgeable opponent in a real fighter.

While the modern fighters on the carrier were always difficult to compete against, one of the more equal opponents we would routinely train with were the Navy F-5 fighters stationed at NAS Fallon or NAS Key West. The F-5 was fast and very tough to see, but it was not as maneuverable as the F/A-18C. In fact, the F-5 had a turning radius that was similar to a well-flown Prowler. During one of my favorite squadron adventures we took our EA-6B's across the country, from Whidbey to Key West, downloaded all the external stores, and flew the aircraft "slick." While this would never be the way we flew in combat, it made the EA-6B surprisingly agile and our efforts against the aggressors became much more fun.

Regardless of the mission, there were many little joys associated with flying at sea. One of the best of these was known as "cloud surfing." Most of our flying was done in international waters under flight rules known as "due regard." While we did have our own separation procedures, on the off chance that there was airline traffic in the vicinity, it was usually well above us. This meant that if there were any good-looking cumulus clouds or a nice flat table-top of cirrus, you could use your spare fuel carving through or around them. This was the type of flying that I think many people dream about. Some guys treated the clouds like an obstacle course, whipping their jets through gaps as if they were canyons. I preferred to be as smooth as possible with my air work, pulling up and rolling inverted to get the canopy as close as possible to the cloud. This generated a much better sense of speed and emphasized the three-dimensional character of the environment. It was also great fun to find a nice flat cloud deck. In situations like this, you could skim right into the upper level of the cloud. When you eventually climbed above the layer you could look back down and see where the turbulence from your passage had left marks in the sky. Finally, there were times when you saw isolated rain showers. Every once in a while it was helpful to fly the jet through them to get a "freshwater wash-down" and remove some of the ever-present corrosive sea salt from the aircraft.

Anyway, when I dream about flying, if it isn't some nightmare about being low on gas, then it is usually a dream about cloud surfing over the Caribbean somewhere.

10

USS AMERICA (CV-66) 1993 - 1994

USS America (CV-66) In the Suez Canal, U.S. Navy Photo

The USS America and CVW-1 had completed a wartime deployment in 1990-1991 and a full cruise in 1991-1992. When we got home, we all expected the normal eighteen months of turnaround and another deployment in 1994. Instead, we got the word that we'd be back at sea doing "workups" in a mere seven months; in fact, we'd be heading "back to the boat" in February to start preparing for our next deployment. For some, this was unhappy news; for me, this was awesome. The gas money kept flowing, our flying continued, and life was busy. After about a month or so of time off, the squadron reassembled from post-deployment vacation and began to do the "unit level" flying that was among the most fun that a young aviator could have.

One good example was an air defense exercise with the Canadians. Whidbey Island is very close to the U.S. Canadian border, and in fact, one of our usual weather-divert fields was Comox Air Base, about seventy miles to the north of us on Vancouver Island, British Columbia. During an unusual stretch of glorious summer weather, we got the unique opportunity to fly to the north end of Vancouver Island, take gas from a KC-135, and then run down the Canadian Cascade Mountain range to the south at low altitude, trying to hide from Canadian F/A-18Cs that were trying to find us. While the VR-1355 low-level that follows the Cascade Mountains in Washington State is the most beautiful low-level route in the U.S., the mountains and glaciers in the Cascades of British Columbia are probably the most beautiful places that I have ever flown on Earth. I will never forget how big everything was, and this was nearly my downfall.

On what I think was probably the final event of the series, we took three squadron jets on the mission. We tanked from the KC-135, crossed back onto the Canadian mainland, and descended into the mountains to start our low-altitude flight. The route we had chosen took us over a monstrous glacier that was eight or nine thousand feet up in the Cascades. Well, the trapezoidal shape of the ice field and the massive size of the glacier made me feel like I was much higher than I was, an optical illusion that was uncommon but dangerous. In order to descend, I executed a lazy flaperon roll (the Prowler had flaperons instead of ailerons) to begin what I thought would be a shallow dive to a low level. However, as I began to recover from the maneuver, my radar altimeter went off at 1000 feet above the ground. I instantly realized that I was much, much closer to the earth than my eyes had led me to believe. Unfortunately, there wasn't a lot to be done. After tanking, I had a jet that was heavy and full of fuel, and the air in the high mountains was much thinner than I had initially allowed for, resulting in less lift from the wings. Without panicking, I applied some power and very carefully eased the stick back as far as I could without stalling. As the dive shallowed, we bottomed out at around 500 feet above the huge ice field, right where I wanted to be but not how I wanted to get there. I am not sure that anyone in the aircraft knew how truly exciting that roll was, but it taught me a lesson about "assumptions" that I never forgot.

In September, we spent two weeks flying a "Green Flag" event at Nellis Air Force Base, Nevada. While many people may be familiar with Red Flag, Green Flag was a slightly different program. Today, a Green Flag event is structured around air-to-ground integration, but in 1992 it was primarily centered around Electronic Warfare and Command and Control. From a practical perspective, this meant that there were not quite as many fighter aircraft participating in air-to-air combat and that the Suppression of Enemy Air Defenses effort that we participated in was a big deal. Two things about that trip stick in my memory. The first was that we couldn't find any rooms on the base. I think we were in one of the periods when the Navy decided to cut back on paying per diem for official travel, and we found ourselves sharing rooms in a seedy hotel in North Las Vegas.

Today, this is the area where the awesome light show takes place on a canopy over Fremont Street. At that time, however, that part of town was only notable for the presence of the Clarke County Detention Center. In essence, we were in a hotel that was one step above those that rented out rooms by the hour. Like all the other hotels in the city, this place had a small casino with one-armed bandits at the entrance. I vividly remember walking into the stale, cigarette-smoke-filled lobby every day and seeing the same old people pulling the handles on those machines, cigarette in one hand, a bucket of tokens in the other. This memory has nothing to do with flying or the Navy, but that picture sticks in my mind to this day.

The second thing that comes to mind is the F-4G guys that flew at that event. While we were the only EA-6B squadron in attendance, the Air Force had sent one of the last F-4G Wild Weasel squadrons from the Air National Guard. These guys were a bunch of crazy heroes, most of them were older, and all had seen combat in Desert Storm. They knew the F-4G was being retired, and they flew with a sense of joy that was palpable.

While the exercise was awesome, one of the primary things that I remember from that detachment was an incident in the Nellis Officer's Club. As you would expect from the Air Force, the Nellis club is very nice, serves good food, and has a bar on a lower level where the "Crud" table is. Crud is an Air Force-specific game played around a huge pool table. There are no pool cues employed; it is a game of physical contact, teamwork, and strategy. Well, there was a lot of testosterone in the bar that evening and no distractions, so events began to… accelerate. The battle around the crud table increased in intensity, pitchers of beer rapidly disappeared, and the sense of competition that normally took place in the sky over Nellis transferred itself into the club.

At some point in the evening, one of my friends had a couple of what we used to call "stray electrons" run through his inebriated cranium. In a moment of brilliance, he decided he'd collect all the reddish hot-wing fat from several baskets and take bets from the crowd to see if he could drink it. Not surprisingly, he won this solo contest and, after he returned from the bathroom, was looking for an additional challenge. It was about then that the Wild Weasel guys identified that the bar had a perfect configuration for "carrier qualifications." While most of the bar top was a regular height from the floor, part of the room had a raised floor that put one end of the bar top somewhere around waist height.

The concept of bar-top carrier qualification was a naval aviation legacy from Vietnam. What this event demands is that an aviator runs toward the "flight deck" at full speed, throws themselves horizontally at the bar, and then slides to a halt while still on the top. To be clear, this is not a typical activity for the Air Force, but the F-4G did have a tail hook, and there were even a few old naval aviators in their squadron. Anyway, the bar top is usually lubricated with beer. There might also be washrags used as arresting wires or beer sprayed at the "pilot" to simulate bad weather. When the aviator comes to a halt, the quality of the landing is judged by the reaction of the crowd.

Well, not being able to resist the challenge, a number of my squadron mates decided to participate in this competition. As the evening progressed, there were several rounds of quals. This event is tiring and tends to increase the amount of alcohol consumed. So, it wasn't a surprise that, eventually, things began winding down. Seeing that the crowd's enthusiasm was waning, one of the F-4 guys yelled, "Crew concept!" Since the F-4 is a two-person aircraft, he got one of his buddies to climb up on his shoulders and threw himself at the bar. Both men slammed to the "deck" and were successfully trapped, resulting in much cheering from the observers. Now, my very inebriated friend was never one to back down from a challenge, and since he could not pick up three naval aviators to match the number of crew members in a Prowler, he just picked the biggest F-4 guy he could find, got him up on his shoulders and started running. At approximately four feet from the end of the bar, he tripped. In slow motion, with his arms wrapped around the other fellow's legs, he planted his face directly into the end of the bar with an audible "crunch." The sound of his "ramp strike" immediately quieted the roaring crowd. He was out cold.

In a remarkably quick move of self-preservation, the senior man in the room, an Air Force Lieutenant Colonel from one of the F-15 squadrons, took advantage of the stunned silence and said, "I saw him slip on some beer," therefore establishing the alibi for the rest of the participants. (Even at this point in history, you did not want to be a participant in an "alcohol-related incident" that ended in a casualty.) My friend quickly returned to consciousness but was moaning in pain. An ambulance was called, and before long he was unceremoniously hauled out on a stretcher. Not surprisingly, the party kind of came to an end. After a brief but animated discussion with a cardboard cut-out of an attractive woman (a beer advertisement that was standing in the front of the club), my friends and I navigated back to our rooms.

The next day was a Saturday, and we had established an admin in a lakeside hotel near Lake Powell. After some shenanigans that involved taking several compromising pictures of our CO (he had unwisely chosen to take a nap on the grass in front of the admin and had a few photos taken with a collection of empty booze bottles near his outstretched hand), the admin steadied into a normal pace. We did not see our injured shipmate for almost twenty-four hours until he sheepishly showed up with a face that was almost entirely purple. His injuries included a shattered sinus, broken nose, and other disfiguring issues caused by his glasses. Even worse, he was medically grounded for the rest of the detachment and became a permanent SDO. I have seen many men swear off alcohol, usually when tremendously hungover. I've even known a few that have kept their word, but I am sure that our friend didn't have a single beer for the rest of the almost two years that he was in the squadron - and as far as I know might not have had one in the years since. As I understand it, there are still teeth marks in the wood at the end of the bar.

In December, I got the opportunity for a rare "good deal." Early in my career in the squadron, I decided to pursue my qualification as a Landing Signal Officer. In addition to being a way to learn more about my profession, being an LSO was a good way to avoid some of the duties that the other junior aviators had to support - most specifically, it meant that I would not have to stand SDO on the carrier during flight operations. This was a mildly contentious issue as, for many of my peers, being an LSO looked like fun – and it was. However, as an LSO, I put in a lot of extra hours in addition to my "real" ground job. During my first deployment, I qualified as a Squadron LSO. This endorsement allowed me to conduct Field Carrier Landing Practice for EA-6Bs and certify that the squadron's pilots were ready to go to the boat. This also put me in the running to do something called "LSO Cross Training." In concept, LSO cross-training was implemented so that the junior LSOs could get a sense of the different flying characteristics of a variety of aircraft. This was great, but the problem was that the most common aircraft for cross-training was the E-2D or the S-3B, neither of which was what I was aiming for - I wanted to fly the F-14A.

I don't know how it happened, but at some point that fall, the Senior Air Wing LSO notified me that I had gotten a quota for LSO Cross Training, and in fact, I had received my first choice of the F-14A Tomcat. Awesome. So, the squadron wrote me orders, the maintenance officer gave me a fuel card, and off I went to NAS Oceana to learn to fly the Tomcat. When I arrived at VF-101, I quickly realized that, while this was a good deal for me, it was a pain in the neck for the training department. They were busy, and the last thing the fighter guys needed was a freeloader from the EA-6B community to gum up the schedule.

After waiting around for a week, I finally made it to the flight schedule and, over the next ten days, executed all the same simulator events that a new Tomcat student would fly. Also, because I was bored, I signed up for whatever spare time I could get in their "dome" simulator. Top-of-the-line technology at the time, the dome allowed you to maneuver against other aircraft and gave you a 360-degree view while you did so. As I ran through the emergency simulators, I quickly realized that the systems in the Tomcat were similar to the Prowler. Both were built by Northrup Grumman, and much of the systems architecture was similar. When I finished all the required procedures and emergency simulators, I repeatedly tried to convince the head LSO to let me get 10 hours in the Tomcat and finish my adventure with a NATOPS check (essentially a flight certification). He politely deferred, and I am sure that he probably then contacted the schedules officer and said, "Get Tater into a jet so we can ship him back to Whidbey before he drives me crazy."

So, while it took longer than I imagined, I finally got scheduled to go fly. On the 2nd of December, the squadron put a senior Tomcat LSO in my back seat and scheduled me for two flights in an F-14A. While the intent of the program was only to get me into the landing pattern, the squadron generously gave me two full tanks of fuel. So, after briefing the flight, we walked, manned up the jet, and took off into the working areas off the coast. As a Prowler guy, the first thing I wanted to do was break the speed of sound. So, I climbed to altitude, went to "zone 5" afterburner, and quickly made it to about 1.3 Mach, downhill. Honestly, while it was great to see the airspeed indicator go past the speed of sound, it was as underwhelming as every fighter guy told me it would be.

Next, I wanted to do the aerobatics that I had been denied as a Prowler pilot. I spent most of that tank of gas doing 250-knot loops in Zone 5 afterburner. After about an hour, when we had burned enough gas, we came back into the landing pattern and I flew the ball. Honestly, I discovered that the jet handled much like a Prowler. The biggest practical difference between the two aircraft was that I could not actually hear the engines in the Tomcat, something that was surprisingly important to my flying skills. After landing, we went to what is known as a "hot pit," where we refueled while still in the aircraft, took off again, and essentially did the same thing. In the end, I logged three flight hours and ten landings in the Tomcat. While this was unremarkable in Oceana, it did good things for my "resume" in the Prowler community, enabled me to have a "legitimate" Tomcat patch stitched to the back of my cruise jacket, and it was a blast.

In late February, the squadron headed back across the country and attended ten days of pain on the USS America that was known as "REFTRA." This was a short "refresher training" event that involved a small amount of flying for the air wing, and a lot of drills for the ship's crew. A REFTRA was filled with nearly continuous fire drills, crash drills, and other readiness preparations. For the aviators on the carrier, drills like this usually meant "deep shelter," which was the code word for "return to your room and take a nap." While the real intent was to get us involved in first aid, firefighting, and other drills, there wasn't a lot of voluntary participation from guys in flight suits. Occasionally, a drill would occur while all the aviators were in the Ready Room doing training or, more importantly, watching a movie. Ship's company loved to throw a "flopper" into a squadron space during these training events. A flopper was a sailor with a fake injury. The intent was to have us describe how we would conduct first aid on the injured man. Of course, we thought this kind of thing was a pain in the neck and the door to the Ready Room was always locked when these drills began. On the rare occasion when the SDO forgot to lock the door, it was not uncommon to have a bit of a wrestling match to try to keep a flopper out of the room.

Complete with REFTRA, we headed to NAS Fallon for our Air Wing certification. Now that I was more familiar with the intent of Fallon, it was a lot more fun. The lodging had improved since my first visit, and the flying was good. The planning was still a pain in the neck, but I was more senior and more experienced and got a sense of when it was okay to disappear. It was during this detachment that we got another reminder of how dangerous our job was.

I was scheduled to fly an evening mission in which we were launching three Prowlers to support a strike. At the time I was working towards my "Division Leader Qualification" and got the opportunity to act as the flight lead. We briefed, started, and taxied on time. NAS Fallon has two long parallel runways, one is 14,000 feet (and is the longest in the Navy), and the other one is 11,000 feet and is parallel. Anyway, we taxied across the long runway and set ourselves up for takeoff on the 11,000-foot surface. As we taxied, an A-6E was positioned on the other runway, and as soon as we were across, he was cleared to take off. Unknown to the crew of the A-6, a latch in their forward radome shook loose on the takeoff roll and was ingested into their right engine. The crew noticed an issue, but instead of trying to keep the jet on the ground, the pilot nursed the jet into the air and jettisoned their entire load of ordnance and external fuel tanks on the runway.

Lined up on the other runway a few hundred feet away, we all watched as the A-6 climbed away from the ground, spewing sparks from the critically damaged engine. The A-6 crew declared an emergency and asked to return to the field immediately. Tower quickly ordered us to take off so that we could clear a place for the stricken A-6 to land. It took us only about thirty seconds to roll, and we had just gotten all three aircraft airborne and were starting a right-hand turn when somebody in the damaged A-6 got half of the emergency call "mayday" out. It was at this point that a huge fireball erupted a few miles in front of us. At the time, I was fairly certain we had watched two shipmates perish. The rest of the flight was quiet. Our mission was canceled, so we went into the working area and just held until they had the runways clear enough that we could come back. After our return, we got the good news that the crew had successfully ejected. We didn't know their condition, but they were alive. After a short debrief of the aborted mission, we rode back to our rooms and then met in the O-Club for dinner. I remember the cheer that went up from the crowd as one of the guys from the A-6 eventually rolled into the O-Club. He was a little sore and a bit worse for the wear but alive.

Late April and May found the squadron embarked on the USS America again for our final training period before deployment. Instead of training just off the East Coast, we headed south to work in the Caribbean Sea. Of all the places to conduct such training, the Caribbean was my favorite. The temperature was good, the water was calm, and there was plenty of air space. The downside was that there wasn't much variety for the guys dropping bombs. The attack and strike aircraft could only use the range at Vieques, a small island off the eastern coast of Puerto Rico that the Navy had been shelling or bombing for many decades. While it was eventually closed, at the time, Vieques was the terminus of any strike. For the rest of us, we flew long overwater missions and did a lot of cloud surfing in the amazing cumulous and cumulonimbus clouds that were always in the area.

We also enjoyed one port visit to St Thomas. Our admin was set up at a place called Sapphire Beach Resort. The water was awesome, the beach bar and the food were great, and there were several places to eat that weren't too far away. There wasn't a lot of nonsense during this visit, but there are stories. One of our shipmates woke up on the couch of another guest's room (a civilian!) at the resort after climbing a balcony to enter the wrong sliding glass door. Another ended up urinating in the closet of another squadron's admin. There was a second urination incident at a nearby bar when one of the guys began to pee while simultaneously ordering his next drink. This particular circumstance resulted in some wet feet and some unhappy shipmates.

For my part, I got destroyed by sand fleas when I thought that sleeping on a balcony and enjoying the wonderful weather would be a good idea. I also remember being quite concerned as a very inebriated friend of mine decided to go "for a long swim" very late one night after returning from town. I tried to convince him that it was a bad idea, but he stubbornly disappeared into the dark. It was a very long wait on the beach until he returned. Despite these misadventures, we had a good time and then went back to the ship. Before we knew it, we were done with workups, and after a quick break for some leave, we were soon back on deployment.

The USS America departed Norfolk for my second deployment in mid-August 1993. The ship and battle group headed across the Atlantic and essentially headed straight into the Adriatic Sea. The Adriatic lies between Italy and the coast of Croatia, Bosnia, and Montenegro and is an excellent place to operate. Soon after we arrived, we started flying missions in support of Operation Deny Flight. This operation was intended to keep Serbian military aircraft out of Bosnian air space. This wasn't defined as a "true" combat mission, but despite this, our fighters were flying with live missiles and were prepared to shoot down any Serbian military aircraft in the unlikely event that any could be positively identified and targeted. This mission was initially quite exciting but quickly turned into a game. The Serbs would fly jets into the denied area, and before NATO AWACS could vector a fighter in the right direction, they would turn around and disappear. For us, these missions meant long hours flying as SEAD cover for the fighters. There was much discussion of the possibility of SAM traps and other ways that the Serbs could try to down an Allied aircraft. In fact, in the years to come, there would be several allied aircraft shot down in the area, but during our two months of coverage, the most that I saw were strings of AAA tracers that were fired harmlessly into the sky.

What I remember most about these flights was the fact that we were flying over Western civilization. I don't know how to say it any other way. These were modern towns and villages that were under fire; people were genuinely at war below us. During the daytime, it was difficult to see what was going on, but at night, we'd fly a route that took us by Sarajevo and then on a counter-clockwise trip around the country. During these events, we would frequently see tracers being fired from one hilltop to another, or into the cities, or between towns. There would be flashes of explosions or fires burning in places that looked very similar to the Italian cities that were only a hundred miles away across the Adriatic. It was tragic.

While most of the missions were not particularly exciting, being on deployment in the Mediterranean was much better than the Arabian Gulf, and we all appreciated this fact, especially when we would pull into a town like Trieste. Our first visit to Trieste was fantastic, I love northern Italian food, and the town was full of good places to eat. Some folks took the train and went to Venice, but several of us took the opportunity to visit Salzburg, Austria. One of my favorite cities, and a place that I didn't get to visit long enough, Salzburg had high mountains, narrow streets, and old shops, and was everything I had imagined about the Alps. It was awesome.

Occasionally, a few of the officers managed to bring their spouses over during deployment. In one of the more amusing vignettes from this particular trip, one of my friends had brought his wife to Europe so that they could spend a week together touring the region by train. Now, it might seem obvious, but getting away from the ship and your squadron was a priority for the guys who brought their wives over. In most cases, this was especially true for the spouse, who had no desire to spend an evening drinking with the boys. So, during one glorious afternoon in Innsbruck, several of us found ourselves in a very nice tavern where we had settled in for an afternoon of beer drinking and good food. It was after about an hour of our arrival when our friend and his wonderful wife walked in. Their arrival was greeted with a rousing cheer from the crowd - followed by a happy smile from my friend and a somewhat horrified look from his wife. Not surprisingly, they didn't join us. However, after they departed, there was much follow-on discussion about the statistical likelihood of such a meeting in a foreign city, hundreds of miles from the ship - especially when you remember that there were no cell phones or other communications at the time.

When we left Trieste, we returned to our missions over Bosnia for a couple more weeks and then headed into port at the south end of the Adriatic in Corfu, Greece. Corfu was a great port visit. While I had been to Athens and Souda Bay on the previous deployment, Corfu was very pleasant. It had a cool old town, lots of scenic little restaurants, and the people were very friendly (unlike other parts of Greece). The only adventure that the Air Wing had during our Corfu visit was that a few of the S-3 guys had rented a boat to take just off the coast into the Adriatic. When they didn't return on time, the chain of command got very nervous. It seems a bit silly now, but we were not very far from the coast of Albania, a cloistered, highly armed former Soviet ally that our intelligence was sure still harbored ill will towards us. The fear was that these guys had been taken hostage. The Greek police and an armed Navy helicopter went in search of the boat. However, instead of a hostage situation, this ended up with a true search and recovery. As I seem to recall the aviators were eventually found in the water with a disabled and overturned boat.

Returning to the Adriatic and our trips around Bosnia, we again watched for SAM systems and AAA fire and listened as the fighter guys chased disappearing radar contacts. Before too long, it was time for another port visit, and we were back in Trieste. I am not sure if we knew this was our last port visit for a while, but I certainly remember our last big night in town. During this port visit, our XO had what was known as "Senior Shore Patrol." As such, he was responsible for the shore-based effort to keep our sailors safe and to deal with any disciplinary or legal issues. It wasn't a great job, but it allowed the XO to have a nice hotel room for the entire port visit, which only partially made up for having to deal with drunk idiots like his own aviators.

On the final night in Trieste, we decided to have a big dinner at a restaurant we had frequented a few times. The owners and wait staff seemed to put up with us; they had good food and lots of good wine. I can picture about a dozen of us along a long table ordering food and booze like we were going to prison the next day. We all drank a lot. However, one of my friends went to at least one glass of wine past his physiological limit. During the meal, he had entertained the group by speaking his serviceable Spanish to the wait staff, using it as a proxy for the Italian that, in his defense, did sound similar. After more than an hour of this, there was a round of hysterical laughter when the waitress, clearly frustrated by the use of Spanish, finally told him in very clear English that "Spanish was not Italian."

As we wrapped up the excellent meal with a final round of wine, my buddy decided it was time to leave. As he approached the door on his way out of the restaurant, his "circuit breakers popped," and he fell. At first, it seemed like he had just stumbled, but it quickly became apparent that he was no longer able to walk. It also didn't help that he simultaneously lost the power of language and began speaking in tongues. Knowing that this was a major issue, a couple of us began to walk him back toward the ship. It was a terrible, slow process; he was an angry drunk and was not helping us at all. To add to our challenge, we were approaching the deadline to get back on the ship. This was normally a bad thing, but it would be really bad to be late the night when your own XO was in charge.

As our frustrating return trip across Trieste progressed, I remember propping my friend up against a wall and wondering if we could somehow summon a taxi. We were approaching the point of maximum desperation when a car pulled up and stopped in front of us. It was our XO. Salvation. Of course, I am not sure he thought so. He quickly understood our dilemma and said, "Get in." We crammed our drunk friend into the back seat and soon were headed "back ship." As we got into the port, the XO dropped us off at the pier and then, as if he was hoping not to be identified, raced off.

We were now faced with getting my hammered friend up what was known as "the brow." The brow was a gangway that connected the hangar deck of the ship to the pier. It consisted of two parts, a twenty-foot-tall set of stairs and about a sixty-foot-long walkway. My friend was in no condition to make it across this obstacle alone. So, with one of us under each arm, we began to slowly climb the stairs, trying to bring as little notice to ourselves as possible. Unfortunately, when we got out of the car, our drunk friend's shoes had slipped off. So, as he attempted to help us, his bare feet audibly crunched into each of the stair risers as his time-delayed attempts to walk were opposite of what was required. While he did whimper in pain, we were doing a decent job of keeping quiet. However, once we got onto the walkway, his feet were now being dragged across a rough non-skid surface. With every dragging step, he complained. As the non-skid did an increasing amount of damage to his skin, he yelled ever louder. By the time we got halfway up to the ship, he was screaming at the top of his lungs. So much for low profile. We had now drawn a crowd to the edge of the hangar deck, and dozens of sailors watched as we dragged our drunk and screaming friend the last few feet to the ship.

Upon our arrival at the hangar deck, we discovered that there was one Officer of the Deck and several large Master at Arms (essentially military police) awaiting our arrival. We showed our IDs and hoped that we could just take our friend to bed. The poor Lieutenant who had Officer of the Deck looked at our drunk friend and did the right thing; he ordered us to take him to medical. We resisted. In one of my favorite memories, one of our Department Heads tried to pull rank and quickly discovered the difference between rank and "positional authority." As he protested the Lieutenant's order, we found ourselves surrounded by armed sailors who were not amused. Not wanting to end up in the Brig (ship's prison), we reluctantly agreed to take our friend to medical. This now meant that we had to take him down four sets of steep ship stairs (essentially ladders). In order to make this happen, we had to convince our drunk friend to scoot down one stair at a time on his butt like a two-year-old. While somewhat amusing at first, we were all tired, and this process took a while.

When we finally arrived at the medical, an enlisted corpsman offered to call the Flight Surgeon. In what turned out to be a wise move, the Doc refused to come to the scene and instead told us to do what we had wanted to do the entire time, put our friend to bed and keep him hydrated. Unfortunately, this now required that we take our friend back up six of these steep ladders. As he was still unable to climb the stairs on his own, this effort was undertaken with his arm over my shoulder. Now, with his arm across my back and my shoulder in his armpit, it meant that I had a lot of leverage. It also meant that with each step, I essentially tried to rip his arm out of his socket. The resulting screams of pain were distracting, but by that time, I didn't have much remaining sense of humor. Screaming or not, he was going up the stairs.

After an extended effort by multiple aviators, we finally made it to our room. Our next thought was to seat him in a chair and get him to drink some water in accordance with the doctor's direction. The first cup of water was helpfully delivered by his boss. Unfortunately, our drunk friend was having none of this, he took a mouthful and quickly spit the water back into his boss's face - at which point his boss slugged him. At this point, we all had seen enough. We rolled our friend into his bed, hoping that he wouldn't die. Despite my exhaustion, a few hours later, I was awakened by the sound of running water. This is not a good sound on a ship. Suspecting that someone had left one of the sinks running, I got up to investigate and found our friend, hand against the wall, urinating on a pair of our roommate's running shoes. When I asked, "What the hell are you doing?" he turned to me and essentially growled. I didn't even say a word, just got back into bed and went back to sleep. The drama of the urine-soaked running shoes would last for weeks to come, but Trieste was done, and we were heading a long way south. It was a port visit that I will never forget.

When we left Trieste for the second time, the USS America had been ordered to the coast of Somalia to support Operation Restore Hope, and apparently, we were in a hurry. We cut to the south, went through the Suez, and did minimal flight operations until we arrived off the African coast...and then...did nothing. We spent six long weeks off the coast of Somalia. Not long after we arrived, it became obvious that there wasn't anything for the air wing to do. Somalia became the epitome of "groundhog station;" every day was a repeat of the last. The good news for some adventurous guys was that they were allowed to go to the shore and participate in the operation on the beach. They served as liaison officers in case air support was required and got to experience being in a crazy expeditionary environment. I tried to get the CO to let me go ashore, but he was very reluctant to let one of his pilots leave the ship. Our intelligence officer spent some time in Mogadishu and came back with stories of riding food convoys and employing axe handles to keep people from stealing food. Another officer from our squadron went ashore and managed to have an illicit romance with a female Army nurse, becoming semi-famous throughout the air wing.

While stuck on the boat, we all flew a few missions over parts of Somalia, but most of our flights were off into the Indian Ocean. I stopped flying along the beach after I had a very close call with a UN helicopter that was going in the opposite direction at the same altitude. CAG and the Admiral tried to spice things up for the air wing by implementing something called "Indian Country." This was a dedicated area near the carrier that was fair game for any aircraft to fight any other aircraft. The strike fighters loved this. For us, it was a great opportunity to try to get into the area, sneak a shot at a fighter, and attempt to survive; this outcome, however, was depressingly uncommon.

One of my favorite memories from this period was being involved in a knock-down-drag-out air combat with one of my friends in another Prowler. We were in the midst of multiple horizontal "rollers" when to our total surprise, we realized that we were directly overhead the carrier, a place that we definitely didn't want to be. We instantly broke off the fight and called it a draw. After several weeks of this boredom, the Admiral decided to head south so that we could cross the equator. It took a day or two, but after we arrived, we participated in what I am sure was one of the Navy's last old-school "crossing the line" ceremonies. All of the "Pollywogs" on the ship were fed a wonderful breakfast of garbage, cleansed in a challenging flight deck obstacle course, beaten with shillelaghs made of fire-hose, and transformed into "Trusty Shellbacks" after a "peanut-butter-and-belly" meeting with Poseidon himself.

After six weeks of Groundhog Day, the day we finally headed north was quite a relief. In much the same way as we had sped south, we hurried back into the Red Sea, Suez, and into the Mediterranean. Despite the apparent urgency of our transit, we did pause in the Red Sea to conduct one set of flights in support of the newly established Operation Southern Watch. While not a substantive contribution to the mission, in the "big picture," these flights were a demonstration of the Navy's tactical flexibility. It was always important for the service leadership to be able to demonstrate what a carrier could do.

From a personal perspective, this mission gave me the opportunity to fly my first "green ink" combat flight. While the color of ink in a logbook may seem trivial, this document is critically important in an aviator's life. My log book contains every single flight I conducted in the naval service. It notes the types of aircraft, hours of Pilot in Command, the number of landings, the number of traps, the instrument time, instrument approaches, and whether the flight was in the daytime (black ink) or nighttime (red ink). Having a flight scribed in green ink meant that the flight was combat-coded. The Navy, being the bureaucracy that it is, has hundreds of Flight Purpose Codes that could be used to describe the specific intent of a combat mission, but the only thing that mattered to me was that it would be the first logbook entry in green. In addition, the mission would qualify me for two points towards a "Strike-Flight Air Medal," a combat-related award that could be earned a few ways but generally required 20 points to receive.

Operation Southern Watch had formally swung into gear the year before as the result of a UN resolution. The mission essentially established a "no-fly zone" over southern Iraq so that the Iraqi military could not use fixed-wing aircraft to kill its citizens. This began an eleven-year-long cat-and-mouse game between coalition aircraft and Iraqi air defenses. We'd fly into Iraqi airspace, and our fighters would prepare to respond to any incursions by their fighter aircraft. The Iraqi military would occasionally send a brave fighter pilot to the south of the line to taunt us. Our fighters would scramble in response, hoping for a coveted air-to-air kill, but the Iraqi plane would always turn and head back across "the line" where it would be safe from attack. At some point during this game, Iraq would usually shoot a SAM or fire AAA in a half-hearted attempt to down one of the coalition aircraft that was responding. During the entire period, the Prowler guys were there in order to jam Iraqi radars and suppress their air defenses. Like most combat operations, Southern Watch was 99 percent boredom and one percent excitement.

When we had initially departed Norfolk several months earlier, we had anticipated that we would head straight to the Arabian Gulf and support Operation Southern Watch, but our Bosnian adventure had happily kept us in the Adriatic. That said, it was a great opportunity to be chosen to fly the only Operation Southern Watch mission that the air wing would conduct during that deployment.

Flying an Operation Southern Watch mission from the Red Sea was a little different than flying from the Arabian Gulf. It was a very long way across the massive desert in Saudi Arabia to Iraq. Our route would take us across all of northern Saudi Arabia to the border, where we would meet an Air Force KC-135 and refuel. We would then escort our fighters into southern Iraq, hang out for a while, and wait for the Iraqis to do something. When our allotted time was done, we would return to the tanker, get more gas, and then head back to the ship. Honestly, the preparation for the mission was more intense than the flight. We conducted a large amount of mission planning, considered all possible contingencies, and ensured that we all knew how to respond to any Iraqi activity. Next, we had to take personal steps to prepare. The air wing didn't have as many combat veterans as it did the previous deployment, and the little differences between peacetime and combat, like wearing sidearms, and using special survival radios, were not yet routine, and it took some effort to get squared away. Finally ready, we took off and headed across the desert.

This was a daytime mission, and my first impression was just a sense of amazement over the endless stretches of empty desert. Saudi Arabia is huge and largely desolate. Despite this, even in this desert, there were signs of life. Occasionally, there would be a large green circle of cropland where some farmer was fighting with the sand, trying to make a living, but mostly it was just barren.

As we arrived at the border area, the most critical task we had to accomplish was getting fuel. We followed our fighters to the Air Force tankers that had been dedicated to our support and breathed a sigh of relief when we joined up and successfully filled our tanks.

The flight from the Red Sea across Saudi Arabia was 500 miles each way and didn't leave us many options if we couldn't get refueled. Once we were topped off, we checked in with the AWACS and entered Iraqi airspace. As excited as I was about my first combat mission, it quickly became clear that the Iraqi desert was indistinguishable from Saudi Arabia, and although our navigation told us we were in a "bad guy" country, it was impossible to tell the difference from above. As we flew in the box that we had been assigned, we listened as the AWACS called out contacts, knowing that they would tell us if they saw any Iraqi fighter activity. In our jet, we dutifully looked for threatening Iraqi radar signals and any signs of resistance, but there were absolutely none. In essence, we flew circles over the empty desert, trying not to fly over the same place twice so that we couldn't be targeted. Honestly, I am sure that we saw more actual combat during our "non-combat" missions over Bosnia than we did during that flight over Iraq. In Bosnia, we frequently saw small arms and AAA fire arc into the sky. In Iraq, there was no such activity. I looked down at the small villages and imagined what it was like to live in such a brown and forbidding environment. In the end, nothing was seen, and we went back to the tanker and home to the ship, happy that our next stop would be Haifa, Israel.

Haifa was a relief. We had been at sea for quite a long time, and it was a good opportunity to get some food, have a beer, and just relax. We got an admin at the Hotel Dan Carmel at the top of a hill that overlooked the port and settled in for some time off. Haifa was a port where the ship anchored offshore. The water around Haifa was known to get extremely choppy; in fact, only a few years before, twenty-two sailors from the USS Saratoga had died when their ferry had capsized in rough weather. As a result, it was common for the ferries to be canceled and for sailors to be trapped on the ship or the shore. This time, when the ferries got canceled, I was trapped on the ship. As a result, I missed several "adventures" that soon became famous in the squadron.

The first one is just short and funny. When the ferries got canceled, one of our junior pilots was trapped on the boat along with the rest of us. However, unlike those of us resigned to our fate, he was still determined to get ashore. At first, despite the cancellation, there were still a couple of empty ferries tied to the carrier. Our buddy tried a number of ways to convince the carrier's officers that it would be safe for him to take one of the empty ferries to shore and that he would happily accept the risk. When this gambit failed, he remembered that there was something that was known as a "garbage barge" tied to the side of the carrier. The garbage barge was just that, it was where the carrier's garbage was dispensed with when we were in port. When the barge became full, it was towed away by a tug boat. So, our intrepid friend made his way down to the barge and waited for the next tug boat to arrive. At some significant risk of being caught by the Navy, he climbed off the ship and onto the barge and then convinced the operator of the tug boat to take him to the shore as a passenger. While very risky, this turned out to be a good move, as he was able to spend an extra two days on liberty.

Because I was trapped on the carrier with the rest of the guys who were not willing to risk their careers to ride the garbage barge, I was not present during this next adventure, but this is a story that I have heard a thousand times. One fine evening, a bunch of my buddies found themselves in a Tel Aviv bar. Over the course of the cruise, three or four of them had begun to conduct what they called "medical experiments" on unsuspecting "patients." In essence, they would pick a target and buy drinks for a person until something catastrophic happened. Along the way, they would pretend to keep up with the patient, essentially testing their subject's ability to consume alcohol. At the beginning of this particular experiment, their unknowing patient (a young naval aviator) was handed a set of "special instructions" that he was told to put in his shirt pocket. A few hours later, and after much "medication," the experiment culminated when the young officer accidentally locked himself in the girl's bathroom. In addition to leaving a lake of puke on the floor, he could not manage to escape the facility on his own. After the door was kicked down, he was rescued by the group and escorted outside to the curb.

Now that the experiment had proven to be successful, a cab was waved over. With much ceremony, the patient was told to reveal his "special instructions." While only partially capable of retrieving the document, help was provided and the special instructions were read out loud. As it turned out, the paper contained the address of the hotel where they were staying. For the crowd, the hysterically funny part of the scene was the foresight demonstrated by the "doctor" who had provided the special instructions. The combination of the inevitability of this young aviator's destruction and the drama with which the document was ultimately presented left them laughing and gasping for air. Yes, with friends like these, who needs enemies? Also, as was mentioned many times when the story was retold in the days to come, the address on the paper could have easily been to someplace in the West Bank. Imagining the potential circumstances around the "special instructions" generated gales of laughter for months to come, and despite the massive hangover, we all believed that the young aviator probably should have considered himself lucky.

With Haifa in the rear-view mirror, we headed back to a couple of days of flying over Bosnia, and then as Christmas approached, we found out that we were going to pull into Marseilles, France for Christmas and New Year's Eve. This was a good deal, and there was much horse trading to get duty scheduled on the right days. When we pulled into Marseilles, five of us who had managed to get the first few days off decided that we wanted to go skiing in the Alps. Of course, we had no reservations. These were the days before the internet and the cell phone, so planning was difficult. In addition, none of us had any ski clothing or equipment. What I did have was a brand new American Express Gold Card that I had signed up for before the deployment. As you can imagine, young aviators and credit cards are not a good combination. However, as we tried to figure out how to get to the Alps, I remembered that American Express had offices where a cardholder could arrange such trips, and it turned out that there was one in Marseilles. So, the group followed me to the AMEX office and waited patiently outside while I made reservations at the only place in the Alps that had any vacancies, a tremendously expensive five-star hotel in a mountain town called Val d'Isere. Now victorious, when I emerged from the office I had reservations for two rooms, and directions for the trains and the bus that we would have to take to get there. We departed the AMEX office, provided ourselves with the sustenance that we had learned was essential for such trips - red wine and baguettes - and walked to the train station.

Several hours later, our train arrived in Albertville, France. The wine and bread had been gone for some time, and we were now ready to begin our alpine adventure. This adventure began when we transferred to a tour bus that was driven surprisingly fast through some beautiful and terrifying scenery. While I am sure the driver had followed the route a thousand times, there were points that I was sure we were going over. After about an hour of daredevil driving, we found ourselves dumped off at the bus station in one of the most exclusive towns in the Alps. I have to say that it was post-card-perfect. The mountains were steep and imposing, the town was covered in snow, and it began snowing not long after we arrived. On the downside, it quickly became clear that the hotel was far too exclusive for us (and expensive!) It was the kind of place where the desk staff knew your name - and issued your brass room key when you walked in, and took it from you when you went out. I suspect they would have frowned on anything like an "admin," if they knew we were coming, but I don't remember a single issue while we were there.

With a base station established, we spent some time scouting the town and found a restaurant and a bar for that first night. The objective for the next day was to rent some ski gear and head onto the slopes. In the morning, we found the only ski shop in town that was open and geared up. I bought some gloves and the only ski pants I could find that would fit (an obnoxious purple nylon). We then rented boots and skis, and off we went.

As a veteran of many skiing trips in the Cascades and Canada, I confidently believed that I could hold my own on almost any slope. We bought our tickets and, after riding a series of ski lifts, found ourselves on a glacier thousands of feet above the town. I quickly became quite sure that I was going to die. After hacking around on the easy parts of the glacier for a while, the guys who were wearing blue jeans were cold, wet, and ready to get home. We attempted to ask several locals for an easy way down the mountain, but nobody would speak to us. It was frustrating. The terrible irony of the question was that we could see our objective; the only problem was that it appeared to be a straight down a terrifyingly steep double-black-diamond cliff. While a couple of guys in the group could actually ski, I will never forget the rest of us sliding, tumbling, and otherwise having an unhappy and very wet and cold experience for a long way down the sheer face of the mountain.

With one of the most expensive six hours of skiing on record complete, it was now Christmas Eve. Having recovered from our mountain adventure and refreshed ourselves in the hotel, it was time to venture out to find a place to eat and drink. There weren't a ton of options, but we did find a bar with a sign that said there would be live Christmas Carols that evening.

The following scene is a little fuzzy in my mind's eye, but in my memory, the bar was on the lower level of a larger building. It was a classic alpine room. The tables were large wooden platforms, and we had staked out the middle part of one of them. There was a stage a few feet away from our table, and the singer had yet to show up. The room was full; there were people of all ages, including at least a few children. A table or two away, there were a few attractive women who were sitting closer to the stage. As I recall, we proceeded with our consumption at a furious pace. When the male guitarist/singer finally arrived, it turned out that he was also an American and was visiting from Miami, of all places. Well, he began to sing the Christmas Carols he knew, interspersed with other pop songs. It didn't take long for us to discover that his library of carols was limited to "Twelve Days of Christmas," "Jingle Bells," and "Silent Night." The Twelve Days of Christmas was a sing-along, and this was fun as the singer assigned parts to the crowd and everyone in the room participated. However, it definitely got old after the third or fourth time, especially since he kept assigning our group "Eight Maids a Milking." This had been funny the first time, but it quickly became clear that he was also competing for the attention of the women in the front row, and "maids a milking" was a targeted gibe. At this point, "the doctors" in our group decided that the next patient to be experimented on was the guy from Miami with the guitar.

There are flashes of other events intermingled with my memory of this evening. One of my favorite moments of lucidity came when some of the guys in our group decided to do a round of "Statue of Liberty" drinks that, for some reason, had become popular with our squadron during that deployment. A Statue of Liberty starts with a large shot of Sambuca or other similar liquor. You dip two of your fingers into the glass, get a helpful friend to light your hand on fire, hold up your flaming digits, and down the shot before your appendages start to burn. Ideally, you then blow the fire out before you feel any pain. Get these steps out of order, and you can turn into a screaming ball of fire, but there were no critical failures that night. What I vividly remember, however, were the kids sitting around us, watching with big eyes as the Americans lit themselves on fire for fun - while singing Christmas carols. I am sure that it appeared to be some kind of magic trick, and, in a sense, I guess it was.

Once the medical experiment began, the doctors began to buy shots of tequila and have them sent to the guitarist. At first, he was a reluctant participant. It was clear that he wasn't thrilled by the drinks, but we were vocal, the rest of the room urged him on, and our behavior appeared non-threatening. Just a group of fellow Americans helping him celebrate the holiday. After the second or third shot was delivered, he was much less happy. The advantage that the doctors had was that the entertainer was trying to impress the girls, and the peer pressure from a group of guys was hard to resist. To add to this contest of wills, we had been requesting "Margaritaville" by Jimmy Buffet pretty consistently since he began to sing. He insisted that he didn't know it at first and then said it wasn't a Christmas song. The musical requests and the flow of alcohol continued. As the night wore on, most of the crowd finally wandered out. The girls had become disenchanted with the singer and us, and yet the consumption continued. The culmination of the night and a moment that will, as they say, live in infamy, came when the last shot was delivered to the stage. The subject of the medical experiment looked at us, looked around the few people in the room, took the shot, and resignedly began singing Jimmy Buffet. Mission complete, we returned to the hotel to pass out and wake up extremely hung over for our Christmas Day in the Alps.

You might think that this would be enough adventure for this port visit. However, we were scheduled to be in port through New Year's Eve. So, this same group went back to the ship, stood duty, cleaned up, and prepared for an event that we all had signed up for, a Navy League party on the Cote de Azure.

The Navy League is an organization of civilian and retired military supporters. It was established by Teddy Roosevelt and has a strong presence in the United States. However, it also has an extension in the French Riviera, and they had invited a busload of Naval Aviators to an exclusive New Year's Eve gathering. Before we pulled into port, there had been some intelligence about this event circulating among the Air Wing, and competition to attend was stiff. When the day approached, four of five guys from my squadron had gotten tickets. On New Year's Eve, we dressed up in respectable civilian clothes, got off the ship, and onto a bus. The bus wound out of the port and up into the narrow mountain roads outside of Marseilles.

At some point, our forward progress stopped. We then watched as the bus driver argued with our escort in very loud French. We, of course, had no idea where we were going, and neither of these individuals spoke English. One or two of the guys attempted to intervene with their limited high-school French, but the hand waving, gesturing and frustrated body language was clear. We were heading to a party, and nobody knew how to get there. Now, as time ticked by and the holiday approached, our dream of attending the high-class event in the hills above the Mediterranean was evaporating. At some point, although the loud argument continued, the bus driver began to navigate the winding roads again. It definitely appeared that we may actually be stuck on a bus somewhere in the Cote de Azure for the new year. I have no idea what the icebreaker was, but at about the two-hour point, the bus came to a halt near what seemed to be a cliff. We were encouraged to get out of the vehicle and then led down a narrow, winding lane to a remarkable house overlooking the sea.

In what would have had to be an interesting scene from inside the house, we wandered down the winding road and all gathered at the front door as if we were trick-or-treating. Our escort knocked and were politely let inside. The house was beautiful. It was a cantilevered design on a steep hillside, straight out of Architectural Digest. The main room had large windows that wrapped around the house and looked over the Mediterranean. There were several members of the local Navy League present, all spoke some English, and they were very pleasant and happy to see us. As we milled about in the room, you could almost smell the desperation of the two dozen aviators who were now in search of alcohol. Introductions complete, we were eventually led across the room to a couple of folding tables that were covered with food and wine, with a small beer keg placed next to them. The first thought that crossed everyone's mind was "finally." The second thought was, "That stuff isn't going to go very far after it has been split among all of us." And so, the competition commenced.

The theme of the night very quickly became "Get what you can before it runs out." Nobody wanted to be sober in such a gorgeous venue for New Year's, but it seemed obvious that some of us were going to be out of luck. The thing about that evening that caught everybody off guard was that our gracious and generous hosts never ran out. The wine flowed liberally and the table seemed as full of food after two hours as it had when we arrived. At midnight we were all totally hammered. I remember singing Auld Lange Syne and giving a rousing cheer of thanks to our hosts. And then, it was time to get back on the bus. As we looked around the room and did a quick head count, we discovered we were missing one of our shipmates. What was also clear was that the bus and its angry French driver would be leaving whether it had everyone onboard or not.

We searched the entire house with no luck. Then, thinking that our friend might have gone outside to take a break in the chilly air, we began to look around the small yard. I eventually found him inside a garden shed, lying among the tools, and he was not very mobile. For the second time during this deployment, I found myself carrying one of my buddies up a hill. This time there was some urgency as we didn't want to be left behind. When we finally got to the door of the bus, the driver stopped us. While we didn't have a word in common, what became clear was that the driver was concerned that my friend was going to be sick, and he would not allow him on the bus. This discussion took a few moments, and based on the grumbles from the back of the bus, the sense from the crowd was that our friend should be sacrificed for the good of all and left behind. After much argument, we somehow convinced the driver that if we placed him in the front seat, he would be okay. Once that issue was solved, the door closed, and we headed back to the ship.

The seating arrangement turned out to be a good call; after about thirty minutes of winding roads, my friend stirred to life and indicated that there was a problem. The driver stopped, and my buddy got out, puked on the side of the road, and got back into his seat. After many more irritated gestures and what was undoubtedly a string of eloquent French curse words, we continued again, finally returning to the ship. The good news was that my friend was now mobile enough to navigate the stairs and get onto the ship by himself. In the days to come, we heard that the group had actually left a few team members behind that night. At least one officer woke up in a downstairs bathroom the next morning, not knowing where he was, and had to be brought back to the ship. Port visit complete, we went back to sea, where thankfully there was no alcohol. Even better, we were now on a schedule that was starting to take us home.

The rest of this deployment breezed by without any notable incidents or accidents. Our last port visit was to Malaga, Spain, the land of sangria and the siesta. I think we were a bit burned out at this point. This does not mean that we didn't have a good time, but we mostly looked for good restaurants, places where we could shop for last-minute presents for those at home, and chilled out a bit. As I recall, one of the guys learned there was a difference between "chica" and "chico" when he was taken by a cabbie to a bar that he did not want to enter, which then made the cabbie laugh his ass off. When we pulled out of port, this time, the USS America headed out of the Mediterranean, did a "turnover" with the carrier that was replacing us, and sailed back across the Atlantic, arriving back in the U.S. the first week of February. It was good to be home.

11

THE MAINTENANCE DEPARTMENT - THE BEATING HEART OF A SQUADRON

EA-6B and Maintenance Personnel, U.S. Navy Photo

While aviators get the headlines and leading roles in the movies, there is an awful lot of hard work by the Maintenance Department that goes into each hour of flight time. The bulk of a Navy squadron is made up of the officers and enlisted maintenance personnel who repair the aircraft and keep them flight-worthy. In an EA-6B squadron, there were usually about 150 troops in the Maintenance Department. This was the largest department in the squadron, and it was run by one of the squadron's most senior Lieutenant Commanders. Here it is worth pausing to explain that the aviators in Navy squadrons essentially always have at least two primary responsibilities. One responsibility is to be a professional aviator, understand your platform and mission, and be able to fly and fight your aircraft. Another responsibility is to be a professional naval officer and to do one of the many administrative or managerial jobs required to keep a squadron running.

A squadron maintenance department is made up of several divisions. The organization's details depend on the aircraft type, but in general, there were Aircraft Division, Avionics/Armament Division, Line Division, and Quality Assurance. Two of these divisions, Aircraft and Avionics/Armament, had multiple branches below them. Depending on the size of the squadron, there was an aviator leading each of the major divisions, and in a Prowler squadron, there would be three or four officers leading at the branch level. A Maintenance Department would usually have at least one or two commissioned or warrant officers who were career aviation maintenance experts. These experts served in senior positions in the department and were there to keep "the trains running on time." Some of my earliest mentors in the fleet were ground pounders, and these seasoned experts shaped how I thought about the squadron, the maintenance department, and how things were "supposed" to run. I remember many evenings when I would be totally frustrated about how the "big Navy" did or didn't work, and one of these guys would sit down with me and explain what, where, when, and how, providing context and enabling me to find ways to work within the system.

When it came to the troops, the senior enlisted maintenance person in the department was a Maintenance Master Chief or E-9. It was a situation that depended a lot on personality, but in my early years, the Maintenance Master Chief was certainly one of the primary power centers in the squadron. In addition to the Master Chief, each division would have a selection of E-8, E-7, and junior enlisted personnel with a wide range of expertise. Despite decades of trying to avoid the reality of how it operates, the Navy is (and always has been) an apprenticeship-based learning organization. Maintenance personnel go to schools to get a basic understanding of their specialty, show up at a squadron, get lots of hands-on experience, get promoted, and go back to school. This process continued until the sailors assumed leadership positions or decided to get out.

As aviators, becoming a leader in the Maintenance Department was generally the first place that you would have formal, day-to-day interaction with any enlisted sailors. This was different from military services like the Army. After my brother had gotten his commission, he had gone through advanced infantry and Ranger training and then immediately put in charge of a platoon of soldiers. When I was finally assigned the job as the Line Division officer, I had been in the Navy for almost four years without a similar responsibility. The thought of being in charge of a maintenance division was a bit intimidating. Not only did I have to learn all the specifics of the maintenance policy and procedures for that division, but I had to learn to lead people. Fortunately for me, I had a superb Line Division Chief, an E-7, who was the perfect person to teach me the ropes.

Line Division was not necessarily the home of the squadron's superstars. This is not a demeaning statement, I love my "Line Rats" to this day. The jobs that Line Division needed to get done were the "dirty jobs," the jobs out in the weather, and the jobs on the flight deck. They chocked and chained jets. They did aircraft washes. They moved aircraft, cleaned canopies, and helped the other divisions with some grunt work. They gradually worked up to the responsibility of being the sailor who walked a pilot through a start and shutdown sequence, a responsibility known as "Plane Captain." In essence, the Line Division would take new sailors aboard who hadn't been previously designated with a technical specialty and get them accustomed to what life in the Navy was all about. Life in the Line Shack was tough; some days it would be ridiculously busy, and some would be boring, and as a leader, you quickly learned the truth of the phrase "idle hands do the devil's work." My Chief, however, was a superhero. He was enthusiastic and positive, set clear expectations, and, at a time when there was still a certain level of "in-house" discipline, could change a sailor's life for the better with a few minutes of personalized attention out behind "the woodshed."

For me, the easiest parts of Line were learning policy and procedure. One of the first lessons I learned was that I was now responsible for a surprisingly long list of "IMRL" gear. This was the list of support equipment that a division was supposed to have in order to get their job done. I remember sitting down and starting to square away the inventory of chocks and chains. At first, my Chief rolled his eyes, but as we progressed, it was clear that he was learning too. Starting with an inventory sounds simple and basic, but when I did my first survey, I found that we had "lost" lots of equipment or that we "didn't know where it was." Some equipment was never used and was placed in storage containers, and some had been replaced and not marked. My policy was if I couldn't put my hands on it, it didn't exist. In the case of our tie-down chains, we had many that had been "borrowed" from other squadrons that needed to be accounted for and marked with squadron colors. It was a good lesson in bureaucracy. An inventory establishes a foundation and expectation for the future and is the perfect place to start.

With inventories out of the way, the hardest part of leading Line Division was learning to listen. It was easy to visit the line shack and ask my sailors how they were doing; it was very hard to hear what they were trying to tell me. My Chief helped me navigate these issues, ensuring I didn't chase too many red herrings. Sailors who think that their boss will solve anything will soon be asking for all kinds of "help." He helped me to look into the root causes of the problems and challenges of a group of young men (and later women) who were living away from home for the first time and who were potentially not getting off to a good start. If a sailor was always late or showed up drunk, or any of the million other small issues that took place, I learned to "pull the thread" and see if there were issues that we could manage so that sailor could recover. With this in mind, I think we saved more than we lost, and this gave me a foundation of experience I would use in the years to come.

We did have occasional incidents that resulted in stories. For example, on one notable evening, a 6'4" member of Line Division went to a party with his shipmates in Whidbey Base Housing. Upon arrival at the party, he saw that the girl who had just broken up with him had now gotten together with one of his shipmates. The sailor was very upset at this new circumstance. He began to drink heavily and got angrier and angrier at the scene he was watching. The sailor was smart enough to recognize that getting in a fight with his shipmate would result in discipline, so he went outside to blow off some steam. Unfortunately, his chosen method to do so was to repeatedly bash his head against the side of his truck (in the days to come, he was very careful to note that it was his own vehicle). He eventually bashed himself with such force that he bloodied his face and knocked himself out. After he had been gone for some time, and knowing that he had been upset, one of his shipmates grew concerned and went to look for him. He found the sailor lying in the grass, bloodied and unconscious. An ambulance was called. Navy security police arrived. The sailor, still unconscious, was loaded into the ambulance, which then proceeded towards the hospital in Coupeville, a 30-minute drive from the Naval Air Station. At this point, base security notified the SDO, which was me. I attempted to collect more information about the incident and notified the Command Master Chief (CMC), but told him I would find out more.

In the ambulance, the sailor finally woke up. Drunk, dazed, and confused, the sailor decided that he no longer wanted to be in the vehicle. The 6' 4" monster sat up, forced the EMT aside, opened the vehicle's rear doors, and exited the ambulance just as the driver slowed enough so that he would roll to a stop on the pavement instead of dying. Not concerned by his new circumstances, the sailor got up, brushed himself off, assessed his location, and began to walk up the highway, facing traffic. At this point, the ambulance driver had called for help from the State Highway Patrol. The 5' 5" State Highway Patrolman who arrived found the sailor walking on the highway, heading home. The officer exited his patrol car and attempted to convince the sailor to return to the ambulance. Without a word, the sailor continued to walk down the road. Unable to convince the young man to stop and now feeling somewhat threatened, the officer pulled his can of mace and briefly employed it in the face of the sailor. There was no response. He sprayed him again. Again, no response. The officer considered his options and employed the entire can of mace directly into the face of the sailor. Unsure of what he might have to do next, the officer waited for a few moments and then observed the mace slowly have an effect until the sailor "dropped like an axed tree."

The two EMTs and the officer placed the sailor back in the ambulance and handcuffed him to the stretcher, now reeking of mace. The sailor arrived at the hospital, was zip-tied to the bed, and was examined. Faced with this new situation, he was now totally docile and helpful. At this point, I arrived at the hospital and briefly interviewed the now very remorseful sailor. He was very sorry for the trouble that he had caused, but he didn't remember most of it. The Highway Patrolman and the ambulance staff proceeded to give me a fair amount of grief (in a restrained way). The officer relayed the story with the mace and suggested that his next option may have been the use of lethal force. It was at this point that the hospital staff assessed that the sailor had no substantial injuries other than a bloodied face, concussion, and some road rash. They asked to release the sailor into my custody. Having heard the story, I wasn't so sure that was a good idea, so I called the XO to ask for advice. After about two seconds of consideration, the XO told me that the sailor should go to jail, where he could sober up. I relayed this to the officer, and the sailor was taken to the Coupeville jail, where the CMC picked him up several hours later.

This was far from a unique story. Being in the Maintenance Department meant that you were responsible for your sailors twenty-four hours a day. The alcohol-related incidents were endless. Domestic violence was frequent. The number of lower-level issues was never-ending. Sailors with car issues, debt problems, sleeping late, and, oh yes, drugs. The Navy did a random urinalysis on a constant basis, and I always found it surprising just how many sailors would take that risk. While we could manage many issues and decide how to manage discipline, if a sailor was caught on a urine test, they were out, usually with an Other Than Honorable discharge.

Non-judicial punishment became a central part of my life. I prepared legal cases against those who had broken the rules and, along with my Chief, decided if they should be referred to the XO. After a while, you became accustomed to the issues, and you did your best to manage them before they required discipline. Occasionally, some stories made you wonder about humanity. Domestic violence was horrible, especially when it involved sexual assault. In these cases, NCIS would take over, and we'd be happy to let them run with it. One of my friends in another squadron had a sailor who murdered his wife, chopped her up, put her in a suitcase, and threw her over the rail of the Deception Pass bridge. I don't want to dwell on the bad stories, but those are what come immediately to mind. What is more difficult to describe are the hundreds of thousands of hours of expert trouble-shooting and aircraft repair work that was not exciting but which kept the squadron and the Navy running.

One of my favorite maintenance-related episodes occurred when we got a "Prowler in a Box." At some point, the Wing staff came to my squadron and asked if we minded re-assembling a Prowler that had been taken apart, almost to the stage of being a bare frame. When my CO said "yes," the maintenance department grimaced but was game to try. Within hours a portion of the jet was towed over, while the rest literally showed up in several large cardboard boxes known as "tri-walls." This was a huge project, and I do not remember why the jet was in such poor shape but it was one of two times in my career when I watched a maintenance department essentially build a Prowler from scratch (this is something that was technically not supposed to happen). I learned a ton from this major task and watched closely as the jet came together. When it came time to fly the jet for its post-maintenance test flight, I wanted to be the guy who did.

When the jet had been reassembled and was ready to fly, I could tell everyone was a bit nervous. My crew briefed the mission thoroughly, got out to the jet, did a thorough pre-flight inspection, and started it up. While we were going through the flight-control part of the checklist, I extended the emergency flaps and slats. The normal method to extend these flight controls involved using hydraulics, but the emergency method used a powerful electric motor. As the flaps and slats went down, a hydraulic line at the base of the right wing blew apart, spraying 3000 psi hydraulic fluid into the very hot electric motor. The fluid quickly ignited and caused a huge blow-torch-like fire on the right side of the aircraft that extended up past the canopy.

This would be the only time that I have ever seen a person do something that was technically impossible. As the troops rushed to use fire extinguishers, and I shut down the jet, the senior ECMO that was sitting in my right front seat traveled across the cockpit and jumped out of my side of the aircraft. I honestly do not know how he got across me and out of the aircraft without levitating, and his jump from the edge of the cockpit to the ground was equally amazing. The edge of the cockpit was probably at least ten feet from the tarmac, and he executed this leap with all his flight gear on. I wasn't in as much of a hurry. As the jet's engines wound down, the hydraulic fluid stopped, and the fire went out. The fire had appeared alarming but wasn't a huge deal. A day later, now fully repaired, we got back into the jet and took the jet flying. It came back with only a couple of "gripes" and was ready to be put into the regular flight schedule. This was a huge victory for the squadron, and for me, it reinforced my belief that a good maintenance department could do almost anything.

A decade later, when I was the Maintenance Department Head, everything that I learned from my first division officer job helped me to keep our jets in the air. I had learned that the basics of program and policy were the foundation of good maintenance. What also helped (although I am sure some of my Chiefs might have a different opinion) was for me to learn as much about the specific maintenance issue that was causing us a challenge as I could. I didn't do this so that I could micro-manage, and I had no desire to replace their expertise, but I needed to understand core issues so that I could explain to leadership what we needed and why. As a result, over time, I could tell you about the issues related to the replacement of a cracked windshield and the installation of a new one. I could tell you about the bearing material on the main landing gear, the trunnion in the nose landing gear, or the requirements to shim an outboard slat. I knew what it took to replace an engine, change a tailpipe, or fix a radio. I knew about paint, corrosion control, and what it took to replace the parachutes in the ejection seat. Finally, and even more importantly, I learned how to lead the irreplaceable experts in each division and department.

12

USS ABRAHAM LINCOLN (CVN-72)
1994-1995

USS Abraham Lincoln (CVN-72) and Strike Group, U.S. Navy Photo

After returning from deployment in early 1994, the VAQ-137 Rooks were notified that the squadron was scheduled to be disestablished. The Navy was getting smaller, and our squadron "drew the short straw." The process of winding down a squadron is kind of a pain in the neck. The resources that the squadron depended on dried up immediately. The Electronic Attack Wing reassigned "our" aircraft to other squadrons. People started disappearing and were not replaced. Our CO had a "change of charge" instead of a change of command and went off to Europe. The XO was moved to a new squadron and became the XO of

VAQ-135. For some reason, I was one of the last people out of the squadron, so I watched as what had been a living, breathing organism was gradually put to rest.

From an aviation perspective, life sucked. I had enjoyed two and a half years of gangbuster flying and had flown several sorties every week since I joined the squadron. After the decision to disestablish the squadron was made, I flew twenty-two flights between February and June. After that, I did not fly at all from July through December. On the bright side, I had dodged being involuntarily released from the Navy, and I was selected to be an instructor at VAQ-129, the EA-6B FRS. This was great news, and yet, I wasn't satisfied with it.

During my transfer to VAQ-129, I was sent to Naval Aviation Safety School in Monterrey, California. Housed on the grounds of the Naval Postgraduate School, the Aviation Safety School provided a graduate-level collection of courses designed to train participants to be Aviation Safety Officers (ASO). In essence, this material qualified us to be aviation mishap investigators. It was unusual for a junior guy like myself to go to this six-week-long school, but VAQ-129 needed another ASO, and my timing was right. The courses were interesting and included material about aviation physiology, advanced aerodynamics, human factors, investigations, structures, and, last but not least, programs and reporting.

As the school kicked off, the faculty began with an unintentional psychology experiment. On the first day, all of the students filed into a large classroom. There were probably sixty of us in attendance, and we filled all the available chairs. Of course, I had chosen a seat in the back of the room, a habit learned early in my career. The day began with an introduction of the core faculty; the course material was explained, the schedule was discussed, and the faculty told us a little about life in Monterrey. Then we were divided into two seminars so that they could maximize the instructor's time and alternate us between courses. The experiment began with the way they chose to divide the class. Usually, classes like this were divided right up the middle, left and right. However, this time one of the facilitators walked halfway up the room, stopped there and declared that the "front half" of the room was Seminar One and the "back half" of the room was Seminar Two. Even then, I thought it was an odd way to make the cut, and this division had interesting implications for the way each seminar approached the class.

As school progressed, I quickly discovered that the syllabus was more demanding than the average Navy school. Somewhat surprisingly, there was a fair amount of homework, something that almost never happened in previous courses. Despite the workload, it was clear that I was going to have a lot of spare time on my hands. As I got organized, I met a Lieutenant Commander from the Prowler community who was a few years senior to me. He was in my seminar and had a similar outlook on how to manage the course. So, we did our homework and then proceeded to investigate some of the local sights.

Monterrey is an awesome (and expensive) town. There are tons of restaurants, a few good bars, and some great golf. If you know anything about golf, you will probably immediately think about famous courses on the peninsula like Pebble Beach, Spyglass, or Spanish Bay, but those courses were financially out of reach for a naval officer. Instead, the courses we played were Bayonet and Black Horse, in what used to be Fort Ord, and Pebble Beach Municipal, a course that turned out to be a much cheaper alternative to its wealthy neighbors. In addition to golf, we also spent a lot of time at a bar called the Mucky Duck, now closed, but which had a good atmosphere, great beer, and decent food. When we didn't have time to go out, there was always the Trident Room, the bar inside the basement of the BOQ itself. One of the first things that I did was to buy my own mug and place it on a hook above the bar, where it was always ready for my weekday "study sessions."

As the weeks progressed, the results of the psychology experiment became clear. The seminar students who had been selected from the front of the room were a bunch of "stress grenades." They buried themselves in their books and never did anything fun. In contrast, the seminar selected from the "back half" of the room routinely went to the gym after class and played basketball before returning for an hour or two of homework, and then usually proceeded to the Trident Room or the Mucky Duck. The difference in the approach was profound, but the results were exactly the same, and I thought about this lesson a bit as I received my certificate of completion and returned to Whidbey.

When I got back to Whidbey, life was boring. I was now at VAQ-129 as the Assistant Safety Officer but was just killing time in what amounted to another "pool." I was not the only one sitting around, and in retrospect, this was an inexcusable waste of resources. However, the community did not have any easy ways to manage over-capacity, especially as the Navy got smaller. So, I flew simulators, did my ground job, and considered settling down and buying an old house so that I could rebuild it.

After the Christmas holidays, I was sitting at the bar in the Whidbey Officer's Club, drinking a beer and being a bit morose, when my old XO sat down next to me and started to chat. He had been through a few busy months in his new squadron. During an air wing CQ event in October, a female pilot had infamously died in an F-14A mishap, and he had been assigned to run the very high visibility mishap investigation. Next, as if that was not enough, a couple of months later, his own CO had gotten into a drunken brawl at the Whidbey Officer's Club with a more junior aviator from the P-3 community. This was such a high-profile event that the three-star Admiral from the Chief of Naval Air Forces, U.S. Pacific Fleet, flew up to Whidbey to handle it. In a quick meeting, he fired the CO of VAQ-135, and the guy who had been my XO was now the new CO of the squadron. Promotion through attrition - Congratulations!

As he sat with me at the bar, the brand-new CO of VAQ-135 explained that he had yet another problem, one of his senior LSOs had just cut his thumb off during their last CQ detachment. I had heard a little about this through the grapevine, but he told me the details. The guy had been leaving the LSO platform of the USS Abraham Lincoln, and as he reached for the handle to close the huge armored watertight door with his right hand, he placed his left hand on the inside of the door for leverage. When he pulled the door closed, the inner hinge instantly clipped his thumb off. Fortunately, the thumb had been recovered and immediately placed on ice. The LSO was now in the hospital in San Diego with the digit re-attached. In fact, the prognosis was good; there was every expectation that the thumb would heal. However, in the near term, the squadron now needed a senior pilot and LSO; would I be interested? The decision didn't take me a second, "hell yes!"

The next day I found myself in the front office of VAQ-129. The CO of the squadron (whom I had almost no interaction with) listened to the story and clearly thought that there was something wrong with me for wanting to leave VAQ-129 after already completing two busy deployments. Despite his misgivings, he permitted me to transfer. Two days later, I had moved my gear to VAQ-135, was back up to speed in the jet, and had started conducting FCLPs. Even better, not only was I back in the fleet, but I would be getting my next traps on the USS Abraham Lincoln (CVN-72) in only ten days. Life was looking up!

The "Black Ravens" of VAQ-135 was an interesting squadron in an interesting Carrier Air Wing. When VAQ-137 had been disestablished, half a dozen officers had transferred to VAQ-135 along with the XO. While a hierarchical organization knows exactly how to manage brand-new guys, it can be difficult to incorporate people who have a wide range of seniority and expectations to match. It was taking quite a while to re-arrange the "pecking order" of the newly combined squadron. In addition, there were now women in the squadron. Congress had changed the law allowing women into combat crews, and the USS Abraham Lincoln and Carrier Air Wing 11 were now going to sea with female aviators and maintenance personnel, the first such deployment on the West Coast. The addition of women provided a new dynamic to the air wing, and a few male aviators resented this change and resisted it to some degree. So, despite my familiarity with many of the people involved, when I arrived in the squadron everything felt a little off-kilter. Nevertheless, I had several close friends in the squadron, we were going on deployment, and life was good. I had been sitting around Whidbey for so long that I was just happy to be back in a jet, and it didn't matter that things were a little "off."

As I joined them, the squadron was poised to participate in the last major workup period before deployment. This time, however, things were a little different for me. The USS Abraham Lincoln was a San Diego-based carrier, and I no longer had to fly all the way across the county to join the ship. In a bigger picture, this meant that I was about to embark on my first West Coast cruise and operate in the Pacific. This was exciting, and like all new West Coast sailors, I was hopeful that this deployment would include a port visit in Australia. Despite my optimism, however, as the at-sea period progressed, it was clear that all was not well. Some aviators were not ready for deployment, and this included a couple of the new female pilots. Their eventual grounding ended up in national news, in Congress, and sparked resentment in the wing.

In general, everything felt a little rough around the edges. The air wing had lost the F-14A and one aviator in October, and during this exercise, we lost another. A F/A-18C was on the catapult, waiting to launch one night in late January. The pilot selected the afterburner, turned on his lights (the night-time signal that the pilot was ready for launch), and was hurled off the carrier. The takeoff initially looked normal. However, the angle-of-attack measurement devices on his aircraft were broken. The jet's computer thought that it was climbing and automatically pushed the nose down hard, flying the aircraft directly into the Pacific. The young aviator had no chance. I was circling overhead that night, waiting to land, and the chilling calls on the radio after the mishap will always be with me.

A few days later, the carrier was scheduled to pull back into San Diego for a quick "port visit" to give us all a break. As was typical for the area, it was very foggy around the coast, and the ship was driving around looking for an opening in the weather to launch some helicopters. When the USS Abraham Lincoln finally found a hole in the fog, it happened to drive itself right into the middle of the America's Cup sailing race. I have a great picture from the front page of the San Diego Union-Tribune that shows the carrier about to run over a very expensive sailboat. Immediately the word was spread that nobody in the air wing should make fun of the ship's crew for this grievous navigational error.

Now, this order was made in anticipation of an air wing awards ceremony known as "Foc'sle Follies." Follies took place every couple of months at sea and was intended to recognize the pilots with the best landing performance and to distribute "centurion patches" to the aviators who had achieved a hundred or more arrested landings on that carrier. The ceremony was also an opportunity for the air wing to blow off some steam and provide "unofficial" feedback to the chain of command. This feedback typically included off-color skits and songs that often contained scathing commentary. As the name implies, the event is usually held in the foc'sle of the carrier (a large room where the anchor chain comes into the ship), and in my opinion, it should never be held anywhere else.

In this case, leadership decided to hold this ceremony in the Miramar Officer's Club. Keep in mind that the next event we would all be attending was a memorial service for our shipmate who had died two days before. The fact that follies were now scheduled in the O-Club meant that the scathing commentary would be delivered under the influence of alcohol; this is never, ever a good thing. So, when the word went out that we were not to make fun of the ship for the navigation issue, it immediately guaranteed that such feedback would be delivered. In an act of sheer brilliance (and total defiance), once we pulled into San Diego, the S-3 squadron rushed ashore and immediately had t-shirts made. When the Admiral, CO of the ship, and CAG arrived at the O-club to kick off the event, the entire air wing was wearing "USS Abraham Lincoln, America's Cup, Official Crew Member" shirts, and the event went downhill from there.

With workups behind us, we departed on deployment in April. Heading west gave me a real sense of the scale with regard to the Pacific. While a carrier could cross the Atlantic in a week or so, it would take the USS Abraham Lincoln a month to cross the Pacific. On our way across the ocean, we didn't fly much but maintained currency by operating in the vicinity of the Pacific islands that provided us with divert fields. The crossing was not without incident. At one point, VF-213, the "Black Lions," the same squadron that had lost an aviator in October, crashed another F-14. In this case, the aircraft was carrying a TARPS pod. A TARPS pod was essentially a large, very expensive pod filled with cameras designed for aerial reconnaissance. The pilot had apparently disregarded the rule against Air Combat Maneuvering with the pod. This rule was established because the heavy pod was loaded off-centerline, which increased the likelihood of a flat spin. Unsurprisingly, while in the midst of an unauthorized engagement, the pilot lost control of the aircraft and went into an unrecoverable spin. The crew ejected and was safely recovered, but what was interesting to the rest of us was how quickly the pilot's mishap was reviewed and he was released to fly.

In our squadron, we had a bit of an adventure when a crew inadvertently shattered the pilot's armored windscreen. The aircraft had the ability to clear rain from the windscreen with hot air taken straight from the engines. However, if you used this system when there was no rain, it was likely to shatter the two-inch thick layered glass. While it stayed physically intact, the shattered screen was impossible for the pilot to see through. After discussing having the crew fly alongside the ship and eject, CAG decided to give the pilot one chance at landing, which was fortunately successful.

After these aviation misadventures, it was time for a port visit, and our first stop was Hong Kong. What a crazy place. It is one thing to know that Hong Kong is one of the trading capitals of the world; it is something else entirely to anchor out in the middle of the port and watch everything that is in motion. The White Star ferries were all over the bay, and there were ships of all sizes everywhere. It was fascinating. Those who had been to Hong Kong before told us about things we should be on the lookout for. There were a few who desired to get a hand-made suit. Others wanted to get some porcelain or other oriental art. Most of us just wanted to see the sights and have a beer. The truth was that while the visit of an American carrier had a huge impact on many ports, the arrival of the USS Abraham Lincoln didn't even make a ripple in Hong Kong. What I noticed was a typical pattern for the air wing; the first thing we did was locate a British or Irish pub and have some beers. Aside from that, despite the variety of things to do, there wasn't a lot that appealed to me, so I spent a fair amount of time on the ship.

On our way to our next port in Singapore, we did some flying off the coast of Vietnam. During one nighttime event, my crew and I decided we'd go see the lights along the Vietnamese coast. Most of us had grown up on stories from the Vietnam War, and it was quite interesting to be flying in the same region. As we headed to the west, we were just starting to see a bit of the glow from the coast when the guys in the back of the jet started to see an increasing number of military air search radars, followed by some radars that were associated with Vietnamese fighters. While we were well offshore in international waters, we decided that it was probably not a good idea to start a diplomatic incident and turned around and went back to the ship.

Within a few days, we were in Singapore. Before the ship arrived in port, we had been repeatedly advised about some of the unusual laws that we might unwittingly break, like not chewing gum in public. However, once we got into town and took a look around, it didn't seem like any of that would be a problem. The good news for me was that we had an admin in a very nice hotel. Somebody in the squadron was friends with the manager of the hotel from a previous deployment, and we had gotten nice rooms at a very good price. So, while I did not do a lot of touring, there was much fun to be had in the hotel, and it was clear to me that, despite some turbulence, the squadron was slowly coming together.

After Singapore, we drove towards the Arabian Gulf at quite a good clip. We only did enough flying in the Indian Ocean to stay current, and after departing San Diego in mid-April, we finally entered the Arabian Gulf in early June. If there was any good news about being in the Arabian Gulf in the summer, it was only that I was very happy that I was not on the USS America. The USS Abraham Lincoln was a nuclear-powered ship, and the quality of life was significantly better than the old rust bucket. Once we arrived, the carrier went right to a carrier-operating area known as "CVOA-4," and we began flying missions in support of Operation Southern Watch.

By this time, Operation Southern Watch had been underway for a few years, and the ritualized aspect of the mission was well-honed with the Iraqis. They would fly a jet or two south, and we would not be able to catch them. Or, they would fire surface-to-air missiles into the air and attempt to shoot down an unwary coalition aircraft and always miss. The severity of these Iraqi actions was judged by leadership in the Combined Air Operations Center or CAOC, and if they were deemed dangerous enough, they would generate what we called a "response option." A response option was a small-scale strike mission that was intended to be proportional to the Iraqi action. If they fired a surface-to-air weapon, our intelligence would find whatever had shot at us (or something like it). One or two strike fighters would then use laser-guided bombs or GPS-guided weapons and attack the missile site or a AAA piece that intelligence had identified. During these strikes, an EA-6B crew would jam and provide cover. The bombs would explode, the Iraqis would now have one less weapon system, and balance would be restored. Since normal missions were so boring, we all wanted to be part of a Response Option. However, being scheduled to support one was just the luck of the draw. I probably lucked into more than my share, but aside from that, this three-month period was a bit of Groundhog Day.

As I look at my logbook, I flew twenty-five combat missions each month during June, July, and August. I only flew a few non-combat flights. One or two of those non-combat missions had to be the "Blue Two" low level in Kuwait because I clearly remember discussing the towering gas flares off the Kuwaiti coast with my CO. We passed these flares on every single mission, and they were huge. They spewed burning natural gas a couple of hundred feet into the air every minute of every day. When I flew with the CO, he would always say, "Come on, Tater, let's go fly through one of them." From my perspective, there was no way that this was going to happen. Not only did it not appeal to me to fly through a big flame, but I also had no idea what structures may exist inside that tower of burning gas. Now, legend has it that at one point, another pilot in the squadron decided to honor the CO's request. They got low and fast and flew in or very near to the flame. The thing about flying through a big flame is that there is no oxygen available for your engines. As they flew by the flame, they got a huge set of "chugs" from the engines, scared themselves, and agreed that it may not have been a good idea. Despite his apparent death wish, I did enjoy flying with the CO. One of our favorite maneuvers was to get to twenty-five thousand or so feet and start a diving spiral, pulling 5.5Gs until we ran out of altitude. There was one particular ECMO who couldn't take that G loading for such a long duration, and it was amusing to "test" their G-tolerance and temporarily put them to sleep.

One major issue that had emerged from Desert Storm and Operation Southern Watch was the critical importance of the Electronic Warfare mission. The EA-6B and its jamming capabilities went from being a "nice to have" to being a "must-have." No coalition aircraft were allowed across the border unless there was an EA-6B or another SEAD aircraft like the F-16CJ that went over the border with them. After years of "Prowler go long," it was nice to be needed. As a community and a squadron, the fact that we now fell into the category of "can't leave home without us," felt great, and we had t-shirts made that said this. The missions themselves, however, were rather boring. Take off, go to the tanker, and head into one of the dedicated "kill boxes" over Iraq. Fly in this area with random turns so that you couldn't be easily targeted, and look for enemy fire. During that entire summer, I think that I probably only saw a few bursts of AAA and maybe one missile way off in the distance. It was not uncommon for the fighter guys to see more, especially at night, but it was clear that we were not duplicating WWII missions over Germany by any means. After we had completed our allotted time in Iraq, we would check out, head back to the ship, and land - just like clockwork.

Not only were the missions monotonous, but so was the ship's schedule. The theme of "Groundhog Day" resonated throughout our lives. We pulled into Jebel Ali in the United Arab Emirates five separate times, once in June, twice in July, once in August, and once in September. While these visits did give us a break, it wasn't really in the spirit of "join the Navy and see the world." However, pulling into the same port did allow us to get our admin down to a real system. For example, we stayed in the same hotel almost every time.

The hotel's management gave us the same large suite whenever we showed up, well, except for our last visit.

As previously discussed, an admin was always stocked with beer and snacks. Usually, we attempted to finish all the beer we had purchased so that we would not leave anything behind. In the UAE, however, one of the guys discovered that we could store any leftover beer in the false ceiling of this particular suite, and nobody would be the wiser. The fear of buying too much disappeared. This worked great until it didn't. When we arrived for what would be our last visit, we were given a different suite. Horrors! The room we had been using was reserved by "regular" people for the entire duration of our stay. This presented us with a conundrum. A couple of the guys explained our issue to the staff, and with very quizzical looks, they notified us when the room was temporarily unoccupied. At this point, one of the staff (who was very well-tipped) escorted us up to the room and unlocked the door. Very quickly, we got up on chairs, pushed aside the ceiling panels, and retrieved the cases of beer that had been stored there. Now, adequately resupplied, the admin could begin.

These five visits blur entirely together. I remember one dance club that had cages hung from the ceiling and ultimately had air wing officers in them. I remember pouring a shipmate into a cab, minus his shoes, which, for some reason, were required by another aviator. I remember hearing about many of the "intrapersonal" relationships among the air wing. You can't put men and women in confined quarters and not expect that there are going to be some relationships, any more than you can order aviators not to curse. This behavior introduced a level of gossip among the air wing that had never existed before. I also seem to remember a withering hot game of golf on a very expensive course that I was sure was going to kill me.

One of the most stressful specific memories came from the day that I had shore patrol with one of the female F/A-18C pilots. We were unlucky and drew the responsibility of maintaining order at the Seaman's Club. This club was intended to be a respite for the merchant sailors who frequently docked in Jebel Ali. It was popular with our enlisted sailors because it had cheap beer, a good pool, and lots of things to do at a very low cost. Unfortunately, it was also popular with Iranian sailors. Much like Follies, putting alcohol together with American and Iranian sailors was not good. It was all that we could do to keep everyone from beating the shit out of each other. However, what impressed me the most from that day was how fearless she was. There would be a huge argument or a particularly drunk and violent sailor, and this five-and-a-half-foot, hundred-and-twenty-pound aviator would wade right into the middle of the scrum. Of course, I was right behind her, usually standing with my arms crossed, backing her up, but I don't think that was part of her calculus. Honestly, it was quite a good lesson in leadership.

During one of these visits, CAG once again decided to hold Foc'sle Follies on shore. Apparently, nobody had learned anything from the event held in Miramar only a few months earlier. In addition to holding follies on the beach and with alcohol, the order went out that there would be no cursing. Somebody thought that they could put a bunch of Naval Aviators on the beach in hundred-degree weather, give them beer, and ask them to put on a bunch of skits and cynical songs without cursing. Predictably, this order goaded the Junior Officers of the Air Wing into high gear. The good news for our squadron was that it wasn't our turn to put on a skit; the bad news was that we had no energy or desire to put together a good song. Even worse, we were the first ones up in what was known as the "Roll Call."

Now, the LSOs of the squadron are generally the ones responsible for squadron input in Foc'sle Follies. In this case, we failed in the most confrontational fashion possible. When our squadron was called, instead of a song, we all just stood up and yelled, "Fuck You," and then sat down. There was a gasp from the crowd, and every roll call from that point went further across the line. About three skits or songs later, things had gotten very raunchy and exceptionally non-politically correct, and the Admiral and his staff got up and walked out in disgust. The event came to a crunching halt after about thirty minutes of pain, and CAG angrily directed all the COs to immediately head back to the ship. After the ship pulled back out the next day, CAG had all the COs report to his office in their dress uniforms. He then chewed them all out and grounded them for a week. It was not a happy time for anyone, and our CO felt betrayed and was very upset. Honestly, I felt bad, but this was a clear case of air wing leadership not having a clue what was going on outside their office door.

Despite the relative boredom of the constant flow of combat missions over Iraq, there were a few exciting events. One afternoon, I had manned up a jet to fly an Operation Southern Watch mission. We were positioned on CAT 4, the catapult that is the farthest to the port side of the ship. Right next to me, on CAT 3, was an A-6 tanker. The way this would work was that the A-6 would "run up," go into tension, and launch, and my jet would be about a minute behind. All things about the launch were normal until the A-6 went to military power and was just about to be launched. Unknown to us, his port tailpipe exploded inside the fuselage and developed a gaping hole. This hole sent burning-hot, high-pressure exhaust gas throughout the entire rear of the aircraft. The crew got a fire warning light in the cockpit and immediately yelled, "Suspend CAT 3, fire!" over the radio. This radio request always results in an immediate halt to the launching process, but a crew is not allowed to bring the throttles back from max power until they are told to do so, just in case they are subsequently launched. There was a ten or fifteen-second delay, and I could see an immense amount of smoke creeping through the A-6 as they stayed at high power. From my perspective (and theirs), it took a very long time for the Air Boss to tell the crew that they were suspended, and it took a few more moments before they could shut down. During this delay, smoke and fire were visibly crawling up the fuselage and erupting through the gaps in the jet's external panels, moving toward the cockpit. It was like a horror movie.

One of the most amazing things you will ever see is the response to a fire on the flight deck. All of a sudden, "all hands on deck" means something. Men in fire suits appear from nowhere, hoses are reeled out and applied to the fire, and the entire team springs into action. Had they seen this activity, the crew in the A-6 would surely have felt that things were under control. However, they were now hidden in a cloud of dense smoke. The canopy of the A-6 is hydraulically driven, and they started opening it as their engines were winding down. Unfortunately for them, when the engines came to rest, the canopy stopped moving backward after about a foot, leaving them trapped inside. Inside the jet, they had taken their oxygen masks off and were struggling to breathe. Outside, a sailor from the ship's crash and salvage team had crawled up onto the aircraft to pull the emergency canopy release that was to the rear of the canopy. Just as he reached it, one of the aviators found the emergency jettison handle inside the cockpit and pulled it. An explosive squib blew the canopy back at tremendous speed and hit the sailor right on his "cranial," the protective headgear that all sailors wear on the flight deck. The sailor instantly dropped like a rag doll and fell to the flight deck. I was entirely convinced that I had just seen a man die.

It was at about this point that my concern for my own aircraft and crew became more of a compelling interest. Our engines were still turning, and we were sitting next to a flaming jet that was full of fuel. As quickly as they responded, it was taking a fair amount of time for the crash crew to slow the fire since it was hard to reach underneath the aluminum shell. I radioed the Air Boss and asked if we could shut down. After a pause, we were permitted to shut everything down and got out of the jet and away from the firefighting effort. We made it away from the fire and back down to our ready room and then watched as the carrier's flight deck heroes secured the fire and prepared to resume flight operations.

This is always the part that gets left out of a lot of stories about accidents on the carrier. Missions still need to happen, jets are still airborne, and the carrier can't just stop. Instead, the fire gets put out, the jet gets pulled out of the way, and the crew continues working; it is literally amazing. Eventually, we heard that the sailor hit by the canopy was alive. He had lost some teeth and had a bunch of contusions but had been saved by his cranial (and the geometry of the glancing blow). I later met him and shook his hand; it is always the quiet heroes that make things work.

Another incident, not as dramatic from a personal perspective but still kind of amazing, took place during an underway replenishment (or UNREP). An UNREP is one of the keys to the U.S. Navy's success. It involves two, or even sometimes, three ships pulling within a couple of hundred feet of each other while moving at a good clip and transferring fuel and supplies. Now, an UNREP is one of those capabilities that marks a difference between how the U.S. Navy operates and "everyone else" in the world. Routinely pulling two massive warships alongside each other at fifteen or twenty knots, getting fuel lines across, and then exchanging tons of groceries and ammo by overhead wires is an amazing feat, and the Navy does it all the time. That said, we generally didn't fly during an UNREP, so I was in my room doing some work when the USS Sacramento pulled alongside. The USS Sacramento was a huge supply ship designed for this job, but it was aging a bit. In this particular case, something went wrong with the USS Sacramento's steering gear, and this huge ship veered directly into the side of the carrier with a tremendous "bang." While the first impact was severe, the ship then slid all the way down the right side of the carrier, making a huge grinding sound and creating a trail of damage the entire way. Most of the damage to the carrier was superficial, but the collision had caused some significant issues, including the creation of one new "window" in the side of the carrier's tower. The good news was that the flight deck crew had pulled all the aircraft away from the side of the ship as required, or we could have easily lost a dozen or more irreplaceable aircraft.

The fifth visit to Jebel was a real hit to the already low morale. It had been a brutally hot summer, and we were all exhausted. Up until that point, it appeared that we might have time to leave the gulf and return home via a port visit in Australia. Rumors were rife, but as we pulled into Jebel for the fifth time, we all knew that the dream of a visit to Sydney was dead. With our last port call in the Arabian Gulf complete, we steamed non-stop for home. After months of flying once or twice a day, I flew a total of five times on the way home. The ship did make a diversion to the south after heading through the Singapore Straights, and we spent a day crossing the equator, cleansing another batch of Pollywogs in a gentle manner that would be acceptable to a more diverse crew.

Twelve days later found us in Hawaii, where we pulled in for a four-day visit. One of the cooler opportunities that this presented was that we could bring a relative to the ship to participate in what is known as a "Tiger Cruise." The Tigers got a chance to spend a week on the carrier, experience some flight operations, and generally see what we did. I brought my father out, and he had a great time. A couple of days later, however, I was home in Whidbey.

After arriving back in Whidbey, I now had done three deployments in a row and could no longer avoid a shore tour. A normal aviation career requires a naval officer to go to a staff job in between periods of sea duty. I had been requesting a job in Washington, D.C. so that I could be closer to where I grew up, and I had gotten what appeared to be a good job in the Bureau of Naval Personnel. In order to prepare for this move, I was granted "house hunting leave" and was in D.C. looking for a place to live when I got a horrible call from back in Whidbey. One of our squadron jets had crashed into the Pacific, two of my shipmates were gone, and two were badly injured. As I was the squadron's senior ASO, I was asked to return to assist in the investigation.

For me, this mishap capped a string of events in this particular air wing that reminded me that there is a tiny but significant difference between a good unit and one that is not so good. The people were the same, but something about the leadership mix just wasn't working. In this case, the squadron had gone out to sea in February for a few days of operations on the coast of San Diego. This was the pilot's first real carrier mission, and he and his very experienced crew were scheduled to fly what was usually a very fun Defensive Air Combat Tactics (DEFTAC) flight against another EA-6B with a very qualified crew. There was a lot for a young aviator to think about on this flight, and there is no doubt that his "bucket was full."

The two aircraft got airborne and set up for their first pass. When they flew by each other, each pulled several "Gs" to react to the "threat." Unfortunately, the young pilot experienced a "G-induced loss of consciousness," or G-LOC. This occurs when the force of the jet's maneuver causes a person's blood to pool in their lower extremities and cause them to pass out. As I discovered during the investigation, this can be an insidious event. While sometimes it is clear that a victim has totally passed out, at other times they may not appear to be unconscious. As a result, when this young aviator became incapacitated, it probably wasn't apparent to the senior crew member sitting next to him. Without anyone actually in control of the aircraft, the jet rolled upside down and sliced through an overcast layer toward the ocean at very high speed. When they came out of the clouds, someone instantly realized that they were very close to the water and ejected the crew (we will never know who).

In the EA-6B, there is a four-tenths of a second delay between each ejection seat leaving the aircraft, and the pilot's seat always goes last. This means that a pilot does not leave the aircraft until one point two seconds after the ejection handle is pulled. While it may seem tiny, this delay could easily be the difference between life and death. In this case, the two aviators in the back and the guy in the right front seat successfully ejected, but the pilot did not. The speed of the aircraft was such that the two guys in the back survived but were badly injured. One of these aviators heroically saved the other, who was incapacitated with flail injuries (caused by ejecting into the five-hundred mile-per-hour wind stream) and couldn't keep his head above the surface of the water. The aviator in the right front seat died when a heavy part of his parachute harness hit him in the head. This mishap eventually led to a new procedure where all Navy ejection seat crews needed to "hang" in their harness to ensure that this would not happen to them. Memorial services never get easier, and this one was particularly difficult. The officer in the right front seat was a brilliant leader, mentor, and friend, and if he had lived, he would certainly have become an Admiral.

After this investigation, I moved to D.C. and started my new job. In August of that same year, the F-14A pilot from VF-213, who had crashed the TARPS jet in the middle of the Pacific, died in Memphis in front of his entire family. He had flown a Tomcat into town for a good-deal "cross country" flight. On his way out of the airfield, he attempted a "high performance" takeoff on a day with low, thick clouds. After zooming into the sky and straight into the overcast, he instantly had no outside reference. The power of the jet's longitudinal acceleration told the vestibular system in his brain that he was "tilting back," so without referencing his instruments, he apparently pushed forward while still in the afterburner and flew right into the ground, killing himself; the aviator in his back seat and three people on the ground.

Since this story now finds me in Washington D.C., I would suggest that one of the key experiences in a naval career that does not come across at all in popular culture is that Naval Aviators don't just fly - all of them must also endure jobs known as a "shore tour." These shore jobs alternate with sea duty or flying jobs. A shore tour is generally a job teaching, training, or participating in the administration of the Navy. Shore tours can make or break a career, but they are generally not that exciting or interesting (at least from the perspective of sea stories). As you have already heard, my first shore duty was an assignment to the FRS in order to be an instructor. This assignment was as good as it gets for a first-tour Lieutenant. The FRS is the hub of all naval aviation communities. Everybody who will be flying the aircraft needs to cycle through the squadron, and as a result, it is an excellent networking opportunity. In addition, the squadron was huge, and there were a lot of Lieutenants in the mix. If you were competitive among that cut-throat crowd, you were on the road toward command. Many senior officers in Naval Aviation made their first mark on shore duty in the FRS.

However, since I had dodged the FRS and returned to the fleet, my next shot at shore duty was not as clear cut. I was a bit "out of phase" at this point, and the detailer (the human resources officer in charge of all assignments) didn't necessarily know what to do with me. I made it a little easier by asking to go to D.C., a place that most officers avoided but which was near to where I had grown up and was an area that I enjoyed. So, in accordance with my request, I was assigned to the Bureau of Naval Personnel (BUPERS) with the intent to be the Assistant Aviation Community Manager. This would have been a great job if I had gotten it. However, when I showed up, the surface warfare Captain who was my boss, assigned me to be the Assistant Officer Personnel Planner. The first lesson I learned was that I should never believe the guys in BUPERS (and I am only half-joking). Our sour joke would be familiar in a lot of places, "How do you know a detailer is lying? His lips are moving." In essence, the office was using the aviation community management job to bait-and-switch officers into one of the most miserable positions in the Bureau. As a result, I became the assistant budget guy for the entire officer account, with a promise that I could eventually move to the aviation job. My role as an assistant didn't last long, as the primary guy retired and left me as the (acting) Officer Personnel Planner. While the heart of that job is not something that developed any good sea stories, it was a period that allowed me to get an excellent experience about "how the sausage was made." The lessons I learned here eventually helped my career but this value barely made up for the pain.

13

USS THEODORE ROOSEVELT (CVN-71) AND USS ENTERPRISE (CVN-65)

AGM-88 HARM on EA-6B, U.S. Navy Photo

After two years of torture at a desk in Washington D.C., I had been promoted to Lieutenant Commander and learned that I was heading back to Whidbey to serve as a Department Head. This was great news. After having already experienced both East Coast and West Coast deployments, I had asked to be sent to another East Coast squadron. When the assignment list was released, I discovered that my request had been granted. I was now heading to VAQ-141, a squadron that was attached to Carrier Air Wing EIGHT and which deployed on the USS Theodore Roosevelt (CVN-71), out of Norfolk. I was even more excited to find out that I would report to the squadron just as it went into the last big phases of workups. So, in the spring of 1998, I left D.C., drove back to Whidbey, and quickly got settled in. I completed the required refresher training in the aircraft and then arrived at the squadron in October, ready to work. Two weeks later, I was flying across the country in an EA-6B to participate in an exercise known as Joint Task Force Exercise, (JTFEX).

My first cross-country trip from Whidbey to Norfolk in this squadron was with my new XO. A great American, the XO was a very "forward-leaning" person who lived by the "beg forgiveness rather than ask permission" mentality. As we flew the jet east towards Norfolk, we were in the vicinity of Wright Patterson AFB, when we got not just one, but eventually two, fuel filter warning lights. This was not a good warning light to see in a Prowler. If the system was working correctly, this light was an indication of clogged fuel filters and imminent engine failure. We declared an emergency, landed safely at Wright Patterson, got a BOQ room, and called for maintenance support. Having a jet with issues on the way across the nation was not an unusual issue, so within a day or so we had our maintenance guys at the base, working on the jet. Of course, when they looked through the fuel system, they couldn't find anything wrong. So, they did what they could, and told us to go fly.

This was good news. Every day that we were late affected the CQ schedule, and we were frequently reminded by the CO that we needed to get the jet to the carrier as soon as we could. With this in mind, we manned up and prepared to fly to Norfolk. All was well as we taxied out to the runway. After I was cleared to take off, I positioned the jet on the centerline of the runway, went to military power, and started the takeoff roll. Taking off in a Prowler is not the same as zooming into the sky in an F/A-18. It takes time for a heavy jet to pick up speed and we had some strict low and high-speed abort criteria. Below eighty knots we would abort for almost anything. Above that, you'd only attempt to stop for a few critical issues that meant you might not stay airborne for long, one of which was a filter light. So, at about 110 knots, with a heavy jet that was full of fuel, we got another filter light. This resulted in the only high-speed aborted takeoff that I ever had to do in a Prowler. Fortunately, the Wright-Patterson runway is very long and I didn't have to use the brakes while we were at high speed (this was notorious for melting the brakes and blowing tires) but allowed the aircraft to decelerate on its own. Having just executed a very dynamic emergency procedure, we taxied back to the hangar and left the jet with maintenance again. We now expected that we might be stuck there for days. The maintenance crew, having exhausted all other possibilities, simply decided to replace the warning light system in the front cockpit, and our troublesome lights went away.

Flying with the XO was always good for a little trouble. Much like workups on the USS America, the USS Theodore Roosevelt headed south towards the Caribbean to do much of JTFEX. We were operating in the Atlantic somewhere north of Puerto Rico when we were scheduled to fly together again. The air plan had us down for a "Prowler go long" mission that we didn't think was particularly interesting. As we discussed the options, we decided we should circumnavigate Puerto Rico. So, we launched and set a course around the island.

Now, there used to be a time when Naval Aviators flew in international air space operating in "due regard." As long as you didn't break any flight rules and made it back to the ship, life was good. However, over time the Navy had slowly become much more like the Air Force. Both the XO and I were new to the squadron and didn't understand the implications of this trend, so when we were told that there was this airspace called the "Bear Box," that had been designated for the air wing to fly within, we both ignored it. As a result, as soon as we left the Bear Box and headed towards Puerto Rico we got a call from the E-2. I suppose we expected that they would just warn us to return within the boundaries. Unfortunately, this time was different, not only were we ordered to return directly to the ship, but we were told to see CAG immediately after we landed. Shit. After we trapped, I prepared to get my ass handed to me. However, as we walked from the Ready Room towards CAG's office the XO told me that he would handle it and went alone. I don't know how that conversation went, but for the rest of my time in the air wing, I stayed within the confines of the Bear Box like a good Air Force crew.

For me, the rest of this sea period was defined by the fact that our EA-6Bs kept losing leading-edge slats. When I arrived at the squadron I had been assigned the job of Safety Department Head. This was a typical job for a new Lieutenant Commander, and I was an ASO, so I fit fine. The Prowler had leading-edge slats that came down along with a set of flaps in order to put the jet into a take-off, or landing configuration. These surfaces increase lift and enable the aircraft to slow to landing speeds. The thing about these slats was that they needed to be rigged pretty precisely. If improperly fitted, they would not quite come all the way up, and this would be indicated on the pilot's instrument panel with a cross-hatched indication known as a "barber pole."

At the time "barber-polled slats" had become a routine event, and pilots in the squadron had even learned that in order to avoid this indication, they could "bump" the nose of the jet down just as the slats came up, and they would generally not catch. This was good because not only did a barber pole indication mean that the crew needed to run through a set of emergency procedures, but when the jet landed, maintenance needed to try to fix it. It's not that we didn't want to fix things, but after this kind of repair, the jet needed an FCF, depriving the squadron of a normal mission. This did not make CAG happy. So, although the informal "bump" procedure worked for a while, it eventually caused things to break. During one flight one of our jets lost a slat as the pilot climbed away from the ship. This damage created quite a dangerous situation and we were lucky that the crew was able to safely land at the Navy airfield at Roosevelt Roads, Puerto Rico. This repair took several days, and since I was the one doing the safety investigation, I went ashore and brought the aircraft back to the ship.

Over the next few months, I learned a lot more about the structure of the wings than I had ever expected. However, despite a very intensive effort from our maintenance guys, slat incidents kept occurring. One of the good things this challenge demonstrated was how much engineering talent I could get in touch with if I needed it. At this point in history, the ship finally had email connectivity with the world, so we soon had dozens of smart Navy engineers across the U.S. working to help solve this issue. It took months of investigation and maintenance work, but in the end, we discovered that there were essentially two issues. One was that the supply system needed to only provide EA-6B slats when they were ordered. Somewhere along the line it had been assumed that re-worked A-6 slats would fit the similar-but-different EA-6B, but this turned out not to be the case. The other issue was that we needed to re-train maintenance on how to install leading-edge slats. At some point, the community had let "experience" override the maintenance manual, and the workarounds that became common with slats were not helping. Having isolated the root cause of the issue, the Navy sent us a team of Technical Representatives who retrained the department and helped us eliminate this challenge.

This would not be the last issue the community faced as the aircraft aged. We were approaching a period of time when slats, tailpipes, and landing gear were all beginning to fail in dangerous ways, requiring close attention by aircrew and an increasing number of man-hours from maintenance to keep the jet in the sky.

After a couple more weeks of flying, we had a good port visit in St Maarten. I don't remember much about that trip except for a visit to the end of the famous runway where the commercial jets landed just over your head, and to the casino that was up on the hill from there. With this short port visit in the rear-view mirror, we headed back out into the Caribbean, completed our exercise, and headed home for the holidays. After the New Year, we returned to the ship for a final month of flying off the east coast in February. When we left the boat this time, there was already some excitement about the potential for NATO operations over Yugoslavia, and we half expected to be told to head east at that time. To our surprise, however, we returned to Whidbey for another few weeks. When the war started there was some real concern that we might somehow miss the fight and instead be sent back to the Arabian Gulf. However, as described in the prelude, we ultimately left on deployment and headed across the Atlantic to support Operation Allied Force at the end of March.

War is horrible, but as countless commentators have observed over the years, aviators definitely get a different perspective of combat. Operation Allied Force was primarily an air war. Our objectives were to erode Serbian defenses and drive them to the negotiating table. After the first set of strikes, the air wing settled into a bit of a routine. For the first ten days or so, we hit a wide range of infrastructure targets and our strikes were very "formal." We planned, briefed, and flew these missions like we were trained to do in Fallon. The only unique component was that after the first couple of missions we were finally incorporated into the Air Force tanker plan, and we could count on getting fuel from one of several Air Force and NATO tanker aircraft that spent hours circling in one of several dedicated locations in the region.

As I think about the war, I remember a few particular vignettes. During one of the early missions, we were supporting a nighttime strike in the vicinity of Pristina, the major city right in the center of Kosovo. We were heading into the area from the south. Our jamming route took us into Kosovo for several miles, before we would turn around and set up an orbit. Most of us had never seen an enemy missile launch at night before and there were radio calls from the fighters we were supporting that said there were "SAMs in the air." This was concerning because as described previously, we did not have night vision goggles. As a result, most of what we saw were the flashes of explosions and strings of Anti-Aircraft Artillery (AAA). We had pushed pretty far into bad guy country when one of the guys in the jet said "I think I see a missile." Of course, this was not the call we were trained to give. Identifying a threat was great, I needed to know where it was in order to react properly. So, once he told me where he thought he had seen it, I turned to put the threat on my wing as I had been trained and began an evasive maneuver designed to protect my large and relatively slow aircraft. It must be said that SAM evasion maneuvers in an EA-6B at night over the mountains of Kosovo are probably as scary as actually dodging a missile. In the end, there was no missile, but I learned that we had to be pretty darned sure that we were being shot at because the "cure" might be worse than the disease.

On another nighttime mission, we flew to the vicinity of the

Macedonian border again and set up an orbit over a mountainous area north of the city of Skopje. Our jamming orbits were typically long ovals, with legs that were ten or fifteen miles long. These ovals would be oriented towards the target, not necessarily because of jammer limitations (the jammers had steerable antennas), but because it was nice to be looking towards the threat as you jammed it. This particular orbit was oriented mostly north-south, with the north end over the mountains in Kosovo, and the south end closer to Skopje. We were on our first turn of the orbit when I saw a ton of barrage-AAA come up right underneath us. The volume of the fire was mesmerizing. Their rounds came up to a few thousand feet below the jet and exploded, looking somewhat like fireworks. The firing stopped when we flew away. At this point, I was very focused on avoiding any SA-6 or SA-3 missiles that were in the air and was listening intently to the radio as our strikers pressed into the target area. What I didn't consider was the implications of "it came up to a few thousand feet below us." Instead, like any dedicated Prowler guy, I hit my turn point and headed right back over the same area. Just as before, there was an immense barrage of AAA right below us. This time, however, that little "Beavis and Butt-Head" lightbulb came on. It sounds stupid, but it suddenly occurred to me that the Serbs on the mountain below were very definitely trying to shoot us down. Sure, the rounds that I could see were exploding under us, but if somebody with a bigger gun decided to take a shot, it could be a very bad day. Without panic or much discussion, I decided to slide the orbit a few miles to the east, and, unsurprisingly, no more AAA was seen.

VAQ-141 shot a lot of HARM missiles during Operation Allied Force, in fact, we fired 78 of them. When it came to firing HARM missiles, the truth was that most of them didn't hit anything other than the ground. This was not necessarily a bad thing. They served their purpose of keeping the Serbs from turning their radar on, even if it was a pretty inefficient way to do so. The Serbian air defense guys were not dumb. They had been studying our tactics for years, and they were courageous and skilled. In fact, they had managed to shoot down an F-117 stealth fighter along with a small collection of other modern jets in the opening days of the conflict. They had been watching how we operated in Iraq and knew that we jammed and fired pre-briefed HARM to create a temporary sanctuary for our strikers. With this in mind, the Serbs didn't turn on their radar as we were flying into the target area. Instead, they typically waited until strikers were leaving, turned on their radar for twenty-or-thirty seconds, took a missile shot at the retreating aircraft, and then turned their radar back off, packed things up, and drove away.

The fact that our squadron was now flying with two HARM missiles and three jamming pods placed us in the unusual position of being able to fire "reactive" HARM. As a result, we stopped shooting HARM at places where we thought that there "might" be a SA-6 or SA-3 site, and started shooting at them when they actually turned their radar on. This, by the way, was definitely not what the Prowler was designed to do. Our onboard system was a very good tool for guiding our jamming pods, but at the time we didn't have the processing power required to quickly geo-locate a threat system in the time required to shoot back at it. Despite this, we designed some procedural workarounds and when we saw an SA-6 radar on our system, or when a fighter called out a threat, we fired a missile. After my first two pre-briefed shots on the first night of the war, I fired seven more in a "reactive" mode. Normally, when a HARM is fired, you would alert the rest of the strike by calling out "Magnum" over the radio. We would do this because the HARM is a large missile, makes a lot of smoke, and can be easily confused with an enemy SAM. In anticipation that the Serbs might somehow hear these radio calls and turn off their radar, we changed the call to "Go Navy." It was satisfying from both an operational security perspective as well as service pride to pull the trigger on a HARM and then call "Go Navy!" over the radio.

Despite the inefficiency of our HARM shots, there was a day I learned that I might have gotten a "hit" with a missile. As the junior Department Head in the squadron, I had a bit of a transient crew. I had three ECMOs assigned, but it was not uncommon for one of the guys to be required to do something else, leaving an empty seat.

As a result, an ECMO from CAG's staff frequently flew in my jet. He was a very smart guy and had maintained a connection back to the intelligence and engineering world that supported EA-6Bs. Well, unbeknown to the squadron, this young officer had done some actual due diligence and discussed some HARM targeting considerations with a few experts back in the U.S. As a result, they gave him an alternative way to target these elusive SA-6 systems. What this officer didn't do was run this new solution up the chain of command, and this mattered because we were not supposed to change the squadron-approved HARM targeting methodology (something I didn't know).

One day my crew and I found ourselves over the western border of Kosovo covering an F-14B that was serving as a Forward Air Control and was vectoring F/A-18Cs to pick off tanks with Hellfire missiles and laser-guided bombs. At some point, we saw an SA-6 signal in the back seat and the F-14B called out a threat on the radio, so this hard-charging ECMO sent his "special" target package to the HARM, and I fired it. This didn't seem to be a particularly notable event until we got back onto the ship. We were in the intelligence debrief when the pilot of that F-14B walked in the door, grabbed me, and said "You saved my ass." He insisted that our HARM had hit the system just as it was shooting at him. This seemed exceptionally unlikely until our guest ECMO admitted that he had changed the target package and we very well might have hit it. When the word got out that we had success with a HARM, everyone wanted to use this new targeting package. There was resistance from within the squadron, and apparently some major unhappiness over changing the targeting package without permission, but after some consultation, (and behind-the-scenes churn) this was approved, and for the rest of the war we used this method.

Life was not all combat. Early in the operation, our squadron was so busy that senior leadership decided that we needed an additional EA-6B on the carrier, and I volunteered to go pick it up. While we were the only EA-6Bs operating at sea, we were far from the only EA-6B's in the theater. In fact, there were about thirty EA-6Bs working from Aviano Air Base in Italy at the northern end of the Adriatic. The base was hosting two U.S. Marine Corps EA-6B squadrons, two active-duty Navy EA-6B squadrons, and the Navy's only reserve EA-6B squadron. They all had been sent to Aviano before the conflict started and had been flying since the war kicked off.

Anyway, I and two other squadron members left the carrier and eventually made it to Aviano via a variety of helicopters and cargo planes. When we finally got to Aviano, we discovered the group of Prowler squadrons was fighting the war the way I had imagined when I was a kid watching WWII movies. While the Marines were living in tents, the Navy guys were living in the BOQ or in a hotel downtown. They were operating from a camouflage-covered WWII-era building and were getting paid "per-diem" to be there. It was cool. In contrast to a slider and bug juice that we were getting on the ship, after they got home from a mission they could go into town and get a glass of red wine with a homemade Italian dinner, take a shower, and sleep in a real bed. While I would not have traded flying combat missions from the carrier, it was certainly clear there were advantages to expeditionary operations like this. (And I would experience some of this later in my career). After we arrived, we greeted all our friends and acquaintances, got a tour of their setup, and had a glass of wine that night. The next day we picked up the EA-6B that was now assigned to the squadron, took off from Italy, flew it down the entire length of the Adriatic, and landed on the USS Theodore Roosevelt off the coast of Sicily; taken all together this was a very unique experience.

As the war progressed, we gradually flew a lot more "kill box" operations. The fighters would focus on a particular grid area and we would provide general support. The tanker tracks were either south over Macedonia, or west over the Adriatic. Our missions became defined by the number of times that we would need gas. We would take off, fly to a tanker, go set up station over Kosovo until we reached a low fuel state, and return to the tanker – rinse and repeat. In order to get more coverage out of the same number of crews and aircraft, we began to fly across multiple carrier cycles. The length of a normal flight went from about two hours to four or more. This was tiring, it took a lot of concentration to find the tanker, especially at night and in bad weather, and staying alert inside Kosovo or Serbia with the constant threat of enemy fire was a challenge.

As we got into the late spring and early summer, the mountains began to build up thunderstorms. On one particular afternoon, it had been very busy, and we had supported multiple strikes. As the day progressed, the thunderstorms built up around our kill box until we were essentially trapped. With no other way out, we used our radar to try to pick our way through the worst of the weather. As we flew through these tall cumulonimbus clouds, we were covered by the worst icing I have ever seen. Within seconds the jet probably picked up a couple of tons of clear ice. With the jet so heavy, I was now at military power and we were still descending, whether we liked it or not. The good news was that we were soon out over the Adriatic. The bad news was that we descended ten or twelve thousand feet before the ice began to melt off the jet and I could climb again. It was a very odd feeling, and we were very fortunate that we didn't stall, and that no big chunks of ice damaged our engines as it melted off.

Oddly enough, in the middle of this operation the Navy decided that the USS Theodore Roosevelt needed a port visit. It seemed pretty unusual for the carrier just to pull out of a very busy war and take a break while everyone else kept fighting, and rumor suggested that the NATO chain of command thought it was odd as well. In VAQ-141 we were acutely aware of this concern because there was a lot of very serious discussion about flying the squadron off the ship and continuing to support the operation from the beach while the carrier was gone. While the Air Force could take up the slack with strike aircraft, there was still an overwhelming demand for Electronic Warfare support. After much deliberation (and hand-wringing), the Navy decided to keep our squadron on the ship, and we all headed toward Antalya. Many of us had been there before, so, despite the fact that we had been awkwardly pulled out of a shooting war, we definitely enjoyed our time off.

When we got back into the Adriatic a week later nothing had changed. We were continuing to run kill-box missions and try to pick off Serbian armor and troops. Every once in a while, we would support aircraft that were not from the carrier. One of the most amazing things that I remember watching was a B-52 strike that we were tasked to support. We had been hearing that two of these huge aircraft were heading towards our area and got the word that we needed to jam for them. We slid over to the target area and found a good jamming orbit, that just so happened to be a place where we could clearly observe the target. The B-52s were flying at a much higher altitude than we were and made contrails that were visible for a hundred miles, almost a deliberate signal of their intent. We watched as they split up and timed their turns to get the most effect from their ordnance. In fact, we became so mesmerized that at one point I looked up at the bombers, and then down at the target and realized that I probably didn't want to be caught in between the two. In what seemed to be a throwback to an earlier age, they were dropping dumb bombs. They called "release" over the radio and it then took more than a minute before dozens of bombs plastered an open area that was their target. The huge expanse of destruction was amazing. I couldn't imagine being on the ground. I also almost wished that the strike had been at night because we were watching something similar to what had been known as an Arc-Light mission from Vietnam. It was an overwhelming display of conventional firepower.

Slowly, the war came to a close. Like most wars, the end was a bit anti-climactic. One day we were flying combat missions, the next we were not. All was not entirely quiet, however. Once the Serbs stopped fighting, the Russians quietly put together an armored column and proceeded to drive across Kosovo toward the Pristina Airport without telling NATO. My crew and I were part of an "alert" package on the carrier that day and were not expecting to fly. All of a sudden, the call went out to "launch the alert strike package." What was odd about this order was that nobody could tell us who, or where we were going to strike. As we got into our gear and walked toward the flight deck, the word finally got to us that we might be tasked to strike a Russian armored column. With that alarming info in our heads, we got airborne with a good-sized strike package from the carrier. Everything was chaos in the skies over the Adriatic. Nobody knew what we were doing, where we were going, or the exact target. The weather was not great either. The Air Force had scrambled tankers and we chased them through the clouds in order to get fuel. Once we got gas, we sat in an orbit over the Adriatic, waiting for World War III to begin. It was literally surreal. Even worse for me, was that amidst this chaos, the microphone in my oxygen mask was not working. As the SEAD mission commander, there was a lot that I wanted to coordinate if we were going to attack the Russians but was unable to do so. I ended up writing a lot of notes for the poor ECMO in the right front seat and was very happy that he was a good sport about it. In the end, after four hours of preparing to kick off the apocalypse, somebody decided that the Russians were welcome at the airport, and we returned to the ship. It was an "entertaining" flight and a good way to wrap up the operation.

The end of Operation Allied Force kicked off the short "Hollywood" portion of our cruise. Not only were we now seasoned war heroes, but we got to spend the better part of the next five weeks moving from port to port in the summertime Mediterranean. This period began with a trip to Palma de Majorca, Spain. Unlike my first trip there several years prior, which had taken place in the winter, summertime in Palma was awesome. While it is a part of Spain, I was surprised at how few locals I met, instead the island was covered with British tourists, and boy did they drink a lot. The seaside bars were full and there were dozens of carnival-like rides along the road. In the evenings the crowd went to one of the many outdoor cafés and then filtered into the huge clubs with loud dance music, flashing lights, and some kind of foam, or fog that only partially hid the raunchy behavior of those on the dance floor. This was probably the only summertime port in the Mediterranean where American sailors couldn't possibly get in trouble because the Brits were out of hand. They definitely took alcohol-related incidents to a new level; the Brits were clearly professionals, and by comparison, we were enthusiastic amateurs.

Next, we went to Cannes, France. This was a great visit. We had arrived in time for the 4th of July, and the place was hopping. We got a nice admin in a hotel right along the famous street very near where the film festival took place and then went to see what the town had in store. As usual, the air wing searched out the first Irish Pub that it could find, and proceeded to try to make the place its own, with some mixed success. While some of the group stayed in town, many of us decided to head to Monaco. We took the train down the coast and soon found ourselves in the famous harbor. We walked to the top of a hill and wandered through the picturesque narrow streets by the royal palace in search of a beer. After realizing that it was not that exciting a location, we then wandered back down the hill and across the town, stopping to refresh ourselves at a number of the expensive bars and restaurants along the way. After following part of the Formula One Grand Prix route, we eventually made it to the top of the principality's other big hill, where we stood outside the world-famous casino somewhat aimlessly, since we couldn't go in. Tourist "check in the block" complete, we went back to the port where we unsurprisingly found ourselves in a restaurant called "Stars'n Bars." As the day wrapped up, we walked out to the seawall along the Mediterranean. One of the guys in the group helped a couple of folks take a picture, and we then found ourselves talking to a man who owned one of the huge yachts in the harbor. He was an American car salesman and was as interested in our carrier as we were in his yacht.

With our excellent visit complete, our deployment turned south and we headed towards the Suez Canal. The trip was quick. We went through the canal on the 9th of July, with the obligatory Steel Beach Picnic, and found ourselves inside the Arabian Gulf five days later. Although we hadn't been there for some time, not much was new about Operation Southern Watch. We quickly got into a routine of launching from the ship, getting fuel, and establishing an orbit somewhere over southern Iraq. The mission was so routine that these flights were no longer considered "combat" unless you were part of a response-option strike. What I do remember is that it was hot. Within about ten days of our arrival, we pulled into Bahrain. Thankfully, instead of the "Bahrain Bell," we pulled pier-side in the port where the Navy had established the headquarters for Fifth Fleet. Aside from the opportunity to shop at a real Navy Exchange and eat and drink at a few of the facilities in the little base, I don't remember much about Bahrain, other than the brutally warm weather.

For the next six weeks, we flew our regular missions in the Arabian Gulf. My logbook shows that we did a lot of flying, and the period went quickly. As the end of deployment approached, the word finally came out about our last scheduled port visit. Once again, we hustled out of the Arabian Gulf, and through the Red Sea, we were headed to Rhodes, Greece. I am not sure why Rhodes was picked, because it seemed well out of our way, but it was an entertaining visit. The walled city of the old town was awesome. There were dozens of little shops selling a million different crafts. Even better were the little sidewalk cafes that were placed in the shade. We were all pretty burned out at this point, so there was not much effort spent trying to do anything but find some presents to bring home, have a beer and a nice meal, and catch up on our sleep. And then, ten days later we were back off the east coast and heading home.

In retrospect, I was in VAQ-141 for a long time. Typically, a Department Head would only hang around a squadron for eighteen months to two years. However, at the midpoint of the next workup period, the CO asked me if I would extend my tour to make the next deployment. Being a glutton for punishment, I said yes. As this is a collection of sea stories, we are going to fast-forward through the next year or so. In short, life was good and we were flying a lot. By this time, I was now a senior Department Head and was balancing all the responsibilities of middle-management while being one of the subject matter experts on the mission and the aircraft.

One of the biggest changes for this next deployment was that in the middle of workups, Carrier Air Wing EIGHT was transferred to a different carrier. Instead of the relatively new USS Theodore Roosevelt, we moved over to the much older USS Enterprise, (CVN-65). Although the USS Enterprise was also a "nuke," she was the first one ever built. While most modern nuclear carriers have two reactors, the USS Enterprise had eight. The ship had some other peculiarities. It had an actual escalator that took aircrew from the main deck to the flight deck. It didn't work very often, but when it did, it was great. This mattered to us because our Ready Room was in an unusual place for a Prowler squadron. We were well below the flight deck and in the aft part of the ship. It was about as "out of the way" as one could get (I don't think CAG visited more than once). In general, this location was a pain in the ass. Unlike the other ships I had been on, we could not avoid fire drills and other ship activities. On the USS Enterprise we were literally in the heart of the boat, and if there was a drill that required that all the watertight doors were closed, we had to fight our way to the flight deck amid fire hoses and other damage control gear (and sometimes irritated ship's company).

The other unique component of the USS Enterprise for me was that I had a two-man room. Unlike the rooms that were right below the flight deck, this room was always quiet. It was also impossibly dark. There were numerous times when I would awake from one stress-related dream or another and not know where I was, and then hit my head on the bunk, wake up, and remind myself that I was in my bedroom. This room was one level below the main deck, in between reactor spaces. On the deck just above me were signs that warned sailors "No Loitering" because of the threat of radiation, and yet that is where I slept. Occasionally, we could hear the engineering loudspeakers and other things going on that we were normally oblivious to, and I will never forget hearing the sentence "Scram the remaining reactor" over the 1MC (speakers that broadcast to the crew). As I write this today, I am sure that I was not exposed to anything down there that would affect my health.

We deployed again in April of 2001 and proceeded on what started out as an incredible "Hollywood" cruise. We had sequential port visits in Palma, Cannes, Naples, Portsmouth, Portugal, and then back to Rhodes. This deployment was a staggering whirlwind of good peacetime flying and great port calls. After Rhodes, we headed south to support Operation Southern Watch. I suspect that we probably needed a break from all the alcohol, and the good news was that things were heating up over Iraq again. When we arrived in the Arabian Gulf the entire system of "response options" had been perfected. We had good surveillance of Iraq and apparently had solid intelligence when they decided to make attempts at downing coalition aircraft. Despite this, being scheduled to support a response option was still the luck of the draw, and I was lucky enough to find myself supporting a number of significant strikes in Iraq. This good fortune would come back to bite me soon.

The USS Enterprise left the Arabian Gulf on the 10th of September, 2001. Leaving the gulf was a tremendous relief, and even better was the fact that we were going to cap a tremendous cruise by doing something that a carrier had not done in a long time, skip the Suez and head to the south around the Cape of Good Hope. Along the way, we would have a port visit in Cape Town, South Africa. On the 10th, the trip looked like a certainty, I had even bought a guidebook and was busy planning the things that I wanted to see. On September 11, I was in a late evening meeting with some of my maintenance leadership, discussing how we would manage the upcoming transit. We were in the Ready Room when someone came in and turned on the television. We watched news of the attacks in New York and Washington and then felt the ship shudder as it changed direction. It quickly seemed obvious that the nation would be going to war, and we were likely to be part of the response. Oddly enough, however, the first thing that I remember was the isolation. We were in the right place at the right time but were pretty much out of the loop. As the ship circled out in the middle of the Arabian Sea, the CO and I read all the intelligence reports that we could find, especially anything that we could get our hands on from the Pentagon, and tried to anticipate the strategy for the conflict we knew had to be coming. The Admiral had placed the USS Enterprise in a very high state of alert, and we spent the following days keeping a very close eye on all the shipping and air traffic around us. As the weeks went by, we stayed in the Arabian Sea and flew. It gradually became obvious that we were going to be part of the next big event, but what that was going to look like was not very clear.

On the 7th of October, the fight was on. Our air wing participated in the first massive strike against Afghanistan. Unfortunately for me, I had drawn the "short straw." We had several hard-charging aviators who didn't have combat experience, and I had been exceptionally "lucky" over Iraq. So instead of flying the first night, I stood on the signal bridge and watched Tomahawk missiles launch toward Afghanistan from the surface ships in the strike group. While I regretted not flying, watching those Tomahawk missiles launch was amazing. The other thing that I didn't miss was the chaos that was sure to be part of the first night of the operation. One of the very unique aspects of these strikes, and the many years of military activity that the nation would conduct after that, was just how far Afghanistan was from the Indian Ocean. It took more than an hour just to cross Pakistan, get refueled, and head into Afghanistan. We were flying at the edge of our range and had no functional diverts, it was a bit stressful.

As we continued to fly missions into Afghanistan, I got a random email from a civilian friend with whom I had worked in the Bureau of Naval Personnel. His brother had been in one of the two towers and had died in the attack. He asked me if I would have a personal message written on a bomb and dropped into Afghanistan on one of the strikes. He wanted a picture of the bomb if possible. This was an especially poignant request and drove home the point that a great many American families had suffered from the attack. So, I got my ordnance guys to write the message on a bomb and take a picture that I could send back to the States.

In the end, I was scheduled to fly two combat missions into Afghanistan during that deployment. The first flight was an uneventful jamming mission to a location near Kandahar. It took about five hours and required three refueling trips to the tanker. The next time I was scheduled was literally the last strike that the air wing would cover before we left and headed for home. This particular mission was important to me because we were providing jamming cover for Operation Rhino. This was a classic Army Ranger operation. It started with a bunch of special operations activity and included 200 Rangers jumping out of MC-130 aircraft, (in the dark at 800 feet), and taking over an airstrip to the south of Kandahar. My brother was an Army Ranger and even though he was not in Afghanistan at this time, I wanted to ensure that we did everything we could to cover the guys on the ground.

This was a night-time mission and our two EA-6Bs launched into the dark and headed north. I had the lead and was taking one of our newest pilots with me. Things began smoothly and we headed to a tanker track at the northern border between Pakistan and Afghanistan. Unfortunately, by the time we arrived at the tanker, the weather was turbulent and it was very dark. I immediately got fuel, but my wingman was having real difficulty getting into the basket, and it soon became clear that we were running out of time. I asked him to take a break for a while and shake it out. I went in to get a bit more gas and topped off. It was at this point that I decided that I would have to leave him behind. We needed to be there for the attack and if he couldn't get fuel, he would have to head back to the ship.

So, I headed north towards Kandahar and set up an orbit. Despite the delay on the tanker, we arrived on time and watched as a couple of AC-130s suppressed the area around the field. Not long after this, our wayward second aircraft showed up, having successfully taken fuel, and, fortunately for him, leaving him with more gas than I had. With both of us in place, we began to alternate going to the tanker to get gas, so that one of us was on station to provide jamming support at all times. This worked for a couple of trips and then we hit an issue. As the air wing jets went to the tanker track to top off for the last time before we went back to the ship it became clear that one of the dedicated Air Force tankers had not arrived. This began a couple-hour nightmare that still makes me stress when I think about it.

First of all, it was dark over Afghanistan. This seems obvious, but not only was it dark, but there was no "environmental" lighting. No cities. No towns. No moon. This was an issue because the EA-6B still hadn't been authorized to fly with night vision goggles. They were coming but hadn't arrived yet. So, as the Air Force scrambled to find a way to provide us with fuel, we were sent from tanker track to tanker track looking for aircraft that were flying without lights on. The second thing was that there was no real divert field. Fuel is always an issue for tactical aviation. Normally, even in combat operations, there is a place to land if the fuel plan falls apart. This was very early in Operation Enduring Freedom, and there was no suitable divert. The closest potential option was an airfield in Quetta, Pakistan. The Marines had sent a detachment to the base to support any damaged or diverted aircraft; however, we had been warned that it was not particularly safe and that CAG definitely did not want anyone to go there on this last mission. The third and final issue was that it was a very long way back to the Arabian Sea. While we would typically keep enough gas onboard our aircraft to return to the ship, that wasn't possible for this mission. The combination of these circumstances provided three sides of a box that was threatening to trap my aircraft and crew.

As the search for gas commenced, I was not the only aircraft without enough fuel to go home. All the air wing aircraft were now out of gas. We drove from tanker track to tanker track relaying our success (or lack thereof) to each other, but the problem was that none of the tankers could make up for all of the missing fuel. So, the game became to stay airborne long enough to reach the next tanker. With no radar and only intermittent contact with airborne command and control, this was exhausting. At one point I finally found myself alongside a tanker with five or six air wing jets. The senior aviator in the group came on the radio and took stock of our fuel states. He established an order so that the lowest fuel state would go next. When it got to my turn to get gas, I couldn't see the refueling basket. It was too dark. I could barely see the strip lights of the fighters near me. After unsuccessfully requesting the tanker turn on a light, I slid the jet over to where I thought the basket was. It wasn't long before I heard "Prowler, where are you going?" over the radio. I hate to admit it, but I whined, "I don't have goggles and can't see the basket." A brave Hornet pilot took the risk and turned on his lights for a moment. Holy cow, the picture I had in my head was totally different from the real configuration of the jets that I had been flying with. In the dark and with my fatigue I had been looking for the basket in between two fighter aircraft. We were very lucky that there wasn't a mishap. Now correctly oriented, I got into the basket and took enough gas to bring my jet up to about nine-thousand pounds.

It was decision time. We were already going to return to the ship much later than planned, something that I had never done. I now had enough gas to fly an emergency profile back to the Indian Ocean and the location where the ship was scheduled to be. So, rather than try to find more fuel, we headed south. On the way back we flew a "bingo profile." This profile provides the most efficient fuel use for the distance you have to go, but it is slow and flown at high altitude. The irony of this profile was that you were supposed to bingo away from the ship, not towards it. We crawled across Pakistan as the sun began to rise. We became the last aircraft airborne as everyone else, including my wingman from earlier, had found enough fuel to fly a more conventional profile and go faster. As we began to descend towards the ship, I thought that I had seen nothing more beautiful. Until I couldn't see much at all. We were descending out of the frigid temperatures at high altitude into the warm, humid air of the Arabian Sea and our aircraft was cold-soaked. We had turned our defroster on thirty minutes prior, but it took a while for that to work, and we didn't have any gas or time to spare. If everything was perfect, I would be landing with three thousand pounds of gas. This was a figure that was technically "tank" state, but there was no tanker airborne. I needed to trap on the first pass. I flew that pass as the heavily armored windscreen in front of me gradually became opaque from the outside in. As I flew the "ball" I could only see through a couple of square inches where the defrost was hitting the glass. To my relief, I trapped and came to a halt in the wires. I was totally exhausted and as we sat there, the rest of the windscreen fogged up. I could not see a thing. The Air Boss came up on the radio and said "Follow your director." I replied, "I can't see." We were the last aboard, so they shut us down right there. The flight was a little over 7 hours and was the longest combat mission I would fly, and despite the fact we didn't get shot at, it was also the most stressful of my career.

14

VAQ-133 EXECUTIVE OFFICER: BAGRAM AIR BASE, AFGHANISTAN 2006

VAQ-133 Logo, U.S. Navy Photo

Squadron Command is the primary objective of a long naval aviation career. I was selected to command an EA-6B squadron while I was working on my second tour in the Washington, D.C. area. Being selected to lead a squadron was tremendously exciting, and I was very anxious to see which Carrier Air Wing I was going to serve in. So, needless to say, I was a bit surprised when I discovered that I was going to command one of the community's new "Expeditionary Squadrons." Being expeditionary is the Navy's euphemism for "land-based." These EA-6B expeditionary squadrons were essentially established as the number of Carrier Air Wings diminished, and the demand for Airborne Electronic Warfare in places like the Middle East and the Pacific increased. There could be entire books written about this topic, but despite what every public statement will tell you, the Navy is not and will never be happy to have land-based tactical squadrons that are supporting non-navy forces; and yet, I would command one.

While at first, I was disappointed that I would not be able to go back to sea and try to achieve a lifetime total of a thousand traps, there were benefits to being an expeditionary unit. Unlike the squadrons that were attached to Carrier Air Wings and who depended on the carrier for everything, an expeditionary squadron was almost entirely independent. Our chain of command went through our Type-Wing Commander, the Captain based in Whidbey Island, who ran our entire community. This was great. I would have a boss who understood what we were doing, why we were doing it, and most importantly, a person who was too busy to micro-manage. When you were a CO of a squadron that was attached to a Carrier Air Wing, you were all living on the carrier and, as a result, were always within a thousand feet of your boss. As the CO of an expeditionary squadron, we would be ten-thousand miles away from ours. This was both awesome and a bit terrifying.

As I joined VAQ-133, the expeditionary squadrons were running at an amazing pace. They were deploying every six months, coming home, training, and then deploying again six months later; it was a grueling schedule, but I thought it was exciting. In Navy aviation squadrons, Commanding Officers "fleet up," which is to say that when we arrive at the squadron, we do so as the Executive Officer and then, fifteen months later, move into command for a total of a thirty-month tour. I showed up as the new XO in October 2005, just in time to participate in a squadron detachment to Eielson Air Force Base, Alaska. This was great news; going on a detachment was a good way to meet everybody, and all of the officers and sailors greeted me with enthusiasm.

Flying in Alaska is a lot of fun. There is a ton of airspace, good training resources, and excellent facilities to live and work in. While there wasn't a ton to do during off-duty hours, this meant that there were not a lot of ways for the squadron to get into trouble. I do recall several of my Junior Officers going salmon fishing and bringing back a dozen fish that they cleaned and dressed in their Bachelor Officer's Quarters (BOQ) sinks. After hearing some stories about their adventure, it was clear that we were lucky that one or more of them hadn't been washed down the river. It also quickly became clear that October is about the latest you ever want to go to Eielson for a detachment. The weather was starting to get cold, and that resulted in some interesting flying. On one event, I returned to Eielson after a mission, and after I landed, I found that the runway had been coated with a slick film of ice. I probably should have taken an arrested landing, but I kept the jet on the centerline of the runway almost to the end without much problem. As we slowed to a running pace, the jet began uncontrollably turning into the wind and eventually did a 180. I had experienced something like this once before in a hydroplaning jet and ended up increasing power from the engines to slow us down as we slid along backward. It was entertaining. Despite the challenge of the weather, the exercise was good, and I enjoyed being back in a squadron. It was great to be flying again.

Near the end of our detachment, the CO had to leave early and go to a meeting in San Diego, leaving me to bring the squadron home. This was not a big deal, and what I should have done was just let the squadron do what it normally does. In most cases, the jets are flown to and from detachments by the most senior crew. It is a good deal to fly home, as the alternative is to sit in the back of a cargo aircraft. As we were looking at the plans to go back, it occurred to me that I'd like to get some of the junior pilots more time on the tanker. I had tanked from an Air Force tanker thousands of times but wanted my new pilots to get some experience before their first time in Afghanistan. So, I changed the schedule and put our junior pilots in the jets for the trip back. When it was time to go home, we took off on a cloudy day and headed south to rendezvous with the Air Force tanker that would give us enough fuel to get all the way to Whidbey. We quickly found the tanker, but the weather was less than ideal; there was a ton of turbulence, and the basket was bouncing a lot, making it very difficult to get into. For me, this was not unusual, and I got fuel. However, one of our new pilots just couldn't make it happen. He tried and tried, and we were now running much lower on gas than we should have been. At some point, I started talking to him over the radio, trying to help, which it certainly didn't. He eventually turned that radio off. I was literally at the point where we were going to have to declare an emergency and head to a Canadian airport where we would be stuck for days when he finally got into the basket and took fuel. Ironically, this was at the very same time when we broke out from the weather, and the turbulence magically went away. To say I was relieved was an understatement, and I learned that I had better conduct an honest risk assessment of any more "good ideas" before I did any more experimentation.

In January 2006, we deployed to Afghanistan. I quickly discovered that one of the nice things that we avoided as an expeditionary squadron was FCLPs. There was no carrier qualification required to land on nice long Air Force runways, and this gave us back a fair amount of time to prepare to travel before it was time to leave. In fact, we didn't even have to take our jets for this deployment. At this point, our community leadership had decided that instead of flying four aircraft all the way to Afghanistan and back every six months, we would just rotate people. The jets would stay in place for a year. In essence, one squadron would fly them to Afghanistan, and the next squadron would return them to Whidbey. While it wasn't fun to be shipped around the world without the aircraft that your maintenance guys had busted their ass to maintain for the last several months, it was a good way to operate.

As we prepared to deploy, I also learned that as the XO, I was responsible for heading over with "the advance detachment." This detachment would consist of a single C-17 that was full of people and equipment who would all deploy about two weeks before the rest of the squadron. The objective of the advance detachment was to do the maintenance work required to transfer the EA-6Bs to our squadron. Accepting these aircraft required tons of inspections and lots of paperwork. We would also work to establish a good working relationship with the Combined Air Operations Center (CAOC). Although our "real" boss was in Whidbey, we worked for the CAOC. The CAOC was the Joint Command and Control Center that ran air operations over both Iraq and Afghanistan. They published the daily ATO that would tell us which sorties to fly.

When I was flying over Afghanistan from the USS Enterprise in 2001, it would have never occurred to me that five years later, I would be returning to the region with a land-based EA-6B squadron, but in 2006 it seemed like the place to be. The nation was involved in two big fights in Iraq and Afghanistan, and I was ready to support from as far forward as I could get. In early January, my trusty group of advance personnel got on a C-17 and headed east. Traveling on a huge cargo aircraft is definitely nowhere near first class, but it is not horrible. These huge jets can install airline-style seats in the cargo area, but in our case, we had filled most of the jet with our gear, leaving us with the webbed chairs along the fuselage. I quickly learned that these weren't bad. The good news was that you had legroom. In addition, once you were airborne, you could throw down a sleeping bag or camping pad and stretch out. Our trip went well until we got to Germany. We landed at Ramstein Air Base and spent the night. In the morning, we got back on the C-17 and resumed our trip. We had only been airborne for twenty minutes when the C-17 had a major maintenance issue that required the crew to land as soon as possible. As a result, we soon found ourselves stuck at the huge Frankfurt International Airport.

While I totally understood that aircraft broke (ours did all the time), as a Navy guy, I was not mentally prepared for the fact that we would then be abandoned. The C-17 crew taxied the aircraft to an out-of-the-way place on the airport tarmac, apologized, got into a cab, and left. Just like that, I had thirty or so officers and sailors, a bunch of classified material, and some firearms, all stuck on this broken C-17, with no prognosis as to when we would get back on the road. Not only were we stuck at a huge commercial airport in Germany, but most of us did not have any civilian clothes.

This unplanned trip to Frankfurt was a real introduction to expeditionary life. The good news was that I had a bunch of very experienced officers and NCOs working for me. We established a watch over the classified material in the jet, found rooms at a local hotel, and allowed the sailors to get room service because I had been told that American sailors were not desired out in the German town in their uniform. And then we waited for the Air Force. I was pretty pissed by their lack of support. It was at this point that somebody helpfully advised me not to consider myself a "passenger." We were just "cargo" and were being accorded all the consideration that cargo required, which was none. Once I got over this mental hurdle, life was good. We had the resources required to make things work for our sailors, and once I accepted these circumstances, it was a refreshing challenge. It took more than a day before the C-17 was repaired, but after it was all buttoned up, we all loaded back in and headed to our new home in Afghanistan. This leg of the flight was long. As we approached Bagram, I went up onto the flight deck of the C-17 and watched as they prepared to land. We were going to do a combat entry to the field, and the crew would be on night-vision-goggles. I reflected on the fact that there were two O-3s in charge of this massive aircraft, but they did an awesome job. The ride was a bit stomach-churning as we spiraled down to the runway at a huge rate of descent in order to avoid any ground fire, and then they scooped to a landing at the last minute. It was great.

My next set of impressions comes to mind like a highlight reel. Exiting the aircraft was like being in a war movie; it was windy, dusty, noisy, and chaotic. We were met by a few members of the outgoing squadron, and the contrast between their casual demeanor and a base that seemed as busy as an aircraft carrier's flight deck was striking. As part of the transition, the squadron had made arrangements to take care of us in transient facilities until it was time to turn all the spaces over. I seem to recall that I stayed in a shipping container habitat, but honestly don't directly remember. What I do remember is that as we adjusted to the time zone and got familiar with the base, it became clear that I had fallen right into the kind of wartime atmosphere that I had dreamed about as a kid. The display of American military force and national wealth was everywhere, and it was staggering.

Bagram Air Base was an interesting place and is probably a topic that deserves an entire book. It was an old base built by the Soviets during their years of occupation. The field sits 5000 feet above sea level in the middle of a bowl of ten to thirteen-thousand-foot-tall mountains that would look huge anywhere else on the planet but were only foothills of the Hindu Kush mountain range that surrounded us to the north. This particular deployment took place five years after the Northern Alliance had pushed the Taliban out of the area, and the Army and Air Force had been operating out of the field since then. It was still the wild west, but there were hundreds of millions of dollars being spent on infrastructure, and it was slowly turning into a modern facility. I soon learned that Bagram wasn't just an airbase; it was a thriving military city. Despite this, our adversaries still definitely owned the local area around the field. While the base was certainly nowhere near as dangerous as the FOBS scattered around Afghanistan from which our soldiers were conducting the war, the Taliban routinely attacked the field with rockets, mortars, Vehicle Borne Improvised Explosive Devices (VBIED), and human suicide bombers.

The EA-6B squadrons that rotated through Bagram lived in a section of the base known as Camp McCool. Named for CDR "Willie" McCool, an EA-6B pilot and astronaut who had died on the Columbia STS-107 along with my friend Doc Brown, the camp was on the northern edge of the base nestled in an odd rectangular protrusion that extended deeply into some farm fields. The outer walls of the base were made from Hesco barriers, clever wire-mesh-and-cloth containers that arrived flat, but after they were unfolded and filled with tons of dirt, they became excellent fortifications. The outer wall of the camp was two or three Hescos high and was topped with concertina wire. There were two guard towers at the corners of the protrusion where we lived. These towers were manned by full-time Army soldiers when we first arrived, but they were gradually replaced by cameras and rotational guards as the infrastructure became more secure. There was an inner Hesco wall around our camp, and we "owned" a gate into our camp where we stationed a sailor armed with a shotgun or rifle to keep an eye on things.

Life in Bagram was a mixture of ad-hoc expeditionary infrastructure and genuine American excess. For example, there were no sewage lines on the base, so the toilets were large porta-potties that got pumped out and taken away for disposal by sewage trucks. While regularly scheduled, waste disposal generally did not occur until these facilities were nearly full. The ones near our living quarters helpfully contained "shit sticks" so that you could push the waste around and make room for more (one had to be careful not to grab the wrong end of the stick). The showers in our camp were portable structures that were much better than those on the USS America and had warm, propane-heated, but not-potable water (do not drink!)

The buildings we lived and worked from were almost entirely plywood B-Huts. According to Wikipedia, "B-hut" is an abbreviation for "Barracks Hut" and is used to refer to temporary billets. Apparently, this term was borrowed from the British, who commonly used the term when referring to cheaply made temporary shelter or housing. These fragile plywood structures were about 18x36 in size. They could be subdivided into smaller "cells" to increase capacity. The junior troops lived eight or ten to a B-Hut, and as you got more senior, you had fewer roommates. The CO and I each had half of a B-hut to ourselves. We also had a dedicated B-hut for our Ready Room, our Administration offices, and a recreation hut where the troops could watch movies, and the Chiefs had their own building as well. These B-huts had no insulation and were cold in the winter and hot in the summer. There was electrical power in each hut, and we had a "mini-split" heating and cooling system that was always working hard to maintain the interior somewhere near livable temperatures.

The camp where we lived was probably about half a mile from the flight line where we worked. We didn't have many vehicles, so most of the time, our sailors walked. The CO had a nice SUV that had been signed out from the Army, I used an old diesel Toyota

Hilux (that I would definitely love to have again), and we had a separate aircrew vehicle to take folks back and forth to the jets. As you walked towards the flight line from our camp, you passed through dozens of other B-huts from one of the many transient units that were stationed there. You would also pass the DFAC or our dining facility. In typical American fashion, the DFAC was awesome. There were two major DFACs on base and a number of smaller facilities in places that you had to look for. "Our" DFAC was at the northern end of the base and could probably seat a few hundred soldiers, sailors, and airmen. The food was great. Unlike the ship, food was accounted for at a service level, which meant that we didn't have to pay to eat. There were daily entrees, grilled food options, and they always had a fresh salad bar. The holiday meals were impressive. If you were there for Thanksgiving, they put on a huge spread, the same for Christmas and other notable events. Occasionally, they served "surf and turf" or some other special that was good for morale. Much like the ship, ice cream was one of the things that was very much appreciated, and when they set up tubs of real ice cream with all the fixings, there would be a line at the door.

The north DFAC was near a small base exchange, or retail store, where we could get basic needs - new DVDs, snack food, and a selection of goods that made life feel almost normal. Around the corner from the exchange was the barbershop. This was a contractor-run facility that was staffed by women from outside the region. These women also worked at a massage parlor, and before you draw conclusions (like several service members did), they had strict rules that forbade any intimacy. The women were making money hand-over-fist as it was and did not want the Army to send them home for breaking the rules.

There were a few other niche dining facilities that my JOs discovered. The Korean and UAE camps allowed a limited number of Americans into their dining facilities on a weekly basis. I never made it in for a visit, but those who did had a great time and spoke highly of the meals. Along the way to the flight line, there was more of an "expeditionary style" DFAC that was smaller and had less of a selection, but the benefit was that it had fewer lines. The seating area was under a tent, but it was a good place to go if you didn't have time for the main DFAC. Every once in a while, we would collect a group and drive down the flight line to where the Army helicopters were based. The "Aviation DFAC" served the same food, with one exception. They had a cook who was a professional at making Philly Cheese Steaks, and it was worth a visit to stand in line and get one of his sandwiches.

The main road that ran through camp was known as "Disney Drive." It was named for an Air Force trooper who had died early in the effort to make the base functional. The road was partially paved, had huge pot-holes, and was always incredibly dusty. About a mile down the road from us was the "Main Exchange." A mall-like area was set up with one large retail store that was stocked with all the things that could be found on a normal military base, with one exception, there was no alcohol allowed for Americans in Afghanistan. Around the store was a pizza parlor, a coffee shop, and a bunch of vendors that sold items from around the region. You could get a rug, or sword, or an ancient (non-functional) firearm. There was also a shop that made military-style mementos, plaques, flags, and other things that were suitable for mounting on your "I love me" wall at home. Flags turned out to be a big thing. I don't know where the practice began, but at some point, we started flying a parachute bag full of American Flags on every flight. When these flags returned from the mission, they were sent to any one of hundreds of people who were supporting us from afar; families, church groups, fire departments, police, schools, and anyone who wanted a flag flown on a combat mission over Afghanistan (or Iraq with other squadrons). I think that we probably mailed a thousand flags home over each deployment, and we were always happy to sign the certificate of authenticity with a picture of the crew that had flown the flight.

A little further down the road was the main headquarters building. This was a huge building that housed the most senior officers on the base. While the name of the command seemed to change frequently, this building was where many of the decisions were made that affected our lives. Once in a while, the CO and I would come down to the headquarters for a meeting with a senior officer or VIP that we couldn't avoid. However, we generally tried to stay out of the place if we could, mostly on the basis of "out of sight, out of mind." The only other reason that my officers would stop by was to talk to the staff in the Operations and Joint Fires planning cells and try to get our constant targeting issues sorted out.

All the way at the end of Disney Drive was the main gate. When we first got there, the Army would line up dozens of supply trucks on the road for miles outside the gate and do inspections. As time went by, the Army built a formal truck inspection facility and created quite a lot of protective infrastructure to keep any opportunistic terrorists from trying to ram or shoot their way onto the base (which happened a few times while we were there). Next to the main gate was a large, fenced-in area where they allowed a weekly bazaar. While it was eventually closed for force-protection reasons, this bazaar provided everyone with an opportunity to meet some of the locals and purchase things to send home. You could order a custom-tailored suit, buy "valuable" gems (if you knew what you were looking for), find tons of authentic furs and other goods, buy "Persian" rugs, ride a camel around a small enclosure, or purchase black-market DVDs that contained shaky, hand-filmed copies of movies that hadn't made it to the regular market yet. For me, the bazaar was interesting to wander through, but aside from some hand-carved wooden boxes, I never found anything of much interest.

Back at "our" end of the base, our maintenance facilities were right on the flight line, just in front of the base hospital. While the hospital began as a collection of B-huts, shipping containers, and mobile Army equipment, by the time we left on my second deployment, it was a modern facility that was probably the best small hospital in the entire region. We were also a couple of hundred feet from one of the original old hangars. This building was among the last of the original structures left on base and had been built by the Soviets. The Army's Combat Rescue helicopters were based in the old hangar, and the landing pad where all the medevacs unloaded their injured passengers was right next door. The constant flow of wounded made it a bit like living inside the old TV show MASH, and every medevac chopper always reminded me of why we were there. The Air Force had set up their headquarters in the old control tower that was further down the flight line. It was an impressive building with thick walls and lots of battle scars. According to legend (and some written accounts), the tower and the old hangar next to us were the locations of last stands by a few Soviet troops, and both buildings certainly contained evidence of combat action.

This brings us to our mission. Unfortunately, while I think it is a tremendously interesting topic, I still can't write much about it. What I can say is that the expeditionary EA-6Bs were in Iraq and Afghanistan to support the troops on the ground. We did this by jamming things that made them safer. You might think that there wouldn't be a lot that a sophisticated jammer could affect in Afghanistan, but when our capabilities were applied correctly, we could have a real impact on the battlefield. In general, we would fly to an area where our support was required and establish an orbit. While we conducted our mission with our jammers, we would also carry binoculars so that we could watch the events below and notify the right people if something looked out of place. There are plenty of open-source articles in the news about our mission that I can neither confirm nor deny. However, what I can definitely say is that the demand for our support vastly exceeded the supply. We could have kept dozens of EA-6Bs employed if we had them. Despite the persistent demand, one of the ironies of Electronic Warfare is the fact that it is difficult to "prove a negative." If we were supporting a force and nothing happened, we rarely got credit for "nothing happening." This lack of evidence was part of the reason why nobody wanted us around in peacetime. In Bagram, where every gallon of jet fuel had to be trucked or flown in at great cost, we sometimes looked like a very expensive rabbit's foot to senior leadership. To help mitigate this challenge, creating some useful metrics and applying some smart targeting processes became one of my pet projects.

Because our flights were often tedious, the JOs figured out how to hook an MP3 player into the internal communications of the aircraft. The crews routinely voted on the mix of music that would play during the flight, and as a result, we learned a lot about each other's personal tastes (good and bad!) As we flew, we would have ongoing conversations about nearly anything, but as one of the squadron's senior officers, I generally steered away from discussing work.

As each mission progressed, it was not uncommon to break off from a scheduled event and support a Troops in Contact or to go back to the tanker to extend our flight to cover a pop-up task. And then, mission complete, we'd fly back to Bagram, where I would get to execute one of my favorite maneuvers, a "combat recovery." As EA-6Bs began to operate at Bagram, the Air Force learned that they did not like the Navy to come into the pattern via what we knew as "the break" at eight-hundred feet; it was too loud for them to sleep (yes, this is really the reason). So instead, we would fly a combat recovery that involved spiraling down from twenty-five or so thousand feet, staying near the field's boundaries to (theoretically) lower the risk of being attacked by a man-portable anti-aircraft missile. I loved doing this. My combat entries always started with a lazy flaperon roll and then a deliberately planned spiral that brought me to the left side of the field. I enjoyed these entries much more than the break, and it was one of the very few Air Force demands that didn't irritate me.

Life in Bagram had a routine. We would get our tasking, write the flight schedule, and ensure we had aircraft and crew ready to support the events. We flew every single day of the six months that we were deployed, something that no carrier-based squadron would ever do, and it was an accomplishment that made me very proud of our aviators and maintainers. When we got airborne, life was repetitive but not boring. There was not much radar coverage over the country, and de-confliction between aircraft was essentially procedural. The Air Force had set up a communication system that covered most of Afghanistan, but it was intermittent at best. When the weather got bad, the instrument approaches to Bagram were rudimentary and very stressful. We routinely flew in the vicinity of the huge mountains that surrounded Bagram in instrument conditions hoping that we would "break out" of the clouds with the runway in sight (and not the side of a mountain). There were not many places to go in an emergency. At the time, Bagram only had one runway, and if an emergency aircraft shut it down or if we had weather issues, we could jump to Kabul International. The problem with Kabul was that its weather was generally worse than Bagram, and the security was questionable. Kandahar was very secure and had the support equipment that we required. This generally made it the best weather divert. However, Kandahar was a couple of hundred miles away, which meant that we had to keep a lot of fuel onboard as a reserve. Jalalabad was also an option. There were special forces stationed there, but it would have been a sketchy place to land.

Our Electronic Warfare support was desired all over Afghanistan, but we spent most of our time around the key areas, Kandahar, Khost, Mazar-al Sharif, Jalalabad, the Kunar Province, the Pech River, and dozens of others; all places that you would regularly hear about in the news. Sometimes we would go places that weren't in the news. One of the most interesting areas to operate was the mountains to the northeast. One of my first impressions of Afghanistan was just how beautiful it was. There wasn't a lot of green, but the mountains and deserts were staggeringly picturesque. The Hindu Kush mountains were literally jaw-dropping. I remember finishing a mission flying far to the northeast of the country and then returning with a flyby of a mountain called "Kuh-e Bandaka." At about twenty-two thousand feet, the mountain was astonishing. The fact I could just cruise around it and take a self-guided tour was also very cool. When your tour of the mountain was complete, you could just follow the Panjir Valley all the way back to Bagram. To the west, I flew as far as Herat and provided support very close to the Iranian border. To the north, we occasionally flew to Mazar-al Sharif, which brought us near the Tajikistan or Uzbekistan border. And, of course, the southern border with Pakistan was a common place to work. As we crisscrossed Afghanistan, these were definitely places that I never dreamed I would see, let alone from the seat of a Navy aircraft.

At this stage of the war, we were among the limited number of tactical aircraft stationed in the country. In addition to a ton of utility aircraft of all types, during this period, Bagram hosted Army helicopters, cargo aircraft, and special operations aircraft like AC-130s, A-10s, and F-15Es. There were also more A-10s in Kandahar, along with some Marine aircraft, but a lot of the support that was delivered to the troops came from aircraft that were flying from outside Afghanistan. This meant that tactical aircraft were spread very thinly across the country. So occasionally, when some component of ground forces would get into trouble, we would be the only jet aircraft available to do a "show of force." A show of force was requested when the ground force didn't think that lethal force was required; the troops just wanted to remind the Taliban that there were American jets watching over them at all times. A show of force request was sometimes called in with a formal nine-line brief as if we were dropping ordnance, and sometimes we were just given a location and a direction. In all cases, what was desired was a low and noisy demonstration that allied aircraft were nearby.

While we couldn't drop bombs in an EA-6B, we could certainly do "low and noisy." I did probably a dozen of these actions in places along the eastern border between Afghanistan and Pakistan, but the one I remember was somewhere near Tarin Kowt, where some British special forces had declared a "Troops in Contact," or TIC. They were in contact with the Taliban, and the situation sounded urgent. We were the only aircraft in the area and had some fuel to burn, so we were called down to do a show of force. Most shows of force are not particularly low. They are "low" for jets but still a few thousand feet above the ground. You'd fly by, be noisy, and shoot off some flares. The British JTAC requested something more impressive. So, I dropped down to about a hundred feet off the valley floor and zoomed through the target area at about five hundred knots. We could see people and animals scattering in the little villages that we passed. I seem to recall we circled the area at a higher level for a while longer just to emphasize the fact that we were there. The

JTAC reported "good effects," and we were out of gas, so back to Bagram we went. Eventually, some Air Force General heard that EA-6Bs were doing shows-of-force and decided that we shouldn't do this anymore because we were "high value." This was a poor decision that deprived the guys on the ground of what might be the only tactical aircraft in the area and was made without the understanding that our EA-6B crews spent more time training in the low-altitude environment than almost anyone – but orders are orders.

Our relations with the other services were sometimes a little tenuous. As a Navy squadron, we were an orphan. On Bagram, the Air Force was represented by the 455th Air Expeditionary Wing. They had a one-star General in charge, who rotated through about every year or so. All of the Air Force units reported to the General. We, however, did not. We had similar support requirements and were part of the flight line, but we technically reported to a three-star Admiral in Bahrain and were tasked by the rotating leadership at the CAOC in Al Udied, Qatar. If this sounds confusing, it was. It was even more confusing when you consider that there was a NATO component and an Army component also based at Bagram, oh, and don't forget about the Special Forces guys, the Koreans, the UAE, and a variety of other folks, like the Egyptians. From my perspective, the Army protected the base, the Air Force was responsible for the runway and all the support of the aviation units, and we were a guest who relied on them all but had little to contribute to the support of this infrastructure.

This inability to contribute to the functioning of the base was occasionally very awkward. The Army, for example, was desperate for extra manpower. One of the places that they wanted me to put my mechanics was in the guard towers near Camp McCool. At one point, they got so desperate for guards that they put soldiers who were part of an Army band in the towers, leading to an unforgettable afternoon tuba solo from the tower nearest our camp. The problem was that none of our folks had any relevant training. On this first deployment, we had shotguns and pistols. All of my officers and sailors were armed with a loaded 9mm handgun that they wore or kept with them twenty-four hours a day. While they had fired 50 rounds of pistol ammunition to get qualified, giving them a rifle and putting them in a guard tower where trained soldiers occasionally fired at Taliban who were trying to sneak onto the base was irresponsible. What we eventually did allow was that a few of our sailors would guard local nationals as they did jobs inside the confines of Bagram. This task seemed harmless, as my impression was that my folks were just doing the job inside the base. Or at least it seemed harmless until there was a suicide bomber who attacked Bagram just outside the front gate. To my surprise, one of our sailors had almost been a casualty. When I talked to him after the event, he was still shaking. This attack put an end to this adventure, and I withdrew the squadron from this task, not because my sailors weren't brave but because we just weren't trained or equipped to support such missions. What this experience did reinforce was my strongly held opinion that we were not adequately prepared by the Navy, who somehow imagined that our situation was equivalent to living on an Air Force base in Oklahoma or something and that we would be "taken care of" by the other services. During our next deployment, it became my objective to have everyone trained to use an M-16 and establish a designated "quick response force" that had some basic instructions on how to use it.

One of the tremendously sad aspects of being on Bagram was the fact that we commonly represented the Navy during Fallen Comrade ceremonies on base. There were days that you heard about (or might even have supported) a TIC where there were casualties. Since our maintenance facilities were right next to the Medevac helicopters and the hospital, we always had a sense of what was going on when things went bad. When there were American fatalities, these service members were honored in a solemn procession as they were carried from the hospital to the C-17 that would take their remains back to Germany and then home. When it was time for a fallen comrade ceremony, the entire base would come to a halt. A truck would slowly carry the service member from the hospital that was behind us down Disney Drive and then turn onto the flight line. The entire route would be lined by soldiers, sailors, airmen, and marines who were saluting all the way to the rear of the C-17. At this point, the senior officers of the base would have been lined up behind the cargo plane. The casket would be removed from the truck, carried onto the aircraft by an honor guard, and secured. The senior officers would enter the jet and say farewell, a chaplain would say some words, and then the aircraft would take off. This happened far too often, and it was tremendously sad. In fact, over time, I found it to be heartbreaking, and each casualty fed a strong sense of cynicism about our mission in Afghanistan, as it just didn't seem like we had a plan.

While there wasn't much risk associated with being shot down, this didn't mean that flying in Afghanistan was risk-free. Aircraft that flew their missions at low altitudes were routinely fired upon. The helicopters and C-130s that delivered cargo and personnel to many of the outlying bases occasionally came home with bullet holes from ground fire and reminded us that we were probably being shot at when we were in our orbits, even if we couldn't see it. We also had a few close calls with airborne emergencies, including a couple that almost cost us an aircraft and crew.

Despite the dry desert air, the mountain ranges would build up huge thunderstorms in the spring and summer. These huge cumulonimbus clouds were beautiful but dangerous, as they were full of large hail. One of our crews was flying a mission along the Pakistani border one afternoon as the storms began to build up in the vicinity of their orbit. The crew adjusted their route, but at one point, the pilot flew the jet right into the storm. This was a huge mistake. The hail inside this storm was so severe that within seconds the aircraft was nearly damaged enough to bring it down. The nose radome was smashed away, the radar was trashed, the engines were destroyed (but fortunately still running), the leading edges of the wing and tail were full of holes and dents, and the windscreen and refueling probe were all damaged. There was not a single surface on the aircraft that was whole. It was literally a miracle that the guys brought the airplane home, and despite the good airmanship required to get it back on the ground, I was definitely not happy about the "headwork" that this mishap represented.

"When it rains, it pours." As we were out on the ramp looking at the hail-damaged aircraft that afternoon, another one of our crews almost had a mishap right at the field. One of the issues about Bagram was that the field elevation was 5000 feet. While this may not seem significant to most folks, the air at this elevation is much less dense and, as a result, requires a pilot to think hard about takeoff and landing. The combat approaches that we were flying were great fun, but they meant that the engines of the aircraft were at idle for most of the descent. This was okay as long as the pilot recognized that they had to bring the power up well before they needed it because the J52 spooled up much more slowly in the thin air. As this particular pilot came into land, he essentially got trapped with engines at idle while his airspeed decayed. In essence, he stalled the jet and landed hard about ten feet before the end of the runway. The crew was very lucky. Had this incident occurred just a week before, the crew probably would have died because, at that time, the end of the runway was just a three-foot wall of concrete. Fortunately, the Air Force had recently dumped a hundred tons of gravel there, giving it a bit of a sloping approach. There was still a bit of a ledge, but it was "only" big enough to blow a tire and send the jet skidding across the runway. The pilot managed to keep the aircraft on the concrete, but it came to rest a few feet from an exposed fuel pipeline that would have turned the incident into a real mess had it been hit.

 We weren't the only aircraft that had a mishap on the field. We very rarely had more than one EA-6B airborne at a time. Sometimes two missions overlapped, but we tried to keep our schedule to single-aircraft operations to give us the most flexibility. On one particularly unusual day, we had two mission aircraft airborne, and I was flying an FCF. I had finished my checklist and was orbiting overhead the field when an AN-12 cargo plane arrived at the base and landed. Having a Russian cargo plane at Bagram was not unusual; several "discount" cargo delivery services used these old aircraft. Sometimes it was difficult to believe that these museum pieces were still flying. There were few things more amazing than watching an old IL-76 accelerate down the entire length of the 11,000-foot runway in a cloud of smoky exhaust. At the very end of the runway the pilot would gingerly raise its nose so that the aircraft could just barely clear the airfield fence. For several moments all you would see was a cloud of dust, and then the old aircraft would begin to slowly climb away, dodging the mountains as it went.

The AN-12 that had landed below me was a propeller-driven cargo plane similar to a C-130 in size. After landing, the aircraft came to a halt about two-thirds of the way down the runway and for some reason didn't make an attempt to taxi clear. I was wondering why it stopped when I saw a little smoke trickle from the aircraft. This trickle quickly turned into a tower of black smoke and an inferno. As I watched from above, the airplane began to burn itself in half. Now we had three aircraft airborne, and the runway was blocked. Fortunately, we all had enough fuel to divert and ended up flying down to Kandahar. We spent a few hours there, visited Tim Hortons (Bagram had Burger King, but Kandahar was more "international"), got something to eat, and refueled the aircraft. As we consulted with our base, it seemed that the wreckage of the AN-12 would be on the runway for some time. So, two of our aircraft took off and supported missions on their way home. I ended up flying my FCF jet straight back to Bagram, not exactly sure what we would do when we got there. When we arrived, the wreckage was still on the runway, but the tower cleared us to "Land short of the wreckage." In what was a very surreal moment, I touched down and rolled until I could take a good picture of the AN-12 through my front windscreen and then taxied home.

All was not work - there were more than a few good times to be had at Bagram. My Command Master Chief was an excellent organizer, and we managed to host a number of service-related events. This included celebrating the Navy's Birthday in our hangar and, more critically, running the Chief Petty Officer initiation. In the other services, the promotion to E-7 is a major milestone, but in the Navy it marks a real shift in responsibility. Chiefs wear khaki uniforms similar to officers and are the backbone of the fleet. While it has gradually been modified over the years, at the time the transition was accomplished by a several-week period of "indoctrination" that culminated in a heart-felt ceremony where the new rank was awarded. Because we were the only Navy unit available, my team of hard-charging NCO's ran the ceremony for every Chief-Select in Afghanistan that could make it to Bagram. My Command Master Chief arranged the pinning ceremony to take place in the large tent down near headquarters and invited a wide range of senior participants from the other services and our allies. I am not sure they understood what was happening, but they surely understood that the Navy was exceptionally proud of their Chiefs.

At one point, we hosted a squadron barbecue back in Camp McCool. Getting burgers and the rest of the food was surprisingly difficult. The DFAC was a contract organization and giving food in bulk to the units on base wasn't part of their normal operating procedure. I was happy that I had some creative and persistent Chiefs because the event took a lot of paperwork. Eventually, we made it happen and hosted an event that was somewhat similar to the flight deck picnics on the carrier. The burgers were fine, but we were eating amidst our B-huts, lounging on piles of sandbags, and essentially hanging out on what looked like a gravel parking lot. Despite the surroundings, the meal was good for morale and provided a change of pace, but it was definitely not gourmet eating.

If you wanted a gourmet barbecue, you had to go to the Chief's mess. Any veteran will tell you that if you want to find "connections," you should start with your senior NCOs, and I was invited to a couple of cook-outs where they served some amazing steaks on genuine charcoal grills that hadn't been in our inventory. Curious about how they had made this all work, I made myself follow the golden rule of not asking questions that you didn't want the answer to. I was glad to have the steak and also kind of happy that the more things changed, the more they stayed the same.

We quickly adapted to flying out of temporary quarters and living and working in B-huts and tents. Every once in a while, we were reminded that Bagram was in the middle of hostile territory. About every two weeks, the Taliban would lob a few mortars or 122mm rockets onto the base. These were not huge deliberate attacks but usually were set up with a fuse or timer so that the weapon launched in the middle of the night. While at least one of the previous squadrons had had rockets land right in the middle of Camp McCool, these attacks were not a risk so much as they were a pain in the ass. When a rocket exploded somewhere on the field, the "Big Voice" speaker system that was placed all around the base would tell us to take shelter. We would sleepily throw some clothes on and head to one of the many sandbagged bunkers in our camp.

The first attacks were a disaster from one perspective. After an attack had taken place we were required to get a head count of all our sailors and send reports to base headquarters. It was like a man overboard drill on a ship, except that our sailors could be in any number of shelters near the camp or our maintenance shops (that always had someone working in them). It took a while, but we finally figured out a good way to account for everyone using radios, phones, and a lot of good junior leadership. Once we got our headcount down, the remainder of the challenge for these attacks was that it took forever for the base to call "all clear." At some point, we finally got tired of waiting for them and took it upon ourselves to declare our squadron safe and send the troops back to work or bed, and that was that.

One of the more humorous "attacks" we faced took place in the middle of the day. Two of our most senior Lieutenant Commanders, the Maintenance and Operations Department Heads, took an EA-6B on an FCF. This jet needed a "Bravo" profile for engine maintenance. This FCF profile required a climb to forty-thousand feet to complete the checklist. They worked their way to altitude directly above the base and then took advantage of the fact that there was no air traffic control. When they were complete with their checklist, they dived down towards the base with the intent of breaking the speed of sound. This was a great idea until the sonic boom that their jet created hit the base. The Army had set up some artillery tracking capabilities that were intended to locate where rockets landed and where it was launched. When it registered the sonic boom, this system said that the base was being attacked from a location not too far outside the wall. The base went on alert and the Army put together a Quick Reaction Force to see if they could locate the attackers. Back in the Ready Room, my CO had instantly known what had happened, and he was pissed. He knew he should tell the Army General in charge what had happened, and reluctantly got in the truck and drove across the base to do so. He later told me that the General had laughed about the incident and jokingly refused to believe that a jet as ugly as a Prowler could actually break the speed of sound. While the squadron had been let off the hook, the CO didn't laugh when our two chuckleheads got back. He grounded them both for a couple of days and made sure that their headwork failure was paid for.

The deployment went by very quickly. When it was time to head home, we were now responsible to bring the aircraft back to Whidbey. While the U.S. has been doing this for a long time, flying tactical aircraft around the world is not a trivial task. First of all, it requires lots of aerial tanking. Second, it requires good maintenance support. The Air Force calls the mission to bring a squadron to a new location a "Coronet" package, and each leg of the trip home generally required a least a couple of tankers and one C-17 chase plane that would carry spare parts and our maintenance personnel. One of these trips takes longer than you might imagine. In addition to the challenge of making sure that all the right pieces are in the right place and at the right time, the aircrew is required to get 24 to 48 hours of rest between each leg of the mission. While this may sound generous, changing time zones is only part of the issue. Flying long missions while sitting in an ejection seat and conducting multiple aerial tanking evolutions along the way is exhausting.

As the time to depart got closer, we did a lot of work with the squadron that was replacing us to ensure there was a good handover, got the jets into good shape, and coordinated with the Air Force representative that would cover our transit. On the day of departure, we all got airborne and headed south. We met our dedicated tanker over southern Afghanistan, made sure we could take fuel, and headed south and across Pakistan. While my last trip across Pakistan in 2001 had essentially been one long emergency - this time we had plenty of gas, and as a result it was much, much less stressful. Eventually, we crossed out into the Arabian Sea and jettisoned our flares, a remarkable sight when all four aircraft dispensed them all at once. We then headed north across Oman and up into the Arabian Gulf and towards Al Udied Air Base in Qatar. This part of the trip was unremarkable. However, the weather at Al Udied was a little sketchy. Qatar is a peninsula that sits out in the Arabian Gulf, and even though the skies will be clear for a hundred miles, it is not unusual for the visibility around the base to get pretty low with a fog or haze that combines with dust and humidity. However, we got into the field and began what amounted to our first break in six months.

Al Udied was the home of the CAOC, and was another true expression of American military and economic strength. At any one time, there would be dozens of Air Force fighters, bombers, refueling, and cargo aircraft based there. Sometimes these aircraft would take off and head northwest into Iraq; sometimes, they would head to the northeast into Afghanistan. During our stopover, we stayed in reasonably nice Air Force "transient facilities." This meant tents or trailer-style accommodations that were not great, but not bad either - the showers were clean and had plenty of warm water, and there was no need for a shit stick. The DFAC served the same food as could be found elsewhere in the region, but seemed to be more civilized than the ones in Afghanistan for some reason. In addition to the basic necessities, Al Udied had gyms, a pool, and several civilian-style luxuries that included Burger King, Pizza Hut, and ice cream shops. Even better, there was an Officer's Club and an all-hands bar where we could get a beer. While alcohol was forbidden in Iraq and Afghanistan, in Al Udied, you could get four beers a day (and this number was "strictly monitored"). I remember ending up under "the Bra," the rude but appropriate name for the huge tent that had been placed over a concrete pad in the center of the base. The Bra was next to the little club where we could get a beer. The tent itself covered a bunch of picnic tables and chairs. It was hot there, even in the evening, but it was a peaceful place to sit and think about all the things that the squadron had accomplished. The next day, we linked up with the tanker representative for our Coronet Package and began detailing the rest of our trip home.

The next leg back was from Al Udied to Souda Bay, Greece.

Located on the island of Crete, the Greek airbase hosted a large U.S. Navy contingent. I had been there before on previous deployments and knew that it was a good place to stop. The flight from Al Udied was long, but at about five or so hours, it wasn't extremely painful. As before, we got airborne, joined with our tanker, and headed west across Saudi Arabia. This flight went smoothly until we reached our third and final refueling period which had been scheduled over Egypt. As we headed across the Egyptian desert, the tanker's refueling basket had been leaking at an increasing rate. Had this been a normal flight, we probably would have stopped trying, but at that point, we didn't have many options. When it was time to make an attempt, I was the first one into the basket and successfully got topped off. The next jet wasn't so lucky, and the hose came apart as he was tanking, gushing out tons of fuel until the tanker crew could shut it off. This left three out of four EA-6Bs high over Egypt without enough fuel to make it to Greece. There wasn't much that could be done; the only available divert was Cairo International. So, I continued to Greece while the other three jets went to Cairo.

Cue the "circus music." When three American combat aircraft showed up with a fuel emergency in Cairo, the first response of the Egyptians was, "No, go away." When it became clear that our guys would not take no for an answer, the controllers reluctantly allowed them to land and told them to taxi off to the side of the field. As they taxied, my CO passed what I still think was a brilliant order (one that probably would not have occurred to me). He told everyone to shut down one engine and leave the other one running. This was a normal procedure at home when we would do something called "hot refueling," but in Cairo, it presented a significant risk that something might get ingested into the running engine. On the positive side, if they could convince someone to bring them fuel, they would not need any of the other support equipment that would normally be required to get a Prowler started.

While my guys struggled on the ground in Cairo, I made it to the air station in Souda Bay and landed. As soon as we shut down, I got out of the jet and ran to find our Air Force tanker representative in Base Operations. He was a bit surprised to see only one aircraft roll up to the hangar. When I informed him that the rest of the jets were in Cairo, he looked at me with a blank face. Despite the thorough procedures that were arranged for such situations, he clearly had not been notified of the issue by the tanker who had been assigned to "take care of us." We quickly assessed the predicament, and then we both started making phone calls. One of the calls was made to the U.S. Embassy in Cairo, alerting them to the issue and hoping that they could get the military attaché in action to get the guy's help. At some point, we had notified everybody that could be found, and we just had to wait.

In Cairo, the jets were still sitting there at the airport, each with a single engine running, waiting for assistance. The crews were making friends on the flight line, but apparently, nobody had the authority required to help. On a good note, a couple of fuel trucks had arrived, but our guys were unsuccessful at convincing them that it was safe to refuel the jets with the engines turning. This standoff continued until "a guy with dark sunglasses" showed up and spoke what seemed to be the magic words to the truck drivers. Nobody knew who the guy was (I am convinced he was with the Egyptian military or security services), but when he said "jump," the ground crew asked, "How high?" It wasn't long before the jets were refueled...and then were ordered to leave "immediately." While it seemed like forever as I sat in Base Operations, this entire incident didn't take very long, maybe two and a half hours or so. In Souda Bay, the tanker rep and I had been hovering near an air traffic control facility, waiting to be told when the jets got airborne. Before long, we got a call from the air traffic guys; the jets were airborne and headed in our direction. Forty-five minutes later, all three aircraft landed safely. The crews were excited about their Egyptian adventure and ready for life in the town. For my part, I had enough stress for a while and essentially shut down. While everyone had rooms reserved in a nice hotel out in town with a pool and a bar, I decided that I needed some space to myself and just got a room in the BOQ. I was done.

Two days later, we were rested and ready to rock. The jets had been repaired, and our next stop was Moron Air Base in Spain. As before, we launched and met the tanker. The long flight down the center of the Mediterranean was unremarkable, and we landed without incident. Two more days passed, and it was time for the TRANSLANT. Flying across the Atlantic in an ejection seat aircraft is not comfortable; doing it in a dry suit is even less fun. Even though it was the heart of summer, the water in the North Atlantic was cold enough that anyone who had to eject from the jet would not live long. It was probably arguable that anyone in a dry suit would not last much longer, but regulations were regulations. We took off from Moron very early in the morning and headed west. This was my longest flight in a Prowler. We tanked uncountable times and gradually worked our way across the ocean. Before too long, it became clear that we were falling behind our fuel plan. The problem was that there were unusually strong headwinds; at one point, we saw almost 200 knots right off the nose, and this just ate up fuel and time. Just when we thought that we'd have to stop somewhere short of our destination, the winds began to slow. The tanker dropped us off somewhere near New Jersey, and we finally made it to our destination of Andrews Air Force Base 9.2 hours later. It was great to be back in the U.S. The rest of the trip was now just a "cross country," although we did have a tanker, which meant that we wouldn't have to stop on the way back. Two more days passed, and we got airborne one last time and headed to Whidbey. Six hours later, we were home.

15

VAQ-133 COMMANDING OFFICER: BAGRAM AIR BASE, AFGHANISTAN 2007

Tanking the Desert Prowler, Author's Collection

After fifteen months in the squadron, it was time for me to move from Executive Officer to the Commanding Officer of VAQ-133. We held our Change of Command on December 7th, 2006, and now I was in charge. Our schedule had changed somewhat since we had come home. Our six-month break between deployments had been extended into an entire year off, and we learned that we would now be deploying again in July 2007. This was welcome news; there was a lot on my list that I wanted to get done before we deployed. We already had a Red Flag exercise scheduled in Nellis and a Maple Flag event scheduled in Cold Lake, Canada. With the pre-deployment training requirements covered, I added some administrative events that I thought the squadron was missing. We had a formal event known as a "Dining Out," a "Tiger Day" for the families, and I even did a command inspection. Not all of these events were met with enthusiasm by my subordinates, but I felt that these were all necessary parts of the Navy experience and were things that the expeditionary squadrons needed to do, just like their carrier-based cousins.

As we prepared for deployment, there were some specific operational gaps that I wanted to fill. The first issue was force protection. After my initial expeditionary experience in Afghanistan, I had bugged enough people that the Navy eventually sent a security assessment team to Bagram to see where we were living and see if there was a real justification to ask for more training and equipment. Not surprisingly, their report said that we needed to be prepared to defend ourselves with more than the handguns that we had been provided. When combined with my constant badgering of the chain of command, this report resulted in getting issued a couple of dozen M-16s that I felt we needed. It also generated support for a useful force-protection training regimen, including numerous live-fire rifle and pistol events for all our sailors. Eventually, we even procured some rifle and pistol simulators that enabled some of the troops to practice with realistic "shoot, no-shoot" scenarios.

When it came to self-sufficiency, we needed to learn to utilize whatever was available. One of my junior maintenance guys became a Defense Reutilization Marketing Office (DRMO) expert. The DRMO collected excess, unused, or damaged material from across the entire government and either re-distributed it to organizations that requested it, scrapped it, or sold it to the public. Frequently the equipment was in great shape, and as long as you had a reason to order it, they would ship it to your unit for free. Since our expeditionary mission required a bunch of gear that the Navy would not supply, we ordered forklifts, vehicles, and whatever the team could find that would make life in Bagram easier, including stuff like camouflage netting so that we could create some shady spots where the troops could take a break. We also built up a collection of hand tools that were not part of our normal loadout. Life in Bagram often depended on making improvements to your environment, and I wanted to be somewhat prepared to make things better when we got back.

Eventually, we made it through all our training and qualification events, and it was time to return to Afghanistan. As we had done previously, we were scheduled to ride to Bagram on cargo aircraft and accept our jets from the squadron that was currently deployed. This time, however, the XO was leading the advance detachment, and I would travel with the majority of our personnel. Instead of a C-17, the rest of the squadron flew over on a contract passenger flight, essentially just a chartered 767. I remember that the jet stopped in Bangor, Maine, for fuel. We were met by dozens of flag-waving American patriots in the air terminal who were there to greet returning troops but were happy to say hello to us on our way to Bagram. Eventually, we arrived in Manas, Kyrgyzstan. Manas was one of the bases in the region that had been established as a trans-shipment point for personnel who were moving into and out of Afghanistan. Flying a large, commercial passenger plane into Bagram was still deemed too risky, so we would land in Manas and wait for seats on whatever military cargo aircraft was available. This transfer process was a little hit-and-miss, and getting scheduled for seats in Bagram was difficult and required patience. There were stories of units being trapped for weeks, but within a couple of days, we found ourselves on a C-17 to Bagram.

In a way, it was good to be back. When we arrived, it was clear that there had not been much improvement to our camp or maintenance spaces. However, life in the rest of Bagram had changed significantly. While we were back in the States the Air Force had built an entirely new runway and was busy building a new complex of modern airfield facilities on the other side of the base. These facilities were intended to support the F-16s and F-15s that were not that amenable to austere locations. These new buildings were definitely going to be the place you wanted to live and work. The services and creature comforts that seemed to come with American troops were also there in force. There was now a Subway, Burger King, pizza place, and numerous coffee shops. There was also a lot more traffic on base, as every unit seemed to have unlocked the riddle of how to get vehicles into Afghanistan. This meant that diesel fuel was at a premium and that it was increasingly hazardous to cross Disney Drive.

My squadron force protection effort got off to a rocky start. My initial focus was on the mission, getting the jets going, and making sure the maintenance department had what it needed. When I got time to ask for a simple inventory of our new M-16 rifles, the answer was, "There is one missing." This was not good. A search was rapidly commenced. The team went through all our B-huts until one of our Masters at Arms confessed that he had been keeping one of the rifles under his bed in case we were attacked. With this resolved, I asked if we had any volunteers for a "Quick Response Force." Unsurprisingly, we had a couple of officers and about two dozen sailors who were interested. I asked them to set up a training plan and let me know how they were going to move forward. While it never reached a level of capability that would have made it "combat effective," what it did do was focus those members of the team on safe training. Over time our quick response force would take a formal combat medic course, get some Special Operations guys to teach them to sweep and clear a B-hut, and enjoy a few opportunities to shoot at the rifle range. I am not sure we were any more secure than we had been previously, but it gave us a slightly better chance to respond to an external threat than we had before. It is worth noting that a few months after our departure, the Marine EA-6B squadron that took over the mission found themselves engaged in an intense firefight right at the gate to Camp McCool. Two Taliban suicide attackers had jumped the fence and started shooting. Both attackers were killed in an exchange of fire with the Marines, and one Marine was badly injured. I am very glad that this event didn't occur on my watch because I am sure that it would have ended differently.

The most important project I had on my to-do list was establishing a real targeting process. While I can't go too deeply into it here, we took an old scheduling process that essentially provided our Electronic Warfare capabilities to the loudest requestor and instead applied our skills to the places where we could generate the most effective support. I placed relentless pressure on our team to create a reproducible targeting process, and they did a magnificent job, working with the CAOC, the Joint Fires office, and a number of interesting agencies that were part of the fight. As a result of their efforts, we moved our missions to places where there was a threat that we had the technical capability to mitigate. We also began to measure our effects and used these metrics to convince the chain of command that we were doing the right thing. We saved lives and had the data to prove it.

As we got up to speed in August and September, our efforts to build a targeting process involved introducing ourselves to lots of organizations that would otherwise not have heard of us. We invited all the Army battalion Electronic Warfare Officers to Bagram to hear about what we were doing and how they could help us to help them. Eventually, we also got involved in the planning process for "Operation Rock Avalanche." Rock Avalanche was an Army mission to pressure the Taliban in the Kunar Valley. This was already a place over which we spent countless fight hours supporting the troops. It was the wild-west of Taliban country, and there was always a fight in progress. In this case, our support of Rock Avalanche would be deliberate and targeted. One of my hard-charging Lieutenant Commanders got in on the ground floor of the planning and ensured that we were in place to provide targeted Electronic Warfare support for the troops when required. As a result, we spent several days over the Kunar Valley during the operation, doing what we could to contribute to the effort. While we were only a small player in this operation, it felt good to be part of something where we weren't just an afterthought.

Another difference in this deployment was that we provided a lot more support to Special Operations forces. We kept an alert crew on the schedule every evening to support what would usually be late-night missions. Typically, our duty officer at the SPECOPS operations center would get word of impending action in the afternoon and, if they desired support, the duty officer would send us the critical details. To be clear, we weren't necessarily "in the loop" of most of these missions. We would get a target and a time, and sometimes an infiltration/exfiltration route. Our planning team would look at the area and make a list of things that we could do to support the mission and then the crew would take off into the darkness. It was common that these missions would be scrubbed, or times would change, or we'd get sent from one mission that we knew about to another that we didn't. They were always very dynamic events. Once we arrived overhead, we would attempt to contact the JTAC. Sometimes they would have an idea of what they wanted; sometimes, they were just too busy with the kinetics that were being employed. It was common to sit in an orbit overhead while an AC-130 pounded the target area or maybe watch a B-1 dropping JDAMs. It was also common to listen to the raid through the microphone of the JTAC and hear the sound of small arms fire when the team was in contact. We could frequently hear the exhaustion in their voice as they humped through the mountainous terrain in pursuit of their targets. Unlike most of our missions, we genuinely felt like participants in these raids and were always happy to support them.

During this deployment, the maintenance department proceeded on one of my riskier projects. I wanted to generate a unique sense of pride in the squadron and our expeditionary mission, and I decided to do so by having one of our aircraft entirely painted in desert camouflage. The squadron had previously painted the rudder of one aircraft with camouflage, but I thought it would be a good project to paint the entire jet. So, once the guys had sourced the paint, I tested the issue with my boss. I am not sure that he understood my real intent, but I did not hear a "no," so the project was on. We timed this effort with some major maintenance that the aircraft required and the guys did an excellent job painting. Before long, we had the only Prowler that would ever be outfitted in desert camouflage. While I am biased, I think the jet looked fantastic. Our newly painted jet did get some attention from the Air Force F-15E squadron across the field. Apparently, they had a somewhat adversarial relationship with the previous EA-6B squadron and didn't know that there had been a swap. They decided our desert camouflage looked "pink" and posted a few flyers near our spaces poking fun at the jet. This was a bit insulting and made my junior officers angry, so they requested to retaliate (don't ask questions you don't want to know the answer to). I denied permission to retaliate but relayed my dissatisfaction to the Air Force at one of their neverending meetings, and the heckling stopped. The JOs did have some fun with the Air Force on the radio, but that is pretty much where the conflict ended (as far as I know, anyway).

Both of these deployments saw a few VIP visitors to the base and the squadron. We had met with General Abizaid, the Commander of Central Command the previous deployment, along with our three-star Navy boss from Fifth Fleet. During this deployment, I got a phone call from a senior officer telling me that the Secretary of the Navy was coming to Bagram and that he wanted to meet with the squadron. This was great, but anyone who has ever been in the military knows that when the Service Secretary comes to visit, you start jumping through hoops. Since I was a veteran of the Pentagon and Navy Staff, I set up what I considered the typical dog-and-pony show in our plywood Ready Room. We put together a briefing that described our mission, what we were doing well, and what we needed help with. I included one of our expeditionary pet peeves that requested formal acknowledgment in our service records that we were serving in Afghanistan. The Navy had said that it would place special notification in the records of the Individual Augmentees that it sent overseas to work with the other services, but our deployments didn't seem to fit their criteria. I also set aside time for the Secretary to visit with the entire squadron in our big tent-covered hangar bay. The briefings went fine. The Secretary told me that we would get similar credit for our Afghanistan service (which we never did), and then he asked to see the troops. Having completed my staff-officer due diligence, we took him to the hangar, where he had a great meet-and-greet with the rest of the squadron. I was truly impressed by the visit. In my experience, most of the time, a VIP would arrive, take a picture, and leave. SECNAV talked to everyone who wanted to chat, took pictures with dozens of sailors, gave out "challenge coins," shook every single sailor's hand, and posed for a "Go Navy, Beat Army" picture. It was probably the best VIP visit we had during that trip, and despite my slight disappointment over what I thought was an important issue, I was impressed with the demonstration of leadership.

When it came to improving our living and working environment, the DRMO facility on Bagram was full of the most amazing stuff that you could imagine. You can tell the U.S. is wealthy by looking at our trash, and Air Force trash was definitely someone else's treasure. Anything that an Air Force unit didn't want to bring home, or couldn't economically repair, went to a huge DRMO facility or into the burn pit. While the effects of the burn pits will haunt our bodies forever, I encouraged my guys to find whatever they needed and bring it back to our camp.

Lots of the stuff they found was useful. One of the best things we got was cold-weather gear. It was hard to convince the Navy that life in Bagram wasn't like the boat, and no matter how hard we tried, I could not get the entire squadron outfitted with cold-weather gear. As a result, I was surprised one day when one of my maintenance guys offered me a brand-new, and very expensive camouflage Gortex jacket. During one of their occasional visits to DRMO, our guys had recovered enough brand-new Air Force Gortex gear to outfit the entire squadron of more than two-hundred people. Another large project that kept my maintenance guys busy was the desire to improve the spaces we had. As we considered projects that would make our lives more productive, I asked them to find a shipping container that we could use as a dedicated intelligence space. It took a while, but it wasn't long before we had a shipping container that was already wired for power delivered right to our flight line. The guys scrounged up some plywood and building materials and commenced building a roof over our new facility; it was awesome. Although we didn't get it quite finished before we headed home, the team did a great job. I believed that it was always good to "have a hobby," and even though we didn't get it completely finished, the work was not done in vain.

One of the unique benefits of having an expeditionary squadron was that we were assigned our own flight surgeon, an officer unsurprisingly referred to as "Doc." Squadron flight surgeons essentially come directly from Medical School before they have a chance to specialize and go to a residency. Our Doc was a young Lieutenant osteopath who very much wanted to be an Ophthalmologist. The squadron was very fortunate to have him onboard. He enjoyed flying and spent so much time in the air that he probably could have been considered officially qualified in the back seat. He fit right in with the JOs, and he was great with the troops. Last but not least, he was a great physician. After we arrived in Bagram, he asked me how much leeway he had to set things up. I told him that it was up to his discretion, and he was off like a shot. Doc had a B-hut to himself inside our camp, and he proceeded to set up his own infirmary and massage parlor (part of his osteopath background). At some point, he took the time to give me a tour of his little kingdom. He and his corpsman had done a great job and had created a truly amazing setup. As I was taking the tour, the Doc asked me if I'd like to see his pharmacy, and I said, "Sure." He opened a locked door to display an entire closet full of medicine that he had been provided by the Army clinic with just his signature. The collection was impressive, and I was fully onboard with the project, with one minor exception; I asked him to take the barbiturates and other potentially concerning drugs back to the hospital where hopefully they were a bit more secure.

As the deployment proceeded, Doc asked if I minded that he did some volunteer work with the Egyptian hospital. The base hospital that was near our camp only took care of Americans and the Afghan military. Elsewhere in the base was an Egyptian-run hospital that did volunteer work for the Afghan civilians in the valley. I told him to go ahead but be careful, and off he went. It was not long before he told me that he was assisting an Egyptian Ophthalmologist. He relayed how the Doctor was allowing him to treat some patients and that he was learning a lot. At one point, he came to me excitedly, having worked on his first case of cataracts under the supervision of this Egyptian expert. In fact, he had documented the case and wanted to submit it to a medical journal to see if it could be published. It always strikes me that there are people who make the best of every opportunity, and there are those who just sit around. It was amazing to occasionally catch up with the Doc and hear what he was doing. By the end of this deployment, he had put together a good package for his last shot at his Ophthalmology residency, including some practical experience. I don't remember when he found out, but I do remember how happy he was when he was notified that he was selected to go be an "Eye Doc," and I am also sure that this was one of the better professional results from the deployment.

In our off time, one of the places for the officers to hang out was a B-hut in the main camp. The building contained a bunch of donated paperback books, a refrigerator, a microwave, a TV, and an Xbox. We didn't just watch movies in that room. This was where we had meetings, hosted holiday parties, and lived as much of a normal life as possible. We hosted our own social events that included some pretty humorous skits, including a very good impression of "fat man in a little coat." While I didn't spend a ton of time in there, we had movie nights almost every night, and Call of Duty was on the Xbox for many hours a day. I had donated the Xbox to the Ready Room and was somewhat addicted to the game myself, but I always resisted the temptation to stay for more than a couple of rounds. There was a stretch where I thought that I was pretty good at it until two brand-new pilots showed up during the middle of the deployment. They immediately destroyed everyone and made it clear that most of us were amateurs. Not only would the new guys not need to shoot us, but most of the time, they could just sneak around and knife the rest of us before we even knew what was going on. When I think about daily life in that room, there are two things that will instantly take me back. One of them is the music to the HBO series Entourage. I will admit that I enjoyed that series immensely, but what made it fun was sitting on the couch and watching the latest episode with the JOs. The other related thing that takes me back is, oddly enough, Olympic Curling. Since we were on the other side of the world, when the 2006 Winter

Olympics came on, the only event we could watch always seemed to be curling.

As we approached the time to leave, we learned that the Navy's only Reserve VAQ squadron would be replacing us. They were not scheduled to spend the full six months on station, but the couple of months that they could stay gave the active duty squadrons a good break. As the Reserve squadron traveled around the world to Afghanistan, they had a maintenance issue with an airplane, and it was decided that we would need to leave one of ours behind to fill the gap. This was not optimum from my perspective, every CO wants to bring back the same number of aircraft that they were assigned, but this decision was above my pay grade. The guys arrived, along with a friend that I had known since my first squadron. We had a great turnover, and then it was time for us to head home.

Much as before, we launched our three EA-6Bs from Bagram and headed towards southern Afghanistan, where we met our tanker and were dragged all the way to Al Udied, Qatar. This time there were no tents for us; the facilities had been significantly improved, and we stayed in nice BOQ-style rooms. The rest of our route home was a bit different than our last trip. The fact that we only had three aircraft changed our tanker requirements and enabled us to stretch our second leg a bit. As a result, our first stop outside of CENTCOM was NAS Sigonella, on the Italian island of Sicily. This gave us a great stop where we could relax for a day or so, have a beer, and get some decent food. We then launched from Sigonella and landed at Lajes Air Base in the Azores. This was a location that I'd like to visit again as a civilian. While I was mentally exhausted and touring didn't appeal to me at the time, the islands were rugged, the town was quaint, and the weather was awesome, right up until it wasn't.

The thing about these missions was that it wasn't enough that the weather was good where we were located; we needed to coordinate with the Air Force tankers that were taking off from different bases. In order for us to be approved to fly across the Atlantic, the weather didn't just have to be good at our destination, but it had to be good where the tankers were based, at our potential emergency diverts, and the location where we were departing from. Sometimes this combination seemed impossible, and it was always a bit frustrating when the weather did not seem to align. So, when the scheduled day of departure arrived, the weather was good everywhere but Lajes. We had a bunch of very significant rain showers in the vicinity, and the sky filled with impressive cumulous clouds. So, I took a risk. I had experienced aircrew with me who had just spent six months flying out of an austere base, tanking every day, and flying in the dark in the middle of nowhere. We launched our three aircraft into the rain, and I kept one jet on my wing for a very sketchy section takeoff that was probably ill-advised but was the best way to keep the flight together. Then we had to chase our tanker through a bunch of thick clouds in what turned out to be a very stressful rendezvous. I'd like to say that I breathed a sigh of relief when everyone had finally joined up, but our initial success only meant that we had seven more hours of tanking ahead of us that were required to get across the ocean. Fortunately, the rest of the trip went without issue, and three days later, we were home at Whidbey, preparing for a change of command that would turn the squadron over to my XO and send me back to Washington, D.C. for yet another shore tour.

16

COMMANDER, ELECTRONIC ATTACK WING, U.S. PACIFIC FLEET

Commodore's Last Flight, Author's Collection

After my command tour at VAQ-133, I went back to D.C. and did a job on the Navy Staff for two years, managing the budgetary requirements and resources for the Navy's entire fleet of EA-18Gs and EA-6Bs. While I was working in the Pentagon, I had the good fortune to be promoted to Captain and was selected to command the Electronic Attack Wing, U.S. Pacific Fleet (CVWP). This meant that I would get to return to Whidbey for one last tour and serve as the commander of all the Navy's EA-6B and EA-18G squadrons. Unfortunately, despite the breadth of this responsibility, there aren't many sea stories from this period in my life. This was a cool desk job that allowed me to travel. The issues that had defined the earlier part of my career no longer applied. When I was younger, the aircraft I flew, the people I worked with, and the places I went, were the center of my life. When I got older, these narratives morphed into gripes about bureaucracy, lawyers, senior leadership challenges, and ever-present resourcing constraints. However, this doesn't mean that I stopped flying.

When my Pentagon tour was complete, I packed my things for a cross-country trip and headed back to NAS Whidbey Island to start my new role as the "Prospective Deputy Commander" of CVWP. When I arrived back in Whidbey, it was immediately clear that life was busy in the EA-6B/EA-18G community, and that we had our hands full in the effort to transition fourteen squadrons from the old jet to the new one. While I was ready to dive right into the issues and get to work, as the Prospective Deputy, my orders provided me with about three months to get settled in and to learn to fly the EA-18G. After a couple of years of painful bureaucracy in the Pentagon, learning to fly a new jet seemed like a vacation, and it was really great to find myself back in VAQ-129 as a "student" again, especially as a senior guy.

With the help of a bunch of exceptionally professional young instructors, it didn't take me long before I was back in the cockpit, and let me tell you, the EA-18G is a true sports car. The aircraft is essentially a highly-modified F/A-18F Super Hornet. The major difference between the two aircraft is that the EA-18G has the internal gun removed. It was replaced by a sophisticated Electronic Warfare system that includes a range of receivers that are attached around the airframe, the most identifiable being the pods that are attached to the wingtips.

As my training in the new aircraft progressed, I sat through all the classroom material and then successfully completed the simulator events that were required before flying. As I moved forward, one of the challenges that my young instructors seemed to be most concerned about was the fact that the old Prowler guy might not be quick enough to retract the landing gear before we exceeded their "speed limit." I got a sense of just how fast the aircraft accelerated when I got my first EA-18G flight - in the back seat. I launched on this flight with a Lieutenant who was excited to show the Prospective Deputy what the new jet could do, and as advertised, the performance was eye-opening. It is one thing to hear about the fly-by-wire capabilities of a modern fighter, but totally another to go out and see what a skilled pilot could do with it. It was a wonderful flight, and while I got the sense that my instructor was also testing the G tolerance of the old guy, I had no issues with maintaining consciousness all the way to the limits of the aircraft. A day or so later, when it was finally time for me to fly the jet from the front seat, I'll admit that the acceleration on takeoff was quick, but I was more than up to the challenge, and once I had the gear up, we climbed into the sky over Whidbey at a rate that was eyewatering - it was just as fantastic as I had imagined.

As I got the basics of flying the EA-18G down, it was the systems of the aircraft that were the biggest revelation. At the time we didn't have a lot of ALQ-99 jamming pods to spare for training, so most of the time I flew the EA-18G with only drop tanks. Sometimes I even flew it "slick," with no external stores at all. I quickly learned that not only was the jet ridiculously fast and agile, but the situational awareness that it generated was also almost overwhelming. The combination of the ALQ-218 Electronic Warfare system and the APG-79 radar was amazing and provided a capability that was unmatched by anything else in the fleet. Of course, I will admit that my first few flights in the aircraft were dedicated to doing all the things I couldn't do in an EA-6B. Much like my flights in the F-14A, I started by wearing myself out doing aerobatics. I pulled seven or more Gs for as long as I could take it and fully explored the aerodynamic capabilities of an aircraft that had been specifically designed to be maneuvered. Unfortunately, I didn't have a lot of time to learn the mission systems. I got a very good sense of the opportunities presented by these new capabilities, but I would essentially always remain a Prowler pilot who got to fly an EA-18G. In the big picture, however, one of the most important lessons I learned was that the extremely capable young pilots and NFOs that were coming to this new platform would never be just "taxi drivers." Instead, the new EA-18G crews would need to be masters of Electronic Warfare, experts in air-to-air weapons employment, and be able to conduct a variety of new missions that these modern systems supported. It was very clear to me that the days of "Prowler go long," were over.

After learning to fly the EA-18G, it was time to formally assume my duties as the Deputy Commander. Like my other command tour, this was a "fleet up" role, in which I would serve as the Deputy for eighteen months and then take command for my last eighteen. When it was time for the Change of Command in which I became the Deputy Commander, I sat quietly on the sidelines of the ceremony and then got to work. I was just getting adjusted to the job when the Commodore called me into his office early one morning to discuss an urgent matter. I walked across the hall to find him talking with the CO of the VAQ-129, a gifted officer and friend of mine. The night before, the CO had been arrested for driving under the influence of alcohol in the small town of Anacortes during the three-mile drive from a local bar to his home. Faced with this issue, the Commodore had no choice, he fired the CO for the unprofessional behavior and temporarily put me in command of the squadron until the Navy could find a replacement. It took a few months for the Navy to name a replacement and send him to us, so I was a busy guy. I ran the training squadron of about a thousand officers and sailors in the daytime and caught up on my responsibilities as the Deputy in the evenings. While I was disappointed by the circumstances surrounding this pop-up command opportunity, I did learn a lot more about the FRS training environment and the resourcing challenges of the EA-18G transition.

All was not office work during this tour. I did manage a lot of travel and made it out for a few visits to my expeditionary squadrons in Afghanistan, Iraq, and Australia. On my first trip, I took my senior flight surgeon with me to Afghanistan to document the Air Force's inability to properly take care of one of our squadrons. As usual, it was a very long trip to Bagram. When the Doctor and I finally arrived in Afghanistan, it was nighttime. We were politely greeted by the squadron CO and XO and were delivered to the

"VIP" living quarters. Once we were established in our little cubical, we tried to catch up on our sleep, totally jet-lagged from the trip. Within an hour of settling down, the Taliban rocketed the flight line. Despite my exhaustion, I heard the explosions, recognized them for what they were, and considered going outside and sitting in a bunker. I woke up the Doc and prepared to go find shelter, but it was quickly clear that neither of us had any desire to go outside. So, we decided that we'd either be okay where we were…or would die in our room.

This visit also included the only chance I had to fly a combat mission in the EA-18G. I had briefed the fight and was ready to walk to the airplane when I experienced one of those unfortunate conflicts between "what you know you should do," and "what you want to do." I was in the region so that I could talk to Navy leadership in Bahrain about how the squadron that I was visiting was being taken care of by the Air Force. Travel between Bagram and the transport hub at Qatar was very intermittent, so when the airlift schedule showed a cargo flight out, I decided that I had to catch it rather than fly the mission the squadron had arranged for me. When I eventually got to Bahrain, however, I immediately realized absolutely nobody would have missed me, and I should have just flown the combat mission.

On another trip, I took my Command Master Chief along, intending to visit an EA-18G squadron that had been deployed to Iraq. We made it to our first stop at the International Airport in Qatar without any issues. My trip through customs went smoothly, but my Master Chief was detained and taken off with security. Unfortunately, he had not correctly departed the country on a previous deployment. This was a bit disconcerting, as I had heard that Qatar frequently deported service members who got caught in this paperwork trap. In this case, they let him go free after a couple of hours with a fine. We then made it to the Air Force facilities where we were staying. When it was time for me to proceed to Iraq to visit our squadron, the Master Chief stayed in Al Udied so that I did not risk losing him in a Qatari prison. Aside from this issue, the visit to Iraq was pretty slick. For the first and only time in my life, I got a ride on a business jet. Of course, it was an Air Force business jet, but it felt like I was a rock star. The crew took me to Iraq and then two days later, flew me back to Al Udied. For me it was great to visit the squadron, they were doing fantastic work with the new jet. The visit was also personally gratifying because it was the only time in two decades that I got to put "boots on the ground" in a nation over which I had flown combat missions over nearly two decades.

My final major trip was a visit to Australia. Again, I took my flight surgeon and we headed to RAF Amberley, on the eastern coast of Australia, north of Sydney. The trip was important for two reasons. The first was that the squadron was having a Change of Command, and I was their boss. The second important reason was that the Australians were in the middle of purchasing twelve EA-18Gs. During the visit, I got to meet a number of senior officials and discuss how we were going to assist in their transition. When it came to the ceremony, the Australians seemed to be a bit puzzled by our short, but formal, change of command. Apparently, it was not the way they conducted business, but they listened to my speech with good-natured patience. This squadron was among the first EA-18G expeditionary squadrons to deploy in the Pacific and it was great to see how the squadron was doing; they certainly had a much better setup than life in Afghanistan or Iraq. More importantly, they were changing the paradigm of what "expeditionary" Airborne Electronic Attack represented. Although it was a long trip, it was worth the time spent traveling halfway around the world.

The "nuts and bolts" of this tour were fascinating. After I became the Commander, I spent a lot of time implementing policies intended to maximize the capabilities of the new aircraft and building a solid foundation for what I hoped would follow. We worked on mission planning, simulation, and Electronic Warfare training. We connected with the operational commanders around the world and started changing plans that had been based on Prowler capabilities, and updated them to include Growlers. We honed the policies and procedures for the support of our deployed squadrons. We gave as much assistance as we could to "Havoc," which was the name for the EA-18G equivalent of Top Gun, even though we were continually short of people, parts, and aircraft. All of these were great investments in the future and are paying dividends today.

The VAQ community did experience tragedy during this time. The last Navy EA-6B mishap took place in March 2013. Two VAQ-129 aircraft took off for a training mission into Eastern Washington. The goal was to complete a low-level section flight on the VR-1350, a route that cut through the center of Washington State. One jet was flown by an instructor, the other by a student. Upon entering the low level, the student pilot became overwhelmed, the NFO instructor in the right front seat of the aircraft was distracted, and the student in the back cockpit didn't have enough time in the aircraft to understand the hazards. When the jet impacted the ground, the student pilot, the instructor, and a student in one of the back seats all died instantly. While I had seen several mishaps and had been involved in safety investigations over the years, facing the grieving families of these heroes as part of the chain of command was difficult, and was one of the times in my career that I felt absolutely insufficient for the task.

At some point towards the end of this tour my "bucket" was full. There was much to be done and I was bothered by how much time I had to spend on the minor issues that some of my squadron leadership thought were important. In addition, I had to spend an amazing amount of time with lawyers, as new laws and policies about sexual assault and harassment essentially turned me into a part-time judge. This was not the only friction. I had no interest in the intra-community politics of Naval Aviation and didn't have much time for people whom I felt were prioritizing the wrong issues. Our job was to prepare for combat, and there were very few leaders in my chain of command who seemed to be energized to get things done, and absolutely no one considered saying "no" up the chain. From my perspective, Naval Aviation leadership spent a lot of time re-arranging deck chairs on the Titanic, and they still are. Despite this, it was an excellent tour and tied together a bunch of issues that I had been working on for a long time. When it was time for me to leave, I was ready.

My last flight in the Navy was flown on the 3rd of January, 2014. I flew an EA-18G with CDR "Shaft" Michaels in the back seat and visited the VR-1355 low-level route for the last time. While the entire point of a military low-level route is to avoid being seen by adversary radar systems, on this flight I flew right along the top of the jagged peaks of the Cascades and got a brilliant, and final view of those magnificent mountains. This was not a long flight and after a little more than an hour, we returned to the airfield. While some had urged me to try to get cleared a low flyby at Whidbey or conduct some other exceptional maneuver, I simply came into the break and landed, the same way I had thousands of times in my career. After preaching the necessity of flight discipline for years, there was no way I was going to fall into the trap of thinking that I was special. It was a wonderful flight on a beautiful day, and I remain grateful that I had the opportunity to finish my flying career in such a manner.

At the end of this last command tour, I got orders to go back to the Pentagon for one last time. I worked for the Chief of Naval Operations (CNO) for a couple of years running something called the "CNO Executive Panel." It was a very interesting challenge and I learned a tremendous amount from the senior executives and policy-makers that I got to work with, and for. This tour also included one ambulance trip to the hospital with chest pains which served as a reminder that I wasn't doing a very good job of taking care of myself. When the job was complete, I asked the CNO if I could wrap up my career in a teaching job. It wasn't long before I found myself in the role of Assistant Professor at the Eisenhower School of National Security and Resource Strategy, teaching Defense Strategy Acquisition and Resourcing for my last two years in the Navy. While the combination of academic and defense department bureaucracy at the school was staggeringly inefficient, teaching was more fun than I could have imagined, and I'd be doing it today if they'd let me.

In the end, I completed my flying career with more than three thousand six hundred hours and seven hundred and fifty-five carrier arrested landings in the EA-6B. I flew two-hundred and fifty-nine "green ink" combat flights. During these missions, I fired nine High-Speed Anti-Radiation Missiles and transmitted thousands of watts of energy into adversary receivers in Serbia, Kosovo, Iraq, Afghanistan, and elsewhere around the globe. Finally, in addition to my Prowler time, I got the opportunity to spend my last three years in the cockpit flying the new, and exceptionally capable, EA-18G "Growler," accumulating a little over three-hundred hours in the aircraft, many of them at low altitude and high-speed in the Cascades.

When it was time to retire, I did so without any ceremony and bought a farm in the Shenandoah Valley. At first, I tried working as a defense consultant, but ultimately this had no appeal. There was money to be made in D.C., but I wasn't responsible for anything as a civilian and couldn't influence any change. I watched people who didn't know anything about Electronic Warfare make the same mistakes as all their predecessors, confusing technological capability for the ability to have an impact on, or over the battlefield. So, I shifted into a writing career and here I am, telling stories of the past. The trip isn't over, but what I have seen and done has been amazing. I am grateful to the nation for the opportunity to lead and fly and am proud of all those wonderful patriots with whom I served.

END

ABOUT THE AUTHOR

CAPT J. P. "Tater" Springett II, USN (Ret) is a retired Naval Aviator, combat veteran, author, teacher, and part-time farmer. He lives in the Shenandoah Valley.

ABOUT SELF-PUBLISHING

PLEASE LEAVE A REVIEW OR RATING!

Thank you so much for reading this book!
Reviews and ratings are really the lifeblood of self-publishing. If you enjoyed this book, please leave a review and/or rating on Amazon, Apple Books, Goodreads, Barnes & Noble, Google, or any of the social media sites of the day.

editor@commodoresridge.com
www.commodoresridge.com

www.ingramcontent.com/pod-product-compliance
Lightning Source LLC
LaVergne TN
LVHW020431070526
838199LV00025B/592/J